Gratia Countryman

Gratia Countryman

Her Life, Her Loves, and Her Library

Jane Pejsa

Nodin Press
Minneapolis

Facsimile of embroidered handkerchief monogram,
a gift from Horace Winchell, 1909
Source: Virginia Buffington Shaw

ISBN 0-931714-66-4

Nodin Press, a division of Micawber's, Inc.
525 North Third Street
Minneapolis, MN 55401

This book is dedicated
to my mother,
Irene Melgaard Hauser,
1896–1990

Contents

Foreword 9

Preface 11

Part I. Child of the Prairie

Nininger on the Mississippi 15
Levi, Between Satan and God 19
Gratia, in Thanksgiving 27
At Hastings High School 35

Part II. University Scholar

A House in Minneapolis 41
A Woman's Vocation 49
Horace V. Winchell 57
One Broken Heart 63
Company Q 67
Commencement 74

Part III. Working Girl

The New Library 79
A Restless Spirit 83
From Britain to Bayreuth 92
Family Obligations 105
Marie Todd 111
The Scramble for a Chief Librarian 117

Part IV. Chief Librarian

The New Chief 123
Friends and Colleagues 126
Hancock Point 133
A Home of Her Own 139
The Furnace and Jack Ryan 146
An Aborted Candidacy 155

Part V. Single Mother

The Branch Explosion 157
"Love's Bondage" 165
Wellington Greenway 169

The War 178
T. B. Walker 182
Rules of Conduct 191

Part VI. Benevolent Autocrat
A House for Marie 201
Genevieve Macdonald 213
At Wetoco Lodge 221
The Snake Lady 225
National Prexy: The ALA 229
Farewell 237

Part VII. Librarian Emeritus
"Miss Farmer" 243
Wellington's Marriage 248
The WPA Project 257
Granddaughter Alta Marie 264
Men and Women in Need 270
Birthday Celebrations 277

Part VIII. Compleat Woman
Leave-taking 285
The Buffingtons of Duluth 288
Marie's Legacy 294
Sharing of Gifts 301

Afterword 307

Selected Writings of Gratia Countryman
"The Vocation in Which a Woman May Engage" 309
"Liberty" 312
"Maria Sanford," A Eulogy 317
"Fathers" 319

Library Ann's Cook Book
Gratia's Recipes 325

Notes 327

Bibliography 329

Index

Foreword

This biography of Gratia Countryman is a fascinating account of her success in establishing a position of leadership in the male-dominated world of her time. Her courage and professionalism opened many doors for women in all fields of endeavor.

Gratia's upbringing in a strong and nurturing family prepared her well for the bold course she set in life. She worked with intelligence and passion to forward her career, not just for personal reasons, but to expand the role of the public library in bringing knowledge to those at all levels of the social structure. And she challenged her male counterparts to follow her lead in setting bold new standards for library service.

There is no question that Gratia Countryman made an important contribution toward realizing the city founders' vision of Minneapolis as a haven of culture and learning. The changes she implemented in the public library—the Fine Arts and Music departments, the children's room, the business/factory library outlets—and her expansion of the branch system made library services accessible to citizens of every age, at every economic level, in virtually every neighborhood, and beyond the city limits to many rural areas as well.

Gratia loved life and she gave generously of herself to everyone. She was active in forming and supporting new community organizations, many of them dedicated to the well-being of women and children. Her life is a powerful example of what an individual can accomplish for the benefit of all.

Jane Pejsa has brilliantly researched and written the story of this remarkable woman to whom the library users of Minneapolis—past, present, and future—owe a great debt of gratitude.

—John Harold Kittleson

Mr. Kittleson has been among Minneapolis's premier citizens when it comes to books. He is a past member of the Library Board, was a buyer for Powers book store in its greatest years, and is a long-time benefactor of the Minneapolis Public Library.

Preface

On the third floor of the Minneapolis Public Library, back in the office of the Minneapolis Collection, hangs a large portrait of a woman—Gratia Alta Countryman, third chief librarian of the public library. The portrait is rather somber, not quite suggesting the sparkle and the inquiring spirit that were packed into this woman's small body. I knew her only in her later years, when I was still quite young. What must she have been like in her youth? Each time I have visited this third-floor corner of the library, a curious wonderment has seized me. Why has no one written Miss Countryman's story? Someone really ought to, or has it been done? It never occurred to me that I should be the "someone," for in past years I was deeply involved in research and writing on subjects far removed from Minnesota.

Then one day a fit of decisiveness seized me. I suddenly realized that there will be no one left to write Miss Countryman's story if I don't do it myself and do it now. Otherwise who will share memories of this remarkable woman, for written materials too easily disappear. Then and there I decided to pursue the possibility.

First I looked to see what had been done, and I discovered that Miss Countryman's career has been well documented by two competent researchers—Mena C. Dyste[1] and Nancy J.

Rohde.[2] I read these manuscripts, and I investigated the Countryman papers in the archives of the Minneapolis Public Library and the Minnesota Historical Society. Ample as these materials are, I felt I had nothing to add to Dyste and Rohde unless . . . unless I could locate Miss Countryman's private papers. I knew enough of family lore to believe that in Gratia Countryman's personal life lay secrets that could explain the incredible impact she had on a multitude of people, my own mother included, and on the community at large.

My first inquiry, in the summer of 1992, was to Gratia's grandniece, Virginia Buffington Shaw of Edina, Minnesota. I called on Virginia and explained my mission. She pulled from the family archives boxes and folders of letters, papers, diaries, and pictures, an absolute treasure trove of nineteenth- and twentieth-century family history. Then I asked Virginia the question most important, if I should decide to uncover the life of her Aunt Gratia: "Is Wellington still alive?" The response was positive. Gratia's adopted son, Wellington Countryman, was alive and well in Des Plaines, Illinois. And so I promptly flew down to Chicago's O'Hare Airport, where Wellington, now eighty-five years old, picked me up. I was stunned at first on meeting this man of modest height, with his blue eyes and wisp of curly white hair, for he looked just like Gratia Countryman as I remembered her!

Wellington's first words were, "I have saved everything. I always knew that some day someone would write my mother's story."

At that first meeting, Wellington shared with me the firm, yet tender, letters of a mother to her son. We talked about his childhood and how he was "found" in the Children's Room of the Minneapolis Public Library. Later Wellington gave me documents that told the story of Gratia's determination to adopt the boy and of the immense obstacles she had to overcome. And there was more. Suffice it to say that after this first meeting, on the plane back to Minneapolis, I resolved to research and write the tale of Gratia Countryman before it was too late.

Gratia herself documented much of her life in diaries, in daybooks, and especially in letters to her loved ones. The letters begin in her adolescent years and extend to the last year of her long life. As I unfolded and read letter after letter, intent on understanding Gratia's heart, I realized that she was a child of the Victorian Age. It was a time when men and women wrote letters of friendship to one another that at the end of this twentieth century may be subject to various interpretations. Yet I felt that Gratia was always at my side, communicating to me her hopes and her disappointments. At least twice in her life she burned many letters. Clearly those that survive do so because of her own sense of history. Many of them are presented here—better that Gratia reveal her own heart rather than allow a biographer to "interpret" it. Like Wellington, she knew that "some day someone would write" her personal story.

It has been a wonderful adventure all the way, but without the sharing of memories and materials by Wellington Countryman and Virginia Shaw it would never have happened. To each of them may I here express my deep appreciation. Also to Gratia's grandnephew Edwin Buffington and to others named in the bibliography who shared with me vignettes out of their youth, when the name Miss Countryman was synonymous with the public library.

What binds this tale together is the written record of Gratia's illustrious career at the Minneapolis Public Library. For making available to me the pertinent documents from the library archives, I express my heartfelt thanks to Deborah Struzyk, assistant to the director. I also acknowledge here the immense contribution of my editor, Barbara Field, whose advice and assistance go far beyond the ordinary definition of the word.

A word of thanks also to Margot Siegel, journalist and friend, who gave the first critical read to the completed manuscript, pointing out needed clarification and thereby enriching the tale for a wider audience.

All of the above notwithstanding, this biography of Gratia Countryman might still be an unpublished manuscript had it not come to the attention of Harold Kittleson—that enduring gentleman of books, publishing, and above all the Minneapolis Public Library. With an evangelistic fervor, Harold Kittleson seized upon this tale of Gratia Countryman, passed the manuscript along to Norton Stillman of Nodin Press, and continues to work with the publisher even as the book is now in print. To both of these men I am deeply grateful.

Finally, and foremost, I thank my husband, Arthur Pejsa, for his consideration and his support. These have made possible this book as well as the two books I wrote earlier. He is the first to give praise, where praise is due, and the best critic a writer could have.

Jane Pejsa
Minneapolis, October 1994

Part I. Child of the Prairie

Nininger on the Mississippi

We invite every honest, practical and industrious emigrant seeking a home in the far West, to locate himself at Nininger. Let him join in all its intelligent activity and enterprise. He will find in his fellow-citizens men like himself, who have left the crowded causeways of the East to seek health, happiness and competence in the free air of the West.

Issue 1, December 1, 1856
Minnesota Emigrant Aid Journal

1856. Before the first nail was ever pounded, even before the first spadeful of prairie sod had been turned over, Nininger City could be found on the Minnesota territorial map. In fact across the nation, in broadsides as well as in the most respectable periodicals, readers were learning about this Golden City on the upper Mississippi River, a utopian dream-come-true.

Like all great dreams, Nininger had its origins in the mind of a single man—in this case Ignatius Donnelly, lawyer, politician, would-be farmer, and above all philosopher and writer. In the twentieth century, one might have called Donnelly a Renaissance Man. In the nineteenth century, he was dubbed the Sage of Nininger, compliment or epithet, depending on one's point of view. Donnelly had emigrated from the East, bringing with him the vision of an ideal community, a place where the handiwork of one's physical labor could be augmented by the output of one's intellectual and creative energies. Ignatius Donnelly believed that he, among all his fellow men, should be the one to bring about such a vision.

He had hardly arrived in this frontier territory before he teamed with one John Nininger, a man who not only presumed to understand the intricacies of land speculation, but also claimed as brother-in-law Alexander Ramsey, Territorial Governor of Minnesota. Together, Donnelly and Nininger laid claim to an entire township adjacent to the Mississippi and proceeded to draft plans for a model city on the river bank.

Donnelly's task was to market the land, along with his utopian vision. To this end he created the Minnesota Emigrant Aid Association. The purchase of a city lot or agricultural land bought membership in the association with its road map to the future. The marketing slogan:

> "Dost Thou know how to play the Fiddle?" "No," answered Themistocles, "but I understand the Art of raising a little Village into a great City."

To a thoughtful but restless young man whose life ambition was to raise the hearts and souls of his fellow men, such a motto would prove irresistible.

That young man was Levi Countryman, originally from upstate New York. His family had farmed in New York since the early eighteenth century. Indeed, the Countryman land grant had been signed by England's King George II, father of bad King George in American history. Levi was educated in the public schools and had in fact taught school in his home village before moving on to Indiana. There he entered a college to prepare for the ministry, and along the way married one Alta Chamberlain. The first two years of marriage had produced two children, but both died in infancy, not all that unusual in the mid-nineteenth century. When, by and by, Alta gave birth to a healthy baby boy, Levi deemed it time to move on. With Alta, the child, and Alta's three siblings in tow, he abandoned college to answer Minnesota's siren call.

At Nininger, Levi bought into the Emigrant Aid Association by acquiring eighty acres of township land and a pair of oxen. With his brothers-in-law, he built a log cabin, erected a barn and shed, and proceeded to break the prairie sod. But the utopian promise withered in the nationwide Panic of 1857. Land values plummeted; John Nininger fled the state; Ignatius Donnelly maneuvered to cut his losses; and money virtually vanished. Nininger on the Mississippi—Donnelly's Golden City and Levi's new Jerusalem—having in a single year risen from the prairie like a phoenix, began its gradual decline into oblivion.

For Levi Countryman and for all the others who had bought into Donnelly's dream, Nininger became the land of broken promises. Still life went on, for the land must be farmed and families must be fed. Disappointed townspeople simply picked up stakes and moved their new or half built homes to Hastings, the nearest town downstream. Those who stayed with the land eventually prospered, but the Spirit of Nininger was dead.

Ignatius Donnelly's star, however, had just begun to rise. He was soon elected Lieutenant Governor of the new state of Minnesota and subsequently to the United States Congress. Defeated for a second term, he abandoned the Republican Party and formed his own People's Party, spawning an agrarian revolt. In between his political forays, Donnelly wrote books that were bestsellers of the time: *Atlantis,* the story of the lost continent; *Ragnarok,* a tale of the earth's beginnings; *The Great Cryptogram,* which "proved" that Sir Francis Bacon wrote

Shakespeare's plays; and finally *Caesar's Column*, a novel describing his own dream for a classless society. Until his death in 1901, this Sage of Nininger continued to speak out on whatever issue caught his interest.

Curiously, in this last decade of the twentieth century, the legacy of Ignatius Donnelly finds a serious contender in the legacy of Levi Countryman—failed farmer from Nininger who lived on until 1924. Like Donnelly, Levi's interests encompassed most of this world as well as the next. And like Donnelly, he wrote prodigiously, leaving behind all matter of sermons, essays, diaries, letters, and poems, although few of them were ever published. Among these was a poem—a ballad of sorts—dedicated to Alta, his wife.

"You Shall be Happy"

I've abused you, I've ill used you,
I've been cruel and severe
And misused you, oft suffused you
In the deep reproaching tear.

Still you'd bear it and repair it
By your deep unchanging love
Then I'd tear it, I declare it
All to atoms, by one move.

Thus on yearly, you have dearly
Bought the pleasures of this life
While I nearly, very merely
Looked upon you as my wife.

Now this feeling I'm revealing
Deeply, deeply, do I take
Humbly kneeling, I am sealing
Vows to live for your own sake.

Over the years, Levi often failed in this earnest resolve, but each failure generated a new beginning. And out of this very human struggle to rise above his own deficiencies, Levi's uncommon legacy evolved—that of father extraordinaire. How else to explain the passionate character and remarkable life of his daughter Gratia Countryman?

Read on . . .

Levi, Between Satan and God

> *This is my birthday, and I am twenty-six years old. A little more than a quarter of a century has passed over my head, and to what purpose have I lived? I want to live every day in such a manner that the night may reveal upon the pages of this book that I have not lived in vain . . .*
>
> From Levi Countryman's Diary
> July 11, 1858

1858. So it was chronicled on the first entry in the diary of Levi Countryman. He, who two years earlier had bought into the Golden City on the Mississippi, now found himself trapped in a log cabin with a wife, her sister, and her two brothers, and now his own two sons—Amplius, who had come with them from Indiana, and Theophilus, born at Nininger in 1857, on Levi's birthday.

Still, Levi and his brothers-in-law toiled on, eking out a subsistence living from the soil. The Countryman cabin, overcrowded from the beginning with five adults and two small children, nevertheless became hostel and way station for the steady traffic between Nininger and Hastings, and beyond. Evenings Levi attended lyceum lectures at Nininger City and Sundays he worshiped in any one of several infant church congregations. With services twice on Sunday and also on Wednesday evenings, he had finally found an outlet for one of his many passions—preaching. His companion passion—to complete his higher education— seemed far beyond reach.

July: . . . Mowed hay before breakfast in the dew. . . . wrote on agricultural matters for the *Nininger Journal* . . . tonight my mind has been exercised on the subject of religion in the Soul, and I do not only fear, but I know that I have more religion on my tongue than in my heart. . . . Finished plowing, sowing, and harrowing an acre of Hungarian grass. Commenced cutting wheat again after dinner and continued cutting till supper time. . . . I have not been very happy today. Alta is not always pleasant. Exhibits scarcely any regard for me; and I have hoped and wished and prayed, and looked for her reformation to religion, but she refuses to become what she ought to be and hence betrays the virulence of temper natural to her. But what have I written? I am not without great sin.

August: . . . I forgot to mention that the baby badly burned his face day before yesterday and Alta is laboring with ague in the breast. So they are both in a bad way. . . . I have a hard and an almost uncontrollable heart. It is passionate and impulsive, . . . Stacked millet this forenoon. After noon I went down to Nininger to attend a meeting of the Executive Committee of the Agricultural Society. No one there but myself. Fear that no one has an interest. After supper mowed sod oats. 'Tis a tedious business . . . Every day of my life I am more and more perplexed about my education. I guess it is a settled matter that I am going to study, but it presses on my thoughts. . . . Disturbed all last night. Had to keep the baby all night, and it squalled like a fury. Alta was called away . . . to assist in a childbirth. It seems that besides being disturbed by Alta's being away, Satan disturbed me to wicked thoughts and wicked deeds. Oh God, help me to be a man. . . . "The spirit is indeed willing" to do right "but the flesh is weak." God help me to mortify the lusts of the flesh and flee them. . . . Alta . . . is a good woman for one who has no religion at heart. She believes in me and desires me to go on in the good work I have chosen. She is perfectly honest in regard to giving to everyone his just due, and honest as to the sacredness of the marriage vow. I need fear no rival in her love. She is a notable housewife—frugal and skillful—and lacks but that one thing needful to make her a complete wife.

September: . . . Commenced raining in the night and before noon it rained very hard showers. All threshing operations were put an end to. . . . I have read nearly all day. The delights of reading good books more than pay me for the loss I am to experience from a half crop of grain. I am satisfied that I am to blame for poor farming . . . but a higher sphere calls me. I often think that I shall study for the ministry, but not lose sight of husbandry in order that I may be of advantage to my fellow men in various ways. . . . Got up early in order to go to the mill with a grist of wheat. . . . I commenced digging potatoes with a shovel and after digging two bushels . . . commenced getting out potatoes with the oxen and plow. Slow work and few on the ground. Have ten or twelve bushels dug to take to town. . . .

October: . . . I husked 24 stocks of corn—husked all day. I have no time hardly to study. I must get up earlier, in order to enjoy the silent hours of morning in study. I do not know but that I shall study at home until next June and then graduate at Red Wing. People may think me fickle minded, but no matter, I must do the best I can for my family, and support them. Royal [Alta's brother] is quite unwell, and therefore cannot be depended upon for support to the family. I hope to be directed by Divine grace. . . . Alta has been mad at me all day because I spent 50 cents, of which 20 cents was [Agricultural] Society money which I can easily replace, but it caused her to . . . call me hypocritical. Ah, it is hard for me to bear such burdens, and in fact I can barely bear them. . . .

1859. With Royal Chamberlain ailing badly, and with a poor crop and even poorer prices the previous fall, Levi found his family's material situation quite unacceptable. He and Alta both longed for an adequate home, more land, and at least a few trappings of material comfort. Hence it was more out of necessity than out of choice that Levi became the teacher at the township school.

January: . . . Quite an unruly school to day. I have promised the scholars to have a new set of rules, by which they will not be allowed to whisper. . . . After supper went up to the schoolhouse to consult about making a new and larger schoolhouse. . . . Studied some in *Olmsted's Philosophy.* Had a tolerably quiet school on account of the laws which I made. . . . Started early this morning for Hastings with some eggs which I had hard work to sell. I do not much like to market on account of the vexation they give me—the people. Hastings is no standard market. Every man buys just as he can take advantage . . . The result is to beget distrust and selfishness. . . . May God keep me from a desire to be rich. . . . Measured up 57 bushels of oats and took them to Hastings . . . I handled them over twice and almost the third time. . . . I believe God enabled me to overcome the propensities to dishonesty today. . . .

February: . . . Went down to Nininger to hear a lecture by I. Donnelly on "Composition in Writing as Indicative of Character." . . . Went up to Pine Bend . . . and preached for them. They are having a revival, and the house was crowded all day . . .

March: . . . Royal is very bad with the inflammatory rheumatism, and I have to wait on him. . . . Alta and I went to town today. Little Offie [Theophilus] has long been afflicted with a sore eye, so we went to the doctor. . . . Hauled lumber all day . . . Sleep feels most desirable . . . I have worked very hard all week. Oh how blessed an institution is the Sabbath day. . . .Today is our marriage birthday. We have been married eight years, and I have reflected much upon how little I have accomplished for good, and how much I might have accomplished . . . God grant that I may do better for the next eight years should he grant me life for so long a time. . . .

April: . . . The prairie fires are burning tonight. It is cold and the wind is high. . . . Commenced snowing at daylight this morning and has continued the whole day. Added to this the wind is blowing fiercely from the northeast . . . altogether the worst storm . . . this winter. . . . I work very hard nowadays but I have a laudable object in view. I want to secure a home for my family so that I may attend more exclusively to the business of the Gospel. I sometimes think I am very unworthy. I have a fearful temper, which is exhibited in my daily labor. . . . Alta and I took our little babe, whose eye is very sore, to Dr. Hanchett. We fear it will go entirely out. The sight is nearly gone now I suppose. . . . In the forenoon built a henhouse and in the afternoon delivered a load of oats and a few turnips. . . . Alta went to Hastings with the baby. . . . The end of the week is come, and I am so depraved that I know I have made no improvement in morals. I have gross passions and appetites which govern me. Tonight I have taken one to see how long I may govern it; I wish I might govern it to the end of my life. . . .

May: . . . The boys are breaking up prairie. . . . Afternoon I took some potatoes to Nininger. Came back in rain, and for the first time, for a long period, Alta and I were alone with our own children. Her two brothers and only sister have been with us for three or four years, making us a large family. They are all producers, however, and have richly earned themselves a home, which they have constantly under my roof. . . .

June: . . . Got up very late this morning. I was desponding, owing to a little difference between my wife and me. She is discontented because we are poor, and it reflects upon me. I could be contented in a mud hovel, if all around could be contented, but when discontentment arises, especially in a companion, then forthwith I am seized with the same malady. . . . Royal is getting much worse . . .

July: . . . Alta has very hard work. So much company—six today in addition to our own. If anybody would help her it would make a difference, but she does it all. She is really a noble woman, may God bless her!

1860. Baby Offie did not lose his eyesight. He recovered completely and would live to the age of 93 years! On the other side, Alta's ailing brother Royal finally died. He was just 25 years old. To accomplish Royal's burial, Levi took out membership in the Oakwood Cemetery Association. The small cemetery in the Nininger township was nonsectarian and open to all who joined the association. If Royal was one of the first to be buried there, Gratia Countryman, almost a hundred years later, would be the last.

1861. A year of great portent: In March Alta gave birth to a daughter, Minnie Martha.

Six weeks later, after spring planting, Levi left home by riverboat to complete the education to which he had so long aspired. South of Hastings, at Red Wing on the Mississippi, was located the Hamline University. It had been established by the Methodists in 1854, and it was the first institution of higher learning in Minnesota.

Levi expected to complete the course for a bachelor's degree within two months. In the meantime, Alta was to be in charge of farm and family, including an infant daughter and two small sons. The bulk of the outdoor work—cultivating, milking, feeding the animals, and more—was to be accomplished by Alta's sister, who continued to make her home with the family.

Immersed in the luxury of higher learning, Levi confided to his diary:

> **May:** . . . here I am in Red Wing, thirty miles from home—thirty miles from my dear wife and children. . . . I am lonely indeed . . . I have had enough to withdraw my attention from the blues today. Attended class at nine, public service at 10:30, Sabbath school at one, Bible lecture at three, sermon at night. . . . I was at school in the morning. Have been trying to study some. . . . It seems to me that I would give up everything for home. Why am I here? Just for the purpose of getting a diploma which is of no value in itself—real learning is. . . . I find that study is a little severe to me. My memory is sadly out of practice surely. Butler's *Analogy* is particularly tedious. Logic, though not new, requires such study as a recitation alone requires. Latin is not hard to translate. . . . Another day of extremely hard study has passed, and I am glad since it shortens the days till Friday, when, God willing, I shall go to Alta and the children. . . . Attended class tonight. My soul was blessed. . . . I wrote about four pages today as part of an oration to be delivered at the commencement day, June 20th. My subject is "Washington's Bequeathment." . . . Classes today in Cicero, Euripides, Butler's *Analogy* and Mental Science. . . . Wrote on my graduating essay for two or three hours . . .
>
> **June:** . . . Have been studying severely all day . . . . Heard classes in Latin (Cicero) and Greek (Alcestis). . . . I have much to do to prepare for examinations. . . . finished my oration this morning. . . . Recited my graduating speech to Dr. Crary at noon. . . . This

> has been a high day to my soul, refreshed with the dews of Divine love. God poured out his spirit upon me in a special manner and I was made glad in my soul. . . . Today began the examination of the classes in the College. . . . I have much confidence. My classes will be Latin, Calculus, Butler's *Analogy*, Mental Science and Logic. . . . Tonight I am exhausted, both in body and mind. I have been under the rack all day and by God's grace I am through the tests. . . . Alta came . . . to see the exhibition of tonight, and the commencement exercises of tomorrow. Oh how glad I am that she has come, for the pleasure that she will receive will give me satisfaction. . . . This morning I wished to read my speech rather than speak it from memory, but Dr. Crary would not permit it. . . . I dreaded the thought of speaking lest I should fail. . . . I got through however without failure. I fully believe God helped me . . . Thus ended harmoniously the toils of the Commencement day in which I with two ladies received the degree of B.A. . . . Busied myself also in packing trunk and getting it to the levee. . . .

The same afternoon that Levi and Alta boarded a riverboat for home and children upstream, almost the entire body of Hamline University male students answered the call of Governor Ramsey. Marching as a single unit—Company F of the Minnesota Second Infantry Regiment—they left Red Wing, sailing downstream to fight in the Civil War.

1863. In January Levi and Alta buried their daughter Minnie Martha in the Oakwood Cemetery. She was not yet two years old. Then in spring Alta gave birth to a new life—Jason Melville. With Royal dead and Alta's other brother Octavia long gone to seek his fortune in Missouri, Levi was farming by himself. In winter he taught school, finding little satisfaction in his "recalcitrant scholars." He began once more to dream about higher pursuits.

1864. Leaving Alta, her sister, and two small boys to manage the farm, Levi went down to Red Wing and enrolled again at Hamline University. This time he completed his master of arts within a few weeks.

1865. In March Levi left family and farm for a third extended absence. He put on the blue uniform of the United States Army, having been recruited for Company D of the Minnesota Second Infantry Regiment. In return he received $300, a sum the family could ill afford to pass up.

The bloody Civil War ended on April 9 with General Lee's surrender at Appomattox. Levi had gotten no further than Washington, D.C. On July 11, he was honorably discharged at Fort Snelling, Minnesota. It was his thirty-third birthday. In September the youngest Countryman child died—Jason Melville, just two years old. He too was buried in Oakwood Cemetery.

For Levi, it was again time to move on. There were still two sons to support, two sons to educate, two sons who should not have to suffer and struggle as their father had. Levi also felt he had somehow misused Alta's sister, still with them and as yet unmarried. On her fell the bulk of the household and animal chores. And Alta herself: was she not meant for better things—a house in town, perhaps even a riding horse and a buggy, and surely a husband who wore a top hat not just on Sunday?

1866. Levi sold the farm, put away the entire proceeds, and rented a house at Hastings. In time he would use the money to provide for his sons' education. In the meantime, he intended to support the family by teaching school. Ill paid as teaching was, it was the only career for which he had been academically prepared.

Levi did not sell his oxen. Having been to Washington and seen the miracle of railroads under steam power, he reasoned that Minnesota would not be far behind. Levi reasoned correctly. When the railroad reached Hastings, he hired out with his team to pull the rails, a task that paid far more than teaching school.

For a family rooted in the soil, a rented house in town was hardly a step forward. Yet, curiously, the vibrant Hastings community was to offer the Countrymans opportunities far beyond Nininger's failed promises, and seemingly without effort or pretense.

Gratia, in Thanksgiving

Maiden, when such a soul as thine is born,
The morning stars their ancient music make,
And joyful, once again their song awake.

Lowell[3]

1866. On November 29, Thanksgiving Day, Alta Countryman gave birth to a daughter. She was plump and healthy, and she arrived with a garland of curls around her little face. Levi selected the child's first name—Gratia, the Latin word for thanksgiving. Alta added the second name—her own. Indeed this was a time not only for thanksgiving but also for optimism.

In fact, it was a most propitious time to be a girl child born in America. Across the land a new mindset was emerging when it came to expectations of the female sex. Furthermore, a cultural and economic boom was in the making that would provide multiple avenues for testing these expectations. The industrial revolution had already begun, swiftly and relentlessly unleashing opportunities for great good and also for evil. Likewise, the idea of a special woman's sphere in public life was being defined. *She* was to be the guardian and defender when it came to child labor, education, industrial conditions, prostitution, social welfare among the poor, and, above all, temperance in alcohol, which was viewed as both cause and effect of all other evils.

This was the America that would shape the early life of woman-to-be Gratia Alta Countryman.

We do not know many details of Gratia's youngest years. Alta's lot did not encourage reflection nor leave time for writing. Levi also had his hands full, trying to make ends meet by substitute teaching, preaching on occasion, and working on the railroad. He had long since ceased keeping a daily diary, and if he wrote many letters, they do not survive. Gratia Alta was not yet ready to keep written score on her own, but her time would come.

Still, other records survive: Hamline University in Red Wing, Levi's alma mater, closed its doors in 1869. (The institution would reemerge in St. Paul a decade later.) Another daughter was born in 1870—Lana, or Lany, named for Levi's sister. Son Ampy (Amplius) graduated from Hastings High School in 1873, and Offie (Theophilus) a year later.

As Levi had vowed earlier, he provided for each of his sons a stellar education. For Ampy it was Oberlin College in Ohio. Ampy graduated in 1878 with a degree in the Classics. He taught school at Hastings for a few months and then went on to medical school in St. Louis. Offie, on the other hand, went off directly to St. Louis. He too graduated in 1878, from Washington University, with a degree in mining engineering. Thus began for him a life of high adventure, of which more will be said in due course.

On Christmas Day in 1878, when Gratia was twelve years old, Ampy presented her with a diary. She promptly set its tone by penning a stern warning on the inside cover:

> Take not this book for fear of life,
> for the owner carries a big jack knife.

In this first chronicle of her own life, Gratia revealed her strong familial attachments, especially to Papa and to Offie. In addition, she recorded the ups and downs of her relationship with best friend Lizzie Root, and with the enigmatic Johnnie Gillis. She also kept score on the continuous stream of visitors in and out of the Countryman household. Recorded almost daily were visits from an assortment of friends and relatives, all of whom seemed to live within walking distance winter and summer. At twelve, Gratia's spelling was impeccable, except for the word *havn't,* a spelling she used throughout her entire life. Now, in Gratia's own words:

> **January**: . . . Hurrah. Today is cold and stormy. . . . Ampy is sick and is cross. . . . Lany, Offie and I played Authors. Offie beat. . . . Tonight Papa, Mama, Offie and I . . . went to the Presbyterian Church. Calvin was there. 23zz3L dn1 3 2r1 d1m.* . . . I got my report today. I stood 92-1/2. . . . This afternoon at recess we snowballed with the boys. . . . There are a few sleighs out. . . . At night I went sliding, had a nice time. . . . Johnnie did not come today, it was so cold. Mama went to see about a house to rent. . . . *Tonight there is a party. Calvin told me and he told me not to tell Lizzie.* . . . Helped Mama and cleaned up this forenoon, and this afternoon went out sliding. . . . Offie, Papa, Mama and I went to church. . . . Calvin was up at school this afternoon. . . . Went down and took my music lesson. . . . *Lizzie went up to meet Calvin this noon. She and I are on good terms again.* Walked up to school with Lizzie R. and Calvin. They are awful good to each other. He does just what she tells him to.
>
> **February:** Today is cold. Helped Mama in forenoon . . . Went downtown, bought two valentines, one for Calvin and one for Lany. . . . I got in a fuss with Miss Smith and she scolded me and made me cry. . . . Lizzie R. is not at school today. I am awful lone-

*Translated: Lizzie R. and I are mad. Throughout the diary, Gratia's most private thoughts were in code, namely: each word was written backwards and 1, 2, 3, 4, 5, 6 were substituted for a, e, i, o, u, y, respectively. On these pages the encoded words are printed in the font shown above.

some. I took a popcorn ball to school this morning and gave Miss Smith a bite after she'd been so mean to me. . . . Went to school and wrote to Lizzie R. I have not seen her for three days and am most dead. . . . Tonight we played a game. Offie and Lany beat. . . . I went to school and Lizzie R. was there. Calvin was there too. *I got mad at Lizzie for a little while,* but got over it. . . . Today I took my music lesson. . . . Johnnie told me he was coming after me Saturday to take me riding. . . . Took my valentine for Calvin downtown and put it at the post office. . . . Today is St. Valentine's day. . . . I got one valentine and Calvin showed us the valentine I sent him. . . . Offie has got a violin and makes lots of music. Johnnie did not come today. . . . Lany has not been in school this week and I have got a cough. Don't know if I'll ever speak to Lizzie R. again. . . . I haven't spoken to Lizzie R. hardly this week and I don't know as I ever will. . . . Today Lizzie R. came up. She didn't know what the matter was with me and said she didn't like me. Mama washed today. . . . Mama ironed today. Took my music lesson, went to school, didn't whisper. . . . Teacher asked me today if Calvin was anything to me.

March: Today is a lovely day. Helped Mama this forenoon. . . . Saw Calvin today. . . . Willie told me that Johnnie went past our house every day. I am going to look out for him. . . . Went to school as usual, haven't spoken to Lizzie yet. . . . Offie took back his violin last night and we can't have any more music. . . . Today I took my music lesson. . . . Today is too nice to go to school, but I did go and studied hard too. . . . Calvin came up at recess . . . Got a note from Calvin. Offie started for St. Louis today. . . . Papa went to fix up the house we are going to live in.

April: Today is real cold. Most froze last night. Sewed carpet rags again today . . . Mama went to bookkeeping class. Papa worked over at the other house . . . went down to clean up our new house. I think it is a nice house. . . . We are most ready to move. . . . we all went over to the other house and cleaned upstairs. . . . Mama was over cleaning again. Ampy and I moved his books over. . . . This afternoon moved all our things. We slept in our new house tonight. . . . We are getting settled now pretty fast. . . . Got up, washed, went to church and was a good girl generally. At night I went to bed. (That's the way Mark Twain wrote his diary.) . . . Today I gave Lizzie my ring, to bind a bargain we made with each other, namely: that we would tell each other everything. . . . Today is pleasant. Lizzie and I are in another fuss. I think it is awful funny. I don't get in trouble with any other girls. . . . I cleaned the yard all day today and had a fair tonight. I see Johnnie now about four times a day. . . . Mr. Rich was here all day. . . . Mama won't let me go to the concert. I have cried so much I can hardly see. . . . Lizzie gave back my ring, but I'll never wear it again. . . . Calvin was up to school, and I saw Johnnie and he said he would be up at night, but he didn't come. . . . Went to school. Made up with Lizzie R. and walked partway home with her. . . . Lizzie R. and I spent all our time talking about Calvin and Johnnie, the future that awaits us, our children and the like. . . . Wrote a note to Johnnie and sent it by Lizzie R. . . . I went to the sociable. Had a splendid time. . . . Worked all forenoon and part of afternoon in my flower beds. . . . This afternoon we had no school. Lizzie R. came home with me. Had a nice talk.

May: Today is pleasant. Went to school. . . . Lizzie R. came over this noon and we went downtown. . . . Tonight we saw Calvin. He invited us to go fishing but Lizzie would not. She never does. . . . I went to school. Lizzie and I changed our seats. She is cross all day thinking about Calvin. She thinks she has lots of trouble, but she has not as much as I. Johnnie is so fickle-hearted. . . . Went to church and Sunday School. Saw Calvin after church. Went up behind him and pulled his hair good. It was pretty short though. . . . *Oh dear, I have not seen Johnnie yet. I'm most dead for him too.* Willie G. and I had to stay after school for our history. Mr. Lewis shut us up in the recitation room and I tell you we kicked up a dust. We threw chalk all over the floor and everything. . . . I have not seen Johnnie for I don't know how long. . . . Everything went right today, only that I did not see Johnnie again and had to stay after school. Bet I won't stay tomorrow night. . . . Got a compliment from Calvin, a nice one.

June: Today pleasant. . . . Wore my new dress to school today. . . . We have had examination all day. Today in grammar and arithmetic. Oh dear, I am so glad it is over with. . . . I got my examination paper today. Stood 90. . . . Rained this afternoon. Worked in my flowers. . . . Mama tried to make me sew but I wouldn't. . . . Today pleasant. Tended flowers and practiced. . . . I ironed this forenoon and sewed. . . . Nothing happened today. Took it easy. . . . Lany was sick while I washed the dishes, but as soon as I had them washed she was well again. . . . Worked in my flowers this morning. . . . Calvin asked me to go to the circus with him, but I won't. . . .

July: Today cloudy. . . . Ampy and I had a fuss today and he hurt me but made full atonement. Ampy and Lany both sick tonight. . . . Today we girls walked out on the railroad track a mile. . . . This afternoon we cut up awful, it being a Sunday. *Mama whipped me today. I needed it too.* . . . Oh dear, I am most roasted this forenoon. . . . I played paper dolls out under the tree. . . . This afternoon Lizzie came down. *I wonder if she does love me. I hope so. I told her lots of things I hadn't ought to. She knew about my committing adultery. She wants me to give up Johnnie.* . . . I have been almost sick today. *Won't be long before I will be a woman, something that happens once a month.* . . . I didn't go to church because I wasn't well enough. *I put on my ring today. I hadn't had it on for an awful long time. Lizzie gave it to me Friday.* . . . Went down and took my music lesson. . . . Helped Mama this forenoon and practiced. . . .

August: Today is pleasant, cool. . . . Took my music lesson this forenoon. . . . Ampy went off this noon for Ohio. Oh dear, I don't feel a bit well today. I haven't been anywhere all day. . . . Went to church. Saw two runaway teams. There was a Dutch picnic in town today. Guess that's what scared the horses so. . . . We were downtown twice and tonight went to the sociable. There was an awful noisy set of young folks there, so of course we had more fun. . . . This afternoon Mama and I went downtown but didn't see Johnnie. Tonight after supper we went up to his house and were downtown after him but saw nothing of him. I am about discouraged. . . . Today awful warm. We washed today. This afternoon I went up under the trees and studied History with Emma. She said she had seen Johnnie and he wants me to write to him. You may be sure I will. . . .

September: Today colder than usual . . . Mama and I washed this forenoon and went downtown in the afternoon. Got me a new hat. We looked for Johnnie but he wasn't there. Calvin was there. . . . When we got home Mama was sick. . . . Mama is awful sick. . . . I am almost tired to pieces tonight. . . . Doctor here again. Oh dear, I am so tired. . . . Mama is a little better tonight. . . . I want to see Johnnie so bad. . . . Mama no better. . . . Today school begins. Oh! I am so glad. Mrs. Champlin is my teacher. She's just splendid. I study Algebra, Latin and Rhetoric. Mama about the same. . . . Wrote a note to Johnnie and sent it. Had all my lessons today in school. Changed my seat today. I sit by Lizzie R. . . . Got a note from Johnnie. Makes me feel good. Mama isn't any better, out of her head some. I played pretty near all the afternoon in school. Mrs. Champlin told me "to leave that little girl at home and bring back the young lady." . . . Mama no better. Doctor comes every day. Got a note from Johnnie and wrote one to him. We have got an awful hard Algebra lesson for Monday but I'll make Papa do them for me. . . . Mama a little better. Johnnie fell down today and split his head on a piece of glass. Consequently he wasn't here this afternoon. . . . Mama about the same. Johnnie isn't at school. . . . Mama worse. Johnnie here today. I wrote to him. . . . Mama is a little better today. . . . Mama about the same. Went to church today. Was Mr. Rich's last sermon. Heard about his *committing adultery*. I am going to do it with Johnnie. . . . Today when Mrs. Champlin took the German class out in the recitation room, I wrote to Johnnie. Harry Mead got hold of it and told the whole school. It made me awful mad. I cried too. I am going to have Johnnie fix him. He wanted to apologize but I wouldn't let him.

October: Today rainy. Wrote to J.G. Mama is a little better today. I got a piece of music that Offie sent to me. The name of it is "Silvery Waves." It is awful pretty. Ampy has gone from Ohio down to a medical school in St. Louis. . . . Dear, I am mad at everybody and everything. Walked home from school with Johnnie. . . . Mama is worse again today. . . . I have had to give up Johnnie because Papa got hold of a note to him and he, Johnnie I mean, is so wicked. I heard that he was tempted to drink and that he got drunk. I must give him up, but I love him all the same. . . . Lany and I study German with Papa evenings now. Lots of fun. We are pretty good dutchmen. . . . Today cold. I expect we'll have snow before long and Oh! won't I be glad. . . . Mama has got so much better. . . . Mama went downtown this afternoon and got Lany and me new dresses, new cloaks and new hoods. They are all of them awful pretty. . . . I look like a daisy. Dear! Wanted to go to a sociable tonight but didn't have anybody to go with.

November: Oh! Am I glad. It snowed all day today. . . . Worked on Papa's slippers all afternoon and played dolls with Lany. . . . The snow is all melting off. Papa got a coal stove in the parlor this morning, and when I got home from school, everything was all torn up. Oh! how I hate house cleaning. . . . House cleaning is about done with and things begin to look decent. . . . Minnie Bassett told me today that she has heard something that Johnnie and I had done. Of course it's a fib, but I don't like such stories to get around. . . . Lany and I studied German tonight. . . . I made a cake today because Lizzie R. is coming here to stay all night. . . . I went to Bible meeting this afternoon. Evening I called on Johnnie. Wanted to see him awful bad but couldn't so I will have to write to him. . . . Felt good all day because Lizzie R. was coming to stay all night with me. . . . Wish *she loved me as much as I love her*. . . . Today is a splendid day. Thanksgiving Day and my birthday. . . .

December: Today about the same as yesterday. . . . Oh dear, I want to write to Johnnie so bad, but Papa won't let me. . . . I was downtown twice this evening. Tried to see Johnnie, but couldn't find him. . . . We had rhetoricals this afternoon. I spoke on "only a farmer's daughter." When I got home from school, I worked on Christmas presents and practiced. . . . My new dress was finished today. It is just handsome. . . . Lizzie R. said she would come home with me to dinner, but she didn't. Mean old thing! . . . Mama washed today. I hate wash day. . . . Papa had bookkeeping class tonight. . . . Today colder than blazes. Most froze my ears off. . . . Ampy has entered medical school. . . . Mama took down my old hat to be fixed today and got the laces and ribbons for our new dresses. . . . Went to church. Wore my new hat. . . . I have had written examination in Algebra and Rhetoric this forenoon. This afternoon I stayed home and commenced a Christmas present for Lany. . . . Worked all the afternoon on my Christmas presents. . . . Today cold as fury. It's "merry Christmas" too, but I didn't get up very early for all that. I got a *photograph album, a new diary, a linen handkerchief and napkin*. . . . Dear! I haven't known what to do with myself today. There wasn't any church to go to so I have read pretty near all day. . . . I don't see whatever has become of Johnnie. I don't see him any more nor get any more notes from him. I guess he has gone back on me. Oh! I am sorry if he has.

No doubt Gratia faithfully kept the new 1879 diary, for she would keep diaries much of her long life. The 1879 diary did not survive. Those diaries that did survive are much less open than this remarkable glimpse into the head and heart of a budding adolescent girl.

In the fall of 1879, not yet thirteen years old, Gratia entered high school. Levi was very much at home in this first high school year, overseeing the education of his two daughters and supplementing it as he thought necessary. His income was sparse—substituting as a teacher in the schools of Hastings and neighboring towns, filling vacant pulpits when the opportunity arose, and hiring out as a day laborer when these intellectual activities could not support the family. On the side he was studying bookkeeping. Levi's obsession with educating himself had evolved into a passion to see that his daughters received the education he had been denied. Curiously, this passion required the constant efforts of Gratia's mother, Alta—to manage the household with stern frugality and yet not inhibit the intellectual ambitions of the daughters. If there was sacrifice on the father's part, there was perhaps even greater sacrifice by the mother, whose own formal education ceased back in Indiana when she married Levi Countryman.

At Hastings High School

When I come down in the morning and Mama begins to scold me for something I've done or have not done . . . then I answer her back, and then I feel so bad afterward and ask her pardon, and then do it again first chance I get. . . .

Gratia Countryman
September 17, 1881

1881. For all the family advantages at Hastings, Levi simply could not earn a satisfactory living there. Conditions eventually forced him to embark on a "life on the road," and for the next decade Levi's occupations would require long absences from home. At first these absences were not that far away, in fact, as close as Reed's Landing on the Mississippi, where he had hired out to lay rails for a new railroad. This absence prompted the first of hundreds of letters that Gratia would write to her father over his lifetime.

September 17

My dearest Papa:

Did you think I had entirely forgotten to write to you? I hadn't forgotten. I don't know why I haven't written before. . . .

School commences next Monday. Oh Papa, I want to know if anyone else has such a time trying to be a Christian. I am almost ready to give up and I am bound not to do that. I pray night and morning for strength to do right, but when I come down in the morning and Mama begins to scold me for something I've done or have not done (you know how it is, you have heard her, and I'm not blaming her a bit) then I answer her back, and then I feel so bad afterward and ask her pardon, and then do it again first chance I get. I'm not a bit better a girl than I was two years ago. I must be a Christian if it takes two years or more. Papa won't you write me a good long letter? Your letters always help me and encourage me. I am afraid this letter is rather blue and discouraging.

I think Mama will let me go to school Monday. I feel well enough. My eyes are all that trouble me. I have on Mama's glasses now. I wear them a good deal.

Well, I must close, with love, Your daughter Gratia.

September 29

My dearest Father:

I thank you very much for writing me such a good letter. It is encouragement I need. I know what is necessary for me to do. I do love Jesus, and there is nothing that I can think of but what I would surrender to him. I do not know what the trouble is, for I know I want Christ bad enough.

It is almost my bedtime, and I cannot write a very long letter this time. Papa, do you think I had better keep at school all this year? I think it would be better for me to study up my old studies this winter, and enter the University next year. In looking over the course (scientific) of study, I see that I can enter the second year.

I have been home all the afternoon, for I felt too bad to walk to school. My studies are very interesting this year but I think it would be best for me to stop. Please write immediately and tell me.

Ampy is cutting up capers and I can't write any more. Your loving daughter Gratia Countryman.

October 21

My dearest Papa:

I have been going to school all week, am rather tired when I get home at night, and have hard headaches a good deal of the time, but feel just as well as I did at home.

We had written examination in Higher English today. Do not know what my standing is yet. I have an essay to write for next Friday on the Magna Charta. I am to tell the condition of England at that time and its effect on the nation. I wish you were going to be here to help me. It is so hard to pick it out of a history like Knight's, for it enters into detail so much. We have no other good history of England, for I cannot find Macaulay's. . . .

That man that has the brushes and has been boarding with us went away this noon. He left Mama a full set of brushes. I have been taking writing lessons this week—25 cents for 12 lessons. Most of the scholars are taking lessons. The premium list to our Companion is coming next week. Can't you imagine us poring over its contents, wishing we could have this or that, or the other?

Well good night, it is bedtime for us girls. Wish me good luck with my essay. Your loving daughter Gratia

October 29

My dearest Papa:

I have just been down and got your letter, and Mama thought you would rather hear from part of us today, than from all of us Monday. I am getting along first rate at school, but I wish now that I had taken up German with the entering class, for when I came to get my Caesar lesson [in Latin], I find that I can remember almost every word of it, and can read it almost as fast as if it

> were English. If I could have taken German, I could have been learning something new. . . .
>
> I wrote my essay and read it yesterday. Mr. Lewis said it was splendid, said I introduced and concluded my subject nicely. My next subject is the "Norman Conquest." That is such a broad subject that I don't know but that my essay will be too long, for I don't know when to stop. . . .
>
> We have heard from Ampy twice. . . . Ampy was well . . . Your loving daughter Gratia Countryman.

1882. In January Gratia's brother Offie (Theophilus) was married down in Missouri. He had just returned from a year in Mexico, having surveyed a railway line from Mexico City to the Pacific Ocean. Offie and his wife Ada essentially moved in on the family, for Offie had taken a position with the Burlington Railroad in Minnesota.

Gratia graduated from Hastings High School with her class on June 16, 1882. At fifteen she was not only the youngest in the class, but by far the smallest. In height, Gratia stood under five feet, and she was underweight. Labeled "sickly" all year, she was also suffering from poor eyesight. Yet with her short curly blond hair and piercing blue eyes, Gratia Countryman dominated the scene wherever she went.

High school commencement exercises took place in the County Courthouse, with words and music overflowing. There were seven graduating scholars—six girls and one boy. Neither Lizzie Root nor Johnnie Gillis was among them.

Each of the graduates gave speeches. The subjects: "The Advancement of Civilization in Feudal Times," "Money, Its Uses and Abuses," "Rome Was Not Built in a Day," "War," "Public Sentiment," "What and How Shall We Read," and "The Vocation in Which a Woman May Engage," this last by Gratia Countryman:

> The question is not what vocation can a woman follow by which to gain a livelihood, as if the sphere of woman were so prescribed

and narrow as to admit of little choice, but from so many what one will she choose, through whose channel she may win bread and butter and clothes, possibly happiness and fame.[4]

Gratia Alta Countryman, 1887
Source: Virginia Buffington Shaw

Part II. University Scholar

A House in Minneapolis

When my brothers were ready for college, they were sent away from home; but when my sister and myself were ready, the family consulted together and decided to move where we girls could go to college and still remain under the family roof. So we moved to Minneapolis and settled near the University.

Gratia A. Countryman, undated

1884. Gratia and family were renting a flat in Minneapolis, near the University of Minnesota. Besides Levi, Alta, and the two girls, "family" still included Alta's sister and Offie's wife Ada. Offie was somewhere between Minneapolis and Chicago, supervising bridge construction for the Burlington Railroad. An infant son had died a few months earlier.

Lany attended high school now, and Gratia was taking classes at the University of Minnesota, although somewhat irregularly, for she was also teaching school. Just south of Minneapolis lay Fort Snelling, a military establishment that included a school for the officers' children. There Gratia did substitute teaching, often for weeks at a time. As in childhood, she continued to be subject to vaguely defined illnesses—attacks of weakness—as well as severe headaches. Her mother also seemed to be chronically ill. Nevertheless mother and daughter were in charge of the household, for Levi's work required his living out west in the Dakota Territory.

The family move to the city was part of Levi's grand dream for the education of his daughters. Yet support of a proper city life required income far beyond what he had ever earned in Hastings. He perceived, quite correctly, that there was money to be earned in business, especially in business related to farm mechanization. Thus, with his agricultural background and his newly acquired bookkeeping skills, he had gone to work for the Pitts Threshing Machine Company of Buffalo, New York—"Buffalo Pitts"—taking over their office in Fargo, Dakota. Levi would spend the next eighteen years with Buffalo Pitts, much of it traveling in Minnesota and the Dakotas.

From surviving letters, it is clear that even at a great distance, Levi was in charge of matters at home. Financial support for the family arrived from Fargo by train every Saturday, in the form of money drafts, so that Alta and the girls were kept on a very short string. There is scarcely a letter to Levi, either from Gratia or Lana, that does not include the sentence, "Mother picked up the draft last night."

The mother's letters were few and far between, for Gratia was the designated family correspondent. However, after one troubling week, Alta was moved to report on conditions at home.

Minneapolis, Minnesota
January 30

Dearest Levi,

. . . I imagine you were a little out of humor on receiving my letter. I guess we are no worse off than most others. The pipes have froze and all the water leaked out; most everyone is having ice drawn. The cold comes in where the pipes come through the wall. You know I told you that I did not think they had a mason to fix the wall, or else the cold comes through the pipes. Last Tuesday was the last time I had it open. The ice was about three inches thick. . . .

We are all better of our colds. I have taken plenty of onion syrup. Gratia began school this week, taking two studies. She is not yet strong. Ada was quite sick last Sunday. Had the Doctor, he called on Monday. She is better now, had a letter from Offie today. They are having a cold time of it. Says two days this week they all froze their noses and had to quit work. They only have two weeks of outdoor work. . . . Have not quite used up our hardwood you carried in. Have been burning some of our new pine wood, burns nicely in the little stove. I have heard quite a number say they were on their fourth or fifth ton of coal. That beats us. Yours in much love, Alta.

Thanks to Levi's expanded earnings and Alta's conscientious thrift at home, the Countrymans were able to acquire a building lot in the same university neighborhood. Levi borrowed money from his brother Peter in Hastings and let out to one Mr. Fisher a contract to build the family a house.

July

My dear Papa:

Just got your letter today and as we have not written before, I will hasten to reply, for you think it is treating you unfairly not to have written. . . . I went down to the Fort [Snelling] yesterday to give lessons. Mrs. Smith paid me ten dollars. I just longed to give it to you or Mama as the first money I had ever earned, but I had to pay $3.00 right away to Mrs. Wilson and it will all be gone soon enough. . . . The draft came Saturday. . . . stopped at the house and talked to Mr. Fisher. . . . The roof was almost wholly shingled and they were to paint the cornice today if it didn't rain. But it just poured down last night and has been cloudy all day.

. . . Mama and I went over to the house a couple of hours yesterday. . . . It is lathed upstairs and partly downstairs. They begin plastering Monday. It is mostly weather-boarded. . . . Mama and I thought all flues were to be 8×12 inches, and Mr. Fisher made the kitchen one 8×8 and said you gave him leave. We had the registers put in above the sitting room and Mama's bedroom. We thought every room in the house was heated except that little one over the bedroom, so we put the register there. They have made real pretty gables. It is beginning to look quite like a house. Mama is rejoicing that she has only one more month's rent to pay. . . . Mama is still having that terrible pain in her lungs. I wish you could compel her to go to a doctor with it. . . . Your loving daughter, Gratia Countryman.

August

My dear Papa:

It has been a shamefully long time since anyone has written to you, not since last Friday, and I know you won't approve, but we are all very busy. . . . I have been over to the house twice today. The woodwork is done, except in the parlor, hall and sitting room. . . . The cistern is fixed, but water from the drain in the sink has only been carried under the sink, and over at Mr. Williams's [house] it is carried into a cesspool and the pipe is bent siphon-like just below the sink, so that a little water always stands there to prevent any smell rising through the sink. Mr. Fisher doesn't seem inclined to do it so. How will you like dirt all beneath the cellar steps instead of stone as at Mr. Williams's and no rise to the steps? We don't fancy it and it is the mason's fault, so Mr. Fisher said he couldn't change it for a hundred dollars. . . . We cannot tell yet when it is best for you to come. They are hurrying as fast as four men can do it, and Mr. Fisher acts so nervous and hurried we hate to say anything. . . . Mama isn't one bit well and I think you should compel her to see a doctor. I go to the Fort tomorrow for lessons and expect to get some more money. . . .

I will just write a short hurried letter. We were afraid you would think from our last letter that the house wasn't getting along well and would write to Mr. Fisher, so I will correct any such understanding if you happen to have it. The woodwork is about finished. . . . The paint is all mixed for the outside and I think perhaps it will be ready. . . . Mr. Butturff was to begin moving the wood this afternoon, but the dirt from the cellar had been thrown out of the window right where he wants to throw the wood, so we hired him to throw it on the terrace. They were

> putting in the grate and mantel this morning when I was over. . . . Lana is studying right along for the University. We bought a bushel of tomatoes . . . and are going to make lots of catsup. . . .
>
> The wood is all hauled now and Mr. Butturff made the coalbin this morning. The woodwork will be finished today, then the painters can go to work downstairs. . . . The upstairs is finished and we could go to cleaning, but the window sash isn't painted. Well, we wish it was all finished and we could be almost moved when you get here . . . We won't write anymore now till you come home. In haste, Your loving daughter, Gratia Countryman.

And as planned, Levi returned home just in time to assist in the grand move to the new Countryman home.

In the fall term, Gratia enrolled as a full-time student at the University of Minnesota. With the courses already taken, she was registered as a sophomore, embarking on a course of study that would lead to a bachelor of science degree. Even as a part-time student, Gratia had become a personality on campus. Now she was truly one of "them."

There would always be a circle of friends around Gratia, for her energetic spirit seemed to attract them in droves. In fact, Gratia had been the first initiate in the Delta Gamma Fraternity,[5] at a time when she was not yet fully enrolled at the university.

In this sophomore year, as in every period of her long life, Gratia had a "best friend," and in the fall of 1884 it was Ima Winchell. Ima was the daughter of Newton Winchell, professor of geology at the university and also the state geologist for Minnesota. This was the time in America when the search for iron ore first came into full swing. In Minnesota, a new land rush had been unleashed—a rush for options on mineral rights—and the place to be was in the pine forests of northern Minnesota. Indeed Professor Winchell was becoming a very important man; it was he who six years later would pioneer the development of Minnesota's famed Mesabi Iron Range.*

At least as important as the professor in the tale unfolding here was Charlotte Winchell, his wife. In these early days of the university, there were no dormitories. Students either commuted from home or lived in boardinghouses surrounding the campus. Mrs. Winchell had observed that for lack of suitable housing, women from outstate were discouraged from attending the university. As a result, the Winchells purchased an old hotel near campus and refurbished it to be a combination family home and place where students could board. It wasn't long before the Winchell home was also the center of student social life.

Son Horace, at nineteen, was the oldest of the children and Ima, at seventeen, the next in line. In this fall of 1884, Ima, like Gratia, was a sophomore. These two young women were not only pledged to Delta Gamma but also to each other as best friends. The happy condition would prevail until the eventual undoing for which poor Ima was in no way responsible.

And Horace? This young man had matriculated earlier, taking the full science course with a major in geology. He would be around the University of Minnesota for another two years and would then move on to the University of Michigan, where his uncle Alexander Winchell was professor of geology. Professor Alexander was almost as well known as Professor Newton, but neither professor would ever attain the worldwide reputation that Horace Winchell later earned.

In the fall of 1884, Horace was taking courses at the University of Minnesota and living at home. One can but imagine the

*Although much of the literature gives credit to Professor Newton Winchell and his son Horace as the men who first identified the potential of the Mesabi Range, in fact a decade before them the Merritt brothers of Duluth had already explored and mapped much of the range's rich iron ore deposits (Walker, David A., *Iron Frontier*, p. 76).

scene as Ima and Gratia, with a flock of their friends, breezed in and out of the Winchell house almost daily, between and after classes. It was under these comfortable circumstances that Horace Winchell and Gratia Countryman—Hortie and Grace—became friends.

The friendship began decorously, with a flowered note card delivered to Gratia's home, a signed photo of Horace enclosed:

At home, Monday evening

Friend Grace:

You proved so entertaining that I entirely forgot one of my errands, which was to ask for the pleasure of your company at the festival on Tuesday evening. Have you already been engaged, or will you do me the favor of going with me? Please answer by return mail.

Exchange photos. You wanted a light one.

Not long after, a second flowered note card arrived:

Minneapolis, November 1

Dear Grace:

Have you made an engagement for the Sophomore class meeting at Lil Porter's on Saturday evening Nov. 22? If not, I wish you would consider yourself engaged to me (for that evening), from the time you read this note. Yours, Hortie.

After Thanksgiving, Gratia's eighteenth birthday, she wrote to Levi:

My own dear Father:

I thank you so much for the dear kind letter you wrote me. It was better than any present you could have sent me, and I shall always prize it. Yes, eighteen years of my life gone. I am glad you feel that I am of so much account. It gives me a great deal of encouragement, for my own retrospect did not reveal anything very

Horace V. Winchell, 1886: “Du bist mein; ich bin Dein”
Source: Virginia Buffington Shaw

flattering. However, I look forward more than backward as you advised. A girl of my disposition is apt to do that anyway.

But I am so thankful every day of my life, Papa, that I have had Christian parents and was compelled to do as near right as possible until I was old enough to do the right from my own judgement. There is so much infidelity and skepticism in the University now, and I often think that it would have been possible for me to be just as untrue to myself and my God, had I been in their place. But I have always been guarded so carefully and had a strong sense of right and wrong that I have never as yet fallen into any misfortune.

It seems to me that my real life is only in preparation, that my education is subservient to something better, and I hope that my life will be a useful and noble life just as much as you, my dear father. I appreciate as well as I can your deep love and interest in me and return it with a child's love, and I will try to merit in some degree what you bestow upon me.

We have been having a vacation since Tuesday and I have been doing a good deal. I read your letter to Lana wanting them to get me a nice present, and Mama more than came up to your request. She bought me a beautiful dress. It is a kind of broadcloth and is made up in the very latest style. She is making it. It is ever so much nicer than silk and will last longer. Didn't she do well by me? . . . Ima brought me a marble tile she had painted and Hortie a beautiful diary for next year. . . . Oh, weren't they all so good to me? It made the tears come to my eyes to think how much affection all my gifts represented. Your letter was the most welcome of all and it represented more love than any. . . . Your loving daughter, Gratia Countryman.

A Woman's Vocation

I do so long to be more than an ordinary woman.
I do so want to fill some high position in life.

Gratia A.Countryman
May 22, 1885

1885. January found Horace Winchell absent from Minneapolis. He did not register for the winter semester, for he was in New Orleans, in charge of the Minnesota Exhibit at the New Orleans Exposition. Ima Winchell and others from Delta Gamma went down to visit him, by river boat. For Gratia, such an extravagant trip was out of the question.

At home, in the Countryman household, Alta's sister and household helper had married and gone to the West Coast. Offie was still building bridges in northern Minnesota, and his wife Ada, now pregnant again, was still living in his parents' home. Gratia had taken on teaching Sunday School to a group of Swedish immigrant boys, a missionary venture so to speak.

And she had acquired a new friend—Esther McBride, or Etta, from outstate Minnesota. As with so many friends who would later touch Gratia's life in deep ways, Etta was a friend in need.

January 5, Minneapolis

My dear Father:

None of us wrote to you yesterday, I don't know why, for Mama had all the afternoon. She and I went to church this morning, and in the afternoon I went down to my Swede Sunday School. . . . Mama got the draft this morning. . . .

Papa, they scolded me for not telling you I was sorry for my display of temper before you left. I thought you knew it. I don't know where I get my temper and obstinacy, but I have a good deal of it. You may see a good deal of it before I conquer it, but you may know I am always sorry and repentant five minutes after the words are out of my mouth, and perfectly scorn myself that I am not stronger. However, I make some pretty strong efforts.

I have a good deal to work against—my natural strong will and pride, and I am told so often that I am unreasonable when I know I am right, but never mind—understand that I am exceedingly sorry for my unfilial conduct and will try to make you some good oyster scallop when you return. Your loving daughter,
Gratia A. C.

January 15

My dear Papa:

. . . I felt very well all last week, but Sunday I was taken sick and haven't been to the University at all. I think though I will start next week if I am well. I haven't tried to study any and will get far behind. The gum swelled over my wisdom tooth and has given me quite considerable pain. The swelling went into my throat, but is better now. . . .

Our Delta Gamma fraternity met here this afternoon. It was such a pleasure to me to see all the girls. Some of them had been to New Orleans and told us considerable of the city and exposition. Hortie promised that his next letter should be devoted to description. He has been trying to secure me a position there, but cannot so far. I think the change and rest would do me good, but alas— . . . Your loving daughter Gratia Countryman.

February 6

My dear Papa:

Mama thinks you will be woefully disappointed unless you receive a letter tomorrow. I had just sat down to make some buttonholes, but left them to write to you. . . . There is a very great revival in the University now. Everybody seems to be interested, in some degree at least, and many have been converted. Boys that have hitherto been very hard cases have changed so completely and are helping right along in our S.C.A. [Student Christian Association] prayer meetings, which are held every morning.

It makes me wonderfully happy, and though I am not very loud in speaking and talking, I try to do as much individual work as possible, and some of the quiet workers feel fully repaid.

I am keeping up pretty well going to school. I have little or no brain work to do except my general reading, and though I don't gain my strength as fast as I should like to, yet I feel well.

I have been thinking somewhat about my future vocation lately. You know I wrote an essay once upon the necessity and duty of a woman acquiring the means to earn her own living. Well, I think I have hit upon a scheme that suits me if I am ever left a forlorn old maid. You know chemistry is an elective study through all the rest of my course and I am on my fourth term of studying it now, so if I wish I may have a good idea of chemistry before I leave. Now, why not turn that to some practical good. So today I asked Prof. Dodge if I might lead the study in the direction of Pharmacy and take a course in that. Lady chemists are becoming quite numerous and I should enjoy having some knowledge of Pharmacy even should I never have occasion to make it earn my living. Doesn't that idea meet your approval?

The wood is all sawed and piled in the woodshed and there is a good bunch of it. We received the draft today . . . It has been snowing this morning. Yours lovingly, Gratia Countryman.

March 22

My dear Papa:

. . . I am so much obliged to you for sending that money. It just helped me out of a straight place, for I was terribly in debt and had to keep up a bank account with each member of the family. I was thinking of going into bankruptcy and pay them two cents on the dollar, and I was very glad to get out of it honorably.

School has begun again, after a few days' vacation. Studies this term are Conic Sections, Modern History, Tacitus, and Zoology, all of which I like except Zoology. I would like that, but I have to recite it in the afternoon and that breaks up the day so. Besides, Prof. Hall who teaches it is a very dry, poor teacher. He always goes at his subject wrong end to and branches off every time he thinks of anything new. We have no textbook, but learn the subject from notes badly mixed, taken from the professor. He teaches Botany to Lana, and the poor child has the subject so confused. I am afraid he can never straighten it out.

Do you remember the talk you had with Miss [Esther] McBride when you were home? She has told me since what a terrible state of mind she was in and how your earnest face went with her and helped her. She asked me to thank you for the good you did her. She has such a happy contented face now. We have grown to be quite dear friends. I cannot help but be drawn to anyone I think true and noble.

I am enjoying my Sunday School class so much nowadays. I have got them so under my control that I can spend my strength in teaching them. One of my little boys had been very bad and I couldn't think of any way to conquer him, so last Sunday I made out some cards with the words "Good Conduct" on them. As usual he was bad and I couldn't manage him, so I completely ostracized him and wouldn't let any of the other boys speak to him. So when I gave the other boys their cards, he felt so bad and teased for one. Today he came with a full determination to be good. He was a perfect little gentleman and so were they all. I praised him from the bottom of my heart after Sunday School, and I felt that I had gained his heart. Oh, I do so love to teach the little fellows. I believe I make a good teacher for them. . . .

I hear from New Orleans quite regularly. I hope Hortie will come home before the cholera comes. Papa, I am quite interested in that young gentleman. Is that bad? . . . Your loving Gratia.

In spring Horace was joined in New Orleans by Charles Conger, also a university classmate. As much as Horace was the scientist, so Charles was the classicist, his first love being poetry, followed by Greek and Latin. What Charles and Horace had in common was Gratia Countryman. In Gratia's eyes there was only Horace, yet Charles had already presented Gratia with a book of love poems, and now he dared pursue a correspondence just in case.

New Orleans, April 23

Dear Grace,

What would Hortie say to this salutation? Nevertheless I will brave his displeasure and yield to my impulse to write you, which circumstances at the present moment favor. There can remain but little to be said about Horace or this wonderful Exhibition that has not already been told you. With such a good correspondent as Hortie and such a disseminator of news as Miss Ima [Winchell], you are well informed and can readily see the embarrassment of my position. However I clench my jaws with determination to find something to say, whether it amounts to much or not, and proceed . . .

Won't you allow Horace to reveal to me those things about me in your last two letters which amuse him so and which he would tell me were it not your wish to have letters confidential communications? Any news of whatever character which would not be betrayals of confidence will be gratefully and properly received. . . .

I am sitting, while writing, in the Minnesota Headquarters within a short distance of the miniature Minnehaha Falls, so pretty, so attractive. I am facing the North and with this missive go my thoughts. In fancy, I anticipate the look of disappointment which comes over you when you see my signature instead of Hortie's. Forgive anything which herein contained may offend you. Remember me very kindly to all my friends, your sister (if I may count her one with her permission) and all your family. Reserve for yourself my sincere respect and best wishes. I am in truth Your friend, Charles T. Conger.

Both Horace and Charles would return from New Orleans before the cholera season. The months of separation had only strengthened Gratia's longing for Horace Winchell.

May 22

My own dear Papa:

It is such a quiet pleasant morning. I feel so safe up here in my cosy room where I can hear the noisy, busy world outside. I feel very thoughtful this morning, but then I always do when I am away by myself. I think you don't enjoy my letters. I imagine you would prefer me to write more practical things, but I <u>cannot</u>, <u>cannot</u> write news. I guess I dream and idealize more than is good for me.

Where did I get such a nature? Not from Mama surely. She is so nice and practical and her poor thoughtless child worries her. Did you used to dream about the most impractical, theoretical things—build up theories upon theories and feel as if everything depended upon your decision in mind of certain points? I feel so disturbed sometimes when Mama calls my mind back from its wanderings to the real and tangible.

Papa, I do so long to be more than an ordinary woman. I do so want to fill some high position in life. I suppose I will settle down and let my ambitions rest unsatisfied as so many women do though. But then a woman's position anywhere is a noble one, if she has a true conception of the meaning of life. I hadn't intended writing so to you, but something impelled me. I do believe so in you, Papa, believe that you have such a dear, affectionate, sympathetic, kind nature and that you can understand every feeling that comes to your child.

Now, I'll tell you something else. My love for Hortie has taken such a strong hold of my life. I know this feeling is reciprocated, though he has never said so. Don't fear that I will be foolish, or that a disappointment could overcome me. Some way I feel as if I had been lifted out of my girlhood and was henceforth a woman, with a woman's responsibilities.

If you answer, please write what you have to say to the other folks separately so that I can have a letter all to myself and won't need to read it aloud.

Your remark that I was studying too hard and that you wish the poor girl was stronger touched me. I have so often wished to be strong; my body is frail and delicate—but is well if I take care of it. I never could bear to give up school before. I haven't given up now. I won't use that word. I have only stopped to rest. I try to study here at home, . . . Oh, dear, I haven't made nearly so good a record in school as I wished to, but what do marks mean and what really is graduation.

We have persuaded Mama to go to Hastings. I think it will do her good if she won't worry that the house is getting rotten dirty. . . . Etta [McBride] is still with me. She is such a true pure-minded girl, it does me good to be with her. We speak of you so often, at least I do. . . . Well, I must stop and study. . . . Your loving daughter, Gratia.

June 20

My own dear Papa:

. . . I will not try to answer your other dear letter. I think so much of it, Papa, and have read it over and over. It sounded just like you. I wonder if all men think as much of their children as you do. I don't believe it, at least they don't show it as plainly. I feel your love so much. Some way Mama and I jar once in awhile. I don't know whose fault it is, but our natures are not in perfect harmony. . . .

I liked what you said about my musical abilities. I like to feel that you believe in me and my ambition. I thoroughly believe in myself. I don't believe there is anything in the world I couldn't accomplish as far as brain and ambition go if I set out to do it.

I have almost decided—I guess I told you—to go back a year at school. I have talked with President Northrop about it and he strongly urges it. I could get a year of studies in that none of the rest will have. . . .

Etta is going home Tuesday. I will be lonely when she goes. I have a favor to ask of you in regard to her, and I hope you will grant it for my sake. I will tell you when I can talk with you. . . .

I was at Lake Calhoun yesterday with Etta and Hortie. We had a nice time and came home respectably early. Hortie came home a week ago last Wednesday. I have been with him about as much as ever. He brought two large bottles of perfume. . . . Your loving daughter, Gratia Countryman.

July 9

My dear Papa:

Have just finished my work and cleaned up for the afternoon. We have been working very hard all this week. Probably Mama told you they were papering all day Monday and Tuesday. Then we had a large washing Tuesday. Wednesday we ironed all the forenoon and swept the whole downstairs, and today we ironed again until ten o'clock and washed all the windows. So you see, we have been doing something.

Oh, but Papa, the rooms downstairs look so very pretty. The paper is very pretty. I rearranged the pictures and knickknacks all around, so we are all changed. We hope you will like it. . . .

Mama said she told you about our taking painting lessons; what do you think about it? I think it is quite an idea. I will earn painting lessons by giving music lessons. And you know I earned French lessons that way, so my music is worth money to me. And, my, I would not change my ability to appreciate music for as much money as I have ever seen. If I find I cannot do well at painting, I can give it up, but I like to try everything. . . .

Papa, Mama said she told you what relation exists now between Hortie and me. I didn't write it to you because I thought I would rather tell you, and when you were home, I didn't have any chance to talk to you. You think it is all right, don't you? Of course, we don't think of such a thing as being married for five or six, perhaps more, years. . . . Yours lovingly, Gratia Countryman.

Horace V. Winchell

Sometime I hope to be a wife, but I never will narrow myself down to the four walls of my home, as too many women do. I will try to raise the standard of woman, and I am glad that Hortie is educated and more cultured than I, for he will be a help instead of a hindrance to my lofty ambitions.

Gratia to her father,
September 24, 1885

1886. For all of Gratia's educational ambitions and life dreams, the new year found her anywhere but in the classrooms of the university. She was registered for the entire school year of 1885–86, but she had not taken any coursework in the fall term. Was it illness, or financial needs, or simply distraction that kept her out of the classroom? Illness didn't keep Gratia away from her Delta Gamma activities, nor interfere with her Sunday School teaching, nor prevent her from participating in the church missionary society and diligently practicing on the piano that Levi had finally procured for her. Yet Gratia demurred when it came to signing up for classes in the winter term. Academically she was falling seriously behind.

Clearly the lives of two important friends were on Gratia's mind. First of all, there was Horace, and then there was Esther McBride—Etta. Or perhaps it was the other way around.

Minneapolis, Minnesota
January 8

My dear Papa:

. . . I have been going up to the U. to Anglo-Saxon [History] every day. Today I drew for a couple of hours, it wearies me so to draw. I am making up Tacitus at home and will take an examination in it next week.

Now I have a matter of business to talk over with you. Etta wishes me to ask your advice as to a plan we have originated. Of course you know she has not money enough to continue her studies through next year. But she wishes to borrow the money. To do that she must have someone to sign her note. Then she will have her life insured for double the amount she borrows and the policy made out to the one who signs her note.

We thought perhaps you might be able to borrow from Uncle Peter [Countryman] and that you would sign her note with such security, believing in her honesty to keep up the premiums, or the assessments rather. Do you think the plan feasible? . . . Your loving daughter, Gratia Countryman.

In Horace V. Winchell's rooms
January 17, Minneapolis

My dear Father:

You will wonder at my heading, but the facts in the case are these: Hortie has been quite sick with a severe cold. I went over to see him yesterday and promised to come today to keep off the blues. He has had an abscess in his head and of course doesn't feel very lively.

I told Mama I would come home early, but Hortie insists on my staying. I urged the fact that I must write to you, so he supplied paper, pen, etc., and told me to go to work, and let him watch me. You see I have to humor him because he is sick.

It has snowed all day today. Nevertheless, we all went to church except Etta. She arose this morning with a very sick headache and has kept in bed, or rather lying down, all day. . . . Etta is by no means a strong girl though she is large. I read your letter to her and the big tears gathered in her eyes, and she said she hardly knew how to accept your offer. She felt she was accepting a great deal from you. I represented to her that you knew what a dear friend she was to me, and that you were helping me to do my friend a favor, and were not really giving her anything but helping her over a hard place when she needed it most. And really Papa, I thank you as much, for she is an ideal friend; such a perfect sympathy there is between us. I do truly love her.

We have not spoken at all to Mama about the plan you suggested for Etta. Mama read your letter and felt it to be her place to consent or dissent without any broaching on the subject. . . .

I guess I must close and talk to my boy, Your loving daughter, Gratia.

Minneapolis, January 30

My dear Papa:

What do you think Mama said! She said when you wrote to her, you always were answered promptly, but when you wasted your productions on your worthless daughters, you might wait a long time for a letter, but she didn't care. Now, wasn't that a pretty thing to say, and she didn't say it in quite such gentle terms either. It aroused a spirit of rebellion within me and I determined forthwith to write to you.

It is Saturday afternoon and I have just finished my dinner and in a few moments must wend my way to Missionary meeting. I am President of the Society still and feel it quite a responsibility. I rather dread it as an ordeal this afternoon. I suppose that is wicked, but I should so much prefer to stay at home and practice. I get along quite nicely with my music, I think. I practice quite a good deal. . . . My piano grows sweeter every day. . . .

Hortie has been very sick again this week. The abscess in his head gathered and broke again. He was in school today, however . . .

Etta keeps intending to write, but her studies take her time night and day. She will write soon, however. Your loving daughter, Gratia Countryman.

Etta did write, on February 1, and such a letter it was—page after page of thanksgiving for Levi Countryman's offer to provide board and room during Etta's university studies and in addition to loan her a sum of cash. Still this would not be enough to cover the remaining years of study. Etta would seek out a summer teaching position to augment the Countryman loan.

No sooner had Etta's fate been decided than Gratia bought into the plan. She and Etta would teach summer school together somewhere. Once again, Gratia's university studies were to be put on hold. During the month of February, Gratia and Etta prepared together for their elementary school teacher examinations. In March they took the exams and were certified to teach in Dakota County. Each received a rural school assignment—Gratia's at Pine Bend and Etta's nearby at Rich Valley.

Whereas Etta would begin teaching in June, Gratia's contract specified April 1 as the start date.

Minneapolis, Minnesota
March 5

My dear Papa:

... I do not intend to register at the University this term. I could not do much in a month. . . . Hortie was over last night. He has gotten me some dumb bells and wants me to practice every night, to develop muscles.

Your dear letter, written to the girls, was read with delight. I do enjoy your sermons better than anyone else's I ever heard, and I conscientiously try to follow them. It is uphill work most of the time, but I hope to reach the summit sometime and look with contempt upon my former self. . . .

Write us some more dear sermons, Papa. I shall anticipate the letter you are going to write to me Sunday. Your loving daughter, Gratia Countryman.

Pine Bend, Minnesota, April 5

My dear ones all!

Heavens! I have just come from my school, rather tired, but in first-rate spirits. I have grown five whole years since I assumed the role and dignity of school mistress. I suspect Lana and Etta are just dying to hear about school . . .

We all rode up to see my schoolhouse last night. It didn't strike me as a very nice place, but they are going to put in new blackboards. . . . I am here to stay three whole months, just think of it! I signed the contract and I'll have to keep it. Mr. Hamp looked at my certificate this morning and turned to Mr. Coates with: "That's about as good as anything we've ever had there, ain't it." Mr. Coates told me they had a very poor school last winter, but he thought I would get along nicely.

After they left, I went to work with a will. Firstly ('cause Lana will want to know), I took all their names and ages, found out just exactly what each one had been studying and how far each had gone. I classified them then and had everything in working order, lessons given out, etc., a half-hour before recess.

Before recess I had my programme made out, and at recess I put the programme on the board. Since then till school was closed, we had regular recitations. I found out just about how much they knew and how fast they could go. There! Ask Etta if that isn't pretty good.

I had eleven scholars today and I have about twenty classes. I declare, I can't stand the State books. I shan't use the Grammar at all. And the Arithmetic and History are abominable. Now, I'll give a list of the things I want.

I want my dictionary, my Smith's *English History* and Doyle's *U.S. History,* Mama's book of *Eminent Americans,* a bottle of ink and 10 or 15 cts worth of foolscap paper. I guess that is all. . . . Haven't I told you everything? Didn't tell you I was homesick, did I? Am not going to either. . . . Good night—Your loving daughter, sister, friend, Gratia Countryman.

Gratia returned to Minneapolis the first of July and Horace was waiting. What a reunion! Horace brought with him the loveliest of summer flowers and left his calling card:

[Horace V. Winchell] now feels and confesses the great pleasure and profit that arises from a constant attendance at the throne of Grace.

It must have been one of the loveliest summers in all of Gratia's long life. Both she and Hortie free of studies, each permitted to postpone for the moment anything but themselves and their dreams. How many evenings did Hortie and Grace walk together on Lake Calhoun's* primitive paths? How often

*Minneapolis is blessed with twenty-seven lakes within the city proper. Lake Calhoun, the largest, dominates a cluster of four connected spring-fed lakes that also includes Lake of the Isles. On the other hand, Lake Harriet, less than a mile from Calhoun, connects to a meandering stream, Minnehaha Creek, whose waters flow from Lake Minnetonka, through miles of countryside, over the picturesque and historic Minnehaha Falls, finally emptying into the Mississippi River. Throughout this "Lake District" of Minneapolis there evolved major residential areas that continue to define the life of the city.

did they share Lake Harriet picnics and band concerts with the Winchell sisters? Or excursions to Lake Minnetonka,* joining in sailing regattas with the well-connected Winchell family friends? At this late date one can only guess, but what we know for sure is that the end of the summer of 1886 turned out to be a watershed in the life of Gratia Countryman. A combination of events occurred that would redirect her life journey, though no one recognized it at the time.

First of all, and best of all in Gratia's mind, was the relocation of her father—Levi—from Fargo to Minneapolis. The entire Fargo episode had been a great sacrifice for Levi. His heart was always with his family, especially with his two vulnerable daughters. Finally, Buffalo Pitts—now the Pitts Agricultural Works—appointed him manager in the Minnesota region, with an office in Minneapolis. For the first time in several years, Levi would be at home to fulfill his family obligations. He judged his prolonged absence to have been detrimental to the family and vowed now that changes would be made at home.

In looking back over Gratia's first years at the university, the claim of "illness" did not ring very true, especially in 1885–86, which was to have been her sophomore year. For all of the activity on campus and off, Gratia had not earned a single academic credit. Levi determined that this would change in the new fall term—Gratia would register once more as a sophomore and continue her studies forward toward her bachelor of science degree. Younger sister Lana would enter as a freshman and be equally consistent in her efforts toward a degree in the classics.

---

*Lake Minnetonka is a magnificent meandering body of water well outside the city. Its shoreline measures more than three hundred miles, the nearest shore being about ten miles from the western city limits. In the late nineteenth and early twentieth centuries, the dominant families of Minneapolis established their summer homes at Minnetonka. In the late twentieth century, many descendents of these families along with thousands of other commuters have their permanent homes on these same shores.

Over at Professor Winchell's household, son Horace's academic record was not much better than Gratia's. His education had been repeatedly interrupted—first by an entire term of working in New Orleans, then by illness, and perhaps also by distractions from the opposite sex. The Winchell parents may well have viewed the spirited and uninhibited Countryman daughter as something of a rustic maiden. And her father? Really, wasn't he little more than a traveling salesman? Whatever discussions took place in the Winchell household, the decision was clear. Horace Winchell would transfer from the University of Minnesota to the University of Michigan. There he would complete his geology studies under his uncle, Professor Alexander Winchell. And while attending the university at Ann Arbor, he would live in the Winchell home, with his aunt and uncle, and his cousin Ida Belle.

For Gratia and Horace, this forced parting was taken in stride. Both were ambitious in their efforts to excel. Their courtship had already included long separations, which only strengthened their firm trust in one another. Still, it was time to make promises. Shortly before Horace left for Ann Arbor, they pledged themselves to each other for life. To seal the mutual promise, Horace presented Gratia with a small diamond, set in a hand-wrought gold filigree ring.

Thus Hortie and Grace entered into a marriage engagement!

One Broken Heart

I am going to live and I am going to do all the good that I can.

Gratia Countryman, June 1887

1887. Horace Winchell had just returned from Ann Arbor, having completed his sophomore year under Professor Alexander Winchell. For Gratia, too, finals were over, and she had indeed completed the entire sophomore year. A summer of lightheartedness lay ahead—just the two of them, Hortie and Grace. But then it all blew up.

It is not clear exactly what led up to the undoing one afternoon in mid-June. Possibly Gratia was giving higher priority to her busy lifestyle than to her fiancé. Or perhaps Horace was too taken with his own success, for even as an undergraduate he was becoming well known in geological and mining circles. Most likely, the immediate cause of the debacle was Gratia's own outburst of temper over a seemingly minor disagreement. What is known about the event is that Horace became very angry and went storming off to Ann Arbor, back to Uncle Alexander's.

Though Gratia was prone to temperamental outbursts at those she loved the most, she was immediately repentant afterward and always quick to apologize. Hence, Gratia promptly inquired of Horace's parents as to his return, and when the time came, she was at the railroad station in her most engaging outfit to welcome home her beloved. Horace emerged from the railroad car, not alone as she expected, but with his cousin Ida Belle Winchell on his arm. During his short visit to Ann Arbor, he had proposed marriage, she had accepted, and they were now engaged to be married.

Gratia returned home alone, removed her diamond ring, and took to her bed. For days she refused food and presently became so weak that she could not stand up. Her parents were frantic over this daughter's sudden and rapid decline. It was Levi who guessed the truth of the matter. But only after he promised to reveal nothing of Gratia's broken heart did she consent to be seen by a physician. The good doctor confessed to Levi that there was nothing he could do. Gratia had lost the will to live, and if indeed she lived, she had probably lost her sanity.

Whatever the failings of Levi Countryman, they did not include passivity. He rejected the diagnosis, dismissed the doctor, and promptly put in motion his own plan of action. This was to telegraph Gratia's bosom friend Etta McBride and order her back to Minneapolis from her summer vacation. Of course Etta came flying, both out of friendship and out of duty, for Levi had been her benefactor.

In the arms of her true friend Etta, Gratia Countryman unburdened her grief and thereby willed her own recovery. She relayed to Etta all that the doctor had said, and she concluded with her own resolve: "I am going to live and I am going to do all the good that I can."[6]

In fall, Gratia was back at the university. She had vowed that life would go on, and she intended first to complete her education. Still, she could not shake Horace out of her heart. Perhaps she secretly hoped that Horace would have second thoughts. Like Gratia, he still had two years of study ahead of him, and certainly didn't plan to marry until he had a secure financial position. That would be unlike Horace. Yet the prognosis at best was poor, for Horace was in Ann Arbor, Ida Belle's home, and Gratia was in Minneapolis.

And Levi was back on the road, once again working out of Fargo in the Dakota Territory.

October 30

My dear daughter Gratia:

. . . Gratia, darling, all of the fall I have wanted to appeal to you on another subject. I have been dumb during the past year. You have commanded me to be dumb, and I have obeyed. I have waited to see you assert yourself and to shake off that incubus, that "old man of the mountain," which has been sapping your strength so long. You have been trying hard to carry along two burdens: the burden of study, which seemed to be both desirable and necessary, and that other burden, which grew not less enlightened nor yet more pleasurable. I would not pursue the ignis fatuus any further. Be calm while I speak, darling: you know that

Company Q, University of Minnesota, 1889: Gratia, second from right
Source: Minneapolis Public Library, the Minneapolis Collection

you are to me as the golden light. I cannot endure that you shall follow a phantom. It is not best that you should dream over and over again the past, only to find daily that it turns to ashes—the substance is consumed. Am I rude? No, my precious girl. I know how ruthlessly you were trampled upon. I saw too clearly the shattering of your young hopes—and sorrow, such as I can feel, whose affections are as deep as eternity, possessed my soul for you. Arise and lean no longer on that broken reed. It is unworthy of you. You have nobly breasted the storm, but you have kept hugging the delusion to your heart, until your strength is nearly wasted. . . .

You must know, for you must give me credit for an average degree of discernment, that I have long since come to the conclusion—plainly speaking—that the object of your day and night dreams is as unworthy as your affections were deep and pure. Do not resent this, as you will thereby resent the truth. I know whereof I assert and know that you will do well to forever drop the remembrance of the diamond-idol, which more careful scrutiny has discovered to be mere paste. Get mad at me, if you will, darling. Even that may break the obnoxious spell, but in your anger, do not weave garlands to place on the brow of cowardice.

I will go no further. You know what I mean. Command me to do anything for you (even to silence on this subject from this time) and I will do it. But do not forget the greater duties of your life, and the great claims on you. You have a mission. I will help you fill it. The sun shines brightly for you. It is not obscured. Not a star has been blotted out of the sky. The paths of duty are all lined with flowers if you will but see them. The gratitude of the needy one who is waiting for your smiles and good cheer is deeply inwrought in that crown of life, which the willing toiler shall wear in heaven. Gratia, Gratia, out of a great love have I in these lines approached you. Forever your father and friend, L. N. Countryman.

Company Q

We, the undersigned, respectfully submit the following petition to the President and faculty of the University of Minnesota: That we, the young ladies of the State University, be

> *allowed some form of military drill under Lieut. Glenn, as an aid to physical culture.*
>
> Gratia Countryman
> November 1888

1888. Gratia's new regimen was in place: Delta Gamma Fraternity, Hermean Literary Society, of which Gratia was both vice president and chairman of the Musicale, Methodist Missionary Society, in addition to serious studies, and always under the watchful eye of Levi. So it was in the spring of Gratia Countryman's junior year, and so it would continue until graduation. Her health had improved remarkably, and her energies were now as directed as they were far flung.

In the biennium 1888–90, women represented approximately one-fourth of the university student body. For some reason, perhaps unwritten, the annual oratorical contest had been restricted to male students. The award in this competition was the coveted "Pillsbury Prize," named for the first president of the university. The prize was of modest monetary worth but was considered a great honor throughout the state of Minnesota. Gratia had a profound admiration for those who expressed themselves effectively, hence were persuasive in their dealings with others. One of her own goals in life was to perfect such an ability in herself, and to this end she made inquiry about the university oratorical contest. No reason could be found for the exclusion of women from the competition, and so in the spring of 1888, she set about to take full advantage of the opportunity. The assigned subject to be addressed was "The Influence of a Nation's Character upon History."

On a June afternoon in the university chapel, selected orations were presented and prizes were awarded: First and second prizes to male seniors, third prize to junior Gratia Countryman.

This third-place oration had a quality about it to which later generations might apply words like "nativism" or, even worse, "racism." But such were the times. The educated idealists who looked forward to a nation where child labor, ignorance, unhealthy working conditions, prostitution, poverty—and, above all, drunkenness—would be abolished, had identified a convenient principal cause—or scapegoat. These descendents of immigrants from earlier decades concluded that their kind had charted the course and that this course was being challenged by the new immigrants in their midst. Gratia Countryman was not immune to these nativist theories, and in the spring of 1888 she spoke emphatically of immutable human characteristics based on nationality:

> . . . Should China be surrounded by the same physical and climatic environment as England and be subject to the same circumstances, the Chinese would never become Englishmen as long as the world would stand, because of the radical positive traits inherent in each. . . . Very different were they from the Tartars who swept in on them from the north despite their 1,500 miles of wall, and whose characteristics made them robbers from first choice and drove them as wild marauders toward the West. What was it that produced the height of civilization to which the Egyptians attained? Why was it that Egyptian learning and science eclipsed even the attainments of our present time, if it were not for the love of search and inquiry which characterized the nation.
>
> . . . Someone has said, "we are creatures of circumstance." We are not. We are under the domination of our own wills, circumstances being incidental. So also with the nation, its history is governed by the will and character of its people, who are to blame for its mistakes, and may share in its successes.

In the fall of the year, Gratia's life was fully directed to the university campus. She had finally mastered the skill of balancing academic achievement with the myriad of extracurricular activities to which she was attracted. Her girls' fraternity—Delta Gamma—was growing in size, yet still without a place to house its outstate sorority sisters. Newly pledged Clara Baldwin caught Gratia's eye and promptly moved into the Countryman home, sharing a room with Etta McBride, who was still high on Gratia's friendship list. These two friendships would become ever deeper as the years marched on. Yet they were quite different in nature. In Etta's case, Gratia's maternal instinct ruled—this "child" Etta must be allowed to regain her health and complete her education. In Clara, however, Gratia had found an equal, an ally for the issues accumulating on her reformist agenda.

In university circles across the land, a "New Woman" was being born. At least that was the term the protagonists gave her. Her birth was both quiet and rambunctious, a protest against the thoroughly middle-class notion of protecting women by maintaining their indoor domesticity. The New Woman pursued intellectual goals; she also played outdoors; she exercised; she learned sports; and she was physically robust. It should be no surprise that the first item on Gratia's reformist agenda was to bring the New Woman to the University of Minnesota.

Together, Gratia and Clara identified the ideal vehicle—military drill for women students! This issue had a curious history. The University of Minnesota was established as a land grant university, under the Morrill Act of 1862. This Act turned federal lands over to the various states, allowing the states to sell the land. The caveat was that the proceeds of such sales must be put into a perpetual trust, with the income used solely for the support of a designated state college or university. Furthermore, the curriculum of every land grant institution must include military tactics and training.

The University of Minnesota under President Northrop took this responsibility seriously, at least as it related to male students. In 1888 the university hired a recent West Point graduate, Lieutenant Edward Glenn, to teach military science and provide military drill for the young men. Military drill turned out to be immensely popular among the men, for the university offered no other opportunity for physical education. Many issues had not been worked out in this first year—for instance, to what extent military science was to be required and whether there should be uniforms on campus—but 1888 did mark the beginning of Reserve Officers' Training on the University of Minnesota campus.

Prompted by Gratia and Clara, the young ladies of Delta Gamma, along with other female friends, reasoned that they too should be entitled to the physical training regimen that was available to the young men. They consulted with Lieutenant Glenn, who lent his support. Gratia then drew up a petition to President Northrop, in her own handwriting. Her name led the list of signatures that included forty-eight names. These represented one-fourth of the women enrolled at the university.

The board of regents gave serious and extended discussion to the women's petition. Lieutenant Glenn spoke in support of military drill for women. There was no recorded objection to the idea, and without fanfare the women's military drill program was set in motion.

1889. In March, the new "Company Q" went about electing officers—a captain, first and second lieutenants, and first and second sergeants. In this first year Gratia Countryman was elected first lieutenant and Clara Baldwin first sergeant. For Gratia and those of like mind, Company Q was a serious endeavor. The initial report in *Ariel,* the student newspaper, suggested a less respectful appraisal across the campus.

> . . . The first public appearance of the company [Q] was on the afternoon of March 23rd when the Gopher's special photographers invaded the sanctum sanctorum and pronounced it altogether too dark a place to take a picture in. Some of the girls didn't exactly like the idea of going out-doors to be shot, but they were told that if they didn't they would have to keep still while it was being done, so they went, and posed in several different positions. The commissioned officers wore swords borrowed for the occasion, which more than made up for the failure of the chevrons to get finished in time. It was generally supposed that the young ladies would

give an exhibition drill after being photographed, but they didn't. They will do so Commencement week, however, and it is expected that visitors will soon be permitted to witness their daily manoeuvers. The uniform next year will be navy blue, constructed according to nearly the same plans and specifications as heretofore, and all the Freshman girls will wear it unless their complexions make it impossible. The officers will wear gold lace chevrons.

By the end of the term, Lieutenant Glenn's coeducational Military Department was a success story by every standard. Still, the editors of the *Ariel* could not contain a certain mirth when it came to Company Q.

The work of the Military Department of the University has, during the past year, been more or less experimental, and regarding it as such, those in charge are well satisfied. Owing to the long delay of the government in sending guns, the greater part of the year has been spent in squad, company and battalion drill. During the short time which has elapsed since the arrival of the guns, the Manual of Arms has been so well mastered that our companies now compare favorably in all respects with the best militia companies of the state. . . .

Lieutenant Glenn expects next year to be able to muster a battalion of at least two hundred men, and besides this and the ladies' battalion, a company of artillery numbering thirty-six men—all he can drill with his battery of two guns.

And what of Company Q? We were never accused of complimenting the ladies, or of repeating to them those of others; but the truth must be told. In the estimation of Lieut. Glenn, Company Q has been a brilliant success. Attendance has been more regular, interest more general, and results superior to that in the other companies. Physical culture is the main object of their drill, and the tremendous effect of that *plus quam ultra* sub-bass warwhoop, which has made them so famous, fully testifies to the increase of lung power. . . .

Considering the difficulties under which he has labored, Lieut. Glenn may well be proud at having thus four companies of

> young men and young ladies who need not fear competition with the best military organizations in the state.
>
> *Ariel,* June 6, 1889

Years later, at the age of eighty-five, Gratia would write down her own memories of the episode:

> . . . When Lieut. Glenn was engaged to give military drill to the boys, the girls felt that we deserved some attention. We talked with Lieut. Glenn, who was willing to instruct us, and then asked permission of the faculty to form a company, with regular instruction from Lieut. Glenn and the use of the Coliseum for drilling purposes, just as the boys. The old Coliseum . . . was the drill hall and a vast auditorium. It later burned down.
>
> Permission was granted, and I have an idea that neither faculty members nor Lieut. Glenn thought the girls were serious. But enough girls signified a desire to try, to make up a company. They appointed a committee to plan a uniform. . . . It was made of the same material as the boys', a heavy broadcloth of cadet grey or blue. The design called for the skirt to be a certain number of inches from the bottom so that, in marching, the line of the skirt and the band should be a uniform line from the floor. The waist had black trim and a black broadcloth sleeveless zouave jacket for warmth. It was a very presentable uniform, and most of the girls or their families made the uniforms themselves.
>
> Ada Smith of the Class of '89 was the first captain. I was first lieutenant . . . and Clara Baldwin of '91 was sergeant, and how she did "dress" the company and make us stand straight and even, with eyes front.
>
> We followed the regular Manual of Arms, setting up exercises, etc. When it came to gun drill, we were provided with wooden guns, which served perfectly well. We took a lot of teasing from the boys about our wooden guns, but that didn't stop us. I think we did very acceptable drilling, for Lieut. Glenn praised us highly. I think he was much interested in the experiment.
>
> The second year, Miss Baldwin was captain, and a splendid one. I remember one incident. We were giving an exhibition with the galleries packed. The company was marching in fours and seemed to be marching straight into a wall, from which we saw no

> escape, when she suddenly gave an order to wheel, and we made a beautiful wheel with less than a yard to spare. We were greeted with explosions of applause. The audience had thought that we were going to meet disaster. . . .
>
> I do not know of any other college at that time which permitted women to drill, nor of any college group which copied us. I believe we were unique. And I can testify to the fact that we all enjoyed the experience and treasure the memory.

Post Script on Company Q. In 1892, Lieutenant Glenn left his position at the university and went on to other assignments. His successor prevailed on the board of regents to restrict military science and military drill to the male students. The regents obliged, at the same time creating a department of women's "physical culture," which later evolved into physical education for women students.

Commencement

> *Church, School and State must combine to arouse the public conscience, by raising the level of general education, and spreading information throughout the country. When the franchise is based upon a suffrage educated intellectually, morally and politically, as the safeguard of our Republic, then only may America indeed be, "The home of the brave and the land of the free."*
>
> Gratia Countryman
> June 6, 1889

1889. It had been more than six years since Gratia Countryman first entered the University of Minnesota. In truth, her education had been haphazard at best, that is, until the last two years—the post-Horace era. By the middle of Gratia's senior year, her accomplishments had become common knowledge. She was elected to membership in the Phi Beta Kappa honorary fraternity. Of the many honors that would accrue to her later in life, this Phi Beta Kappa key from Minnesota's Alpha chapter would be one of the most dearly treasured. Perhaps Gratia herself recognized how thin the line was that separated success from failure.

In spring, buoyed by her success the previous year, Gratia again entered the annual oratorical contest, with a speech entitled "Safeguards of the Suffrage." Seven students competed—six young men and Gratia Countryman. It was a public event—competition and awards—held in the university chapel on the day before commencement. The orations, in order of their presentations, were "The Labor Problem," "The Times," "John Bright," "Modern Music," "Oliver Cromwell," "Safeguards of the Suffrage," and "Step by Step."

Gratia's oration began modestly enough, in a fine patriotic manner:

> America is the "child of the earth's old age." Our people are the latest-born race on the globe, inheriting the tendencies and characteristics of every nation and every clime . . . We are a democracy, a government of the people and by the people. But who constitutes "the people"? The New Englander, whose forefathers signed the Declaration of Independence, the Russian Nihilist longing to break all human law, the Englishman and Chinese, the German and Negro. All these components, differing in birth and education, in religion and ideas of government, make up the people, whose clashing ideas must be united to form a strong Republic governed by the people. . . .

Gratia continued with an increasingly evangelistic fervor. She enumerated some of the most egregious instances of corruption in government since the Civil War. She called attention to the rapid growth of population in this period of massive immigration and expanded suffrage. She appeared to be less interested in further expanding suffrage, that is, to include women, than she was in restricting suffrage through safeguards:

> . . . The first safeguard, which we believe is necessary, is a radical change in our naturalization laws. There is not a State in the Union but has virtually set aside the U.S. Statute requiring five years' residence before naturalization. This was none too long a time and should be the uniform time of naturalization in every State. A large share of our great population have not been fostered under the benign influences of our democracy; they can have no appreciation of our wants; they are ignorant of our institutions. . . . We have no right to grant this [voting] privilege to the man who cannot speak nor understand the language in which our laws and Constitution are written. . . . Education must be the chiefest safeguard of our suffrage; it will protect us alike from foreign stupidity and viciousness, from the corruption of the wirepuller, and from the illiteracy of our own masses. Our ballot must be intellectually, morally, and politically educated. To this end, at least, three qualifications could be justly demanded by the State: An intellectual qualification, made manifest by ability to read and write; an economic qualification, evidenced by ability to support one's self without the public aid, and a moral qualification made manifest by continual obedience to the laws of peace and order. . . .
>
> Church, School, and State must combine to arouse the public conscience, by raising the level of general education, and spreading information throughout the country. When the franchise is based upon a suffrage educated intellectually, morally and politically, as the safeguard of our Republic, then only may America indeed be, "The home of the brave and the land of the free."

If Gratia could still be called a "nativist," she had nevertheless come a long way in one year. Here she was enunciating a magnificent promise—that through education each human being, no matter of what race or out of which benighted land, had potential for the greatest good in America. In this farewell to her university education, Gratia had laid out a veritable road map for her life journey.

Gratia, alone among the Pillsbury Prize competitors, presented her oration again, at the commencement exercises in the university Coliseum. At the conclusion of the program, President Cyrus Northrop awarded twenty-seven degrees in the

College of Science, Literature, and the Arts. Of these, ten were for bachelor of science. The two women who received bachelor of science degrees were Captain Ada Smith and First Lieutenant Gratia Countryman, both from Company Q.

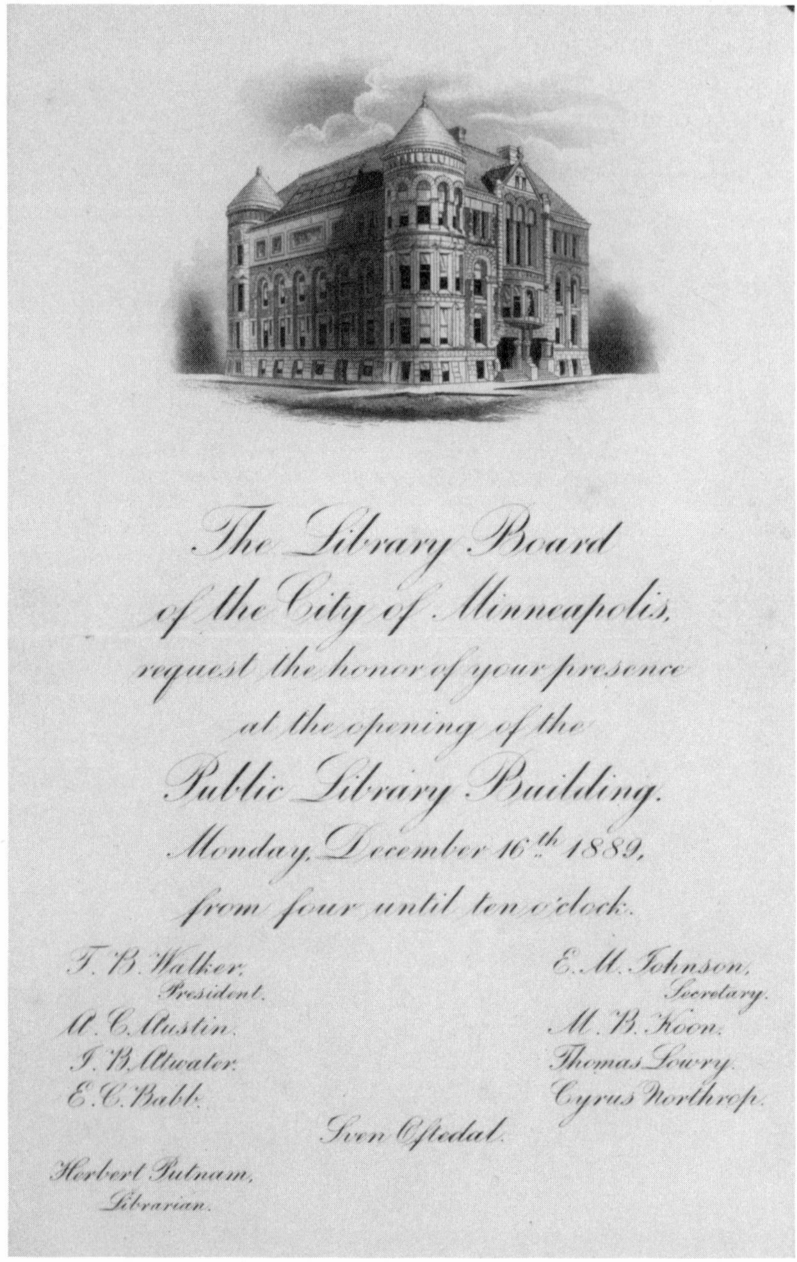
The Library Board
of the City of Minneapolis,
request the honor of your presence
at the opening of the
Public Library Building.
Monday, December 16th 1889,
from four until ten o'clock.

T. B. Walker,
President.
A. C. Austin.
J. B. Atwater.
E. C. Babb.

E. M. Johnson,
Secretary.
M. B. Koon.
Thomas Lowry.
Cyrus Northrop.

Sven Oftedal.

Herbert Putnam,
Librarian.

Invitation to the Opening of the Minneapolis Public Library, 1889
Source: Virginia Buffington Shaw

Part III. Working Girl

The New Library

What was my surprise when a slight little girl in a blue sailor suit and a cap, with a visor perched jauntily on top of her blond curls, very modestly announced herself as Gratia Countryman. I took to her at once, and we have been the best of friends for forty-seven years.

Josephine Cloud, librarian
December 1936

1889. The Minneapolis Public Library opened its doors on Monday afternoon, December 16, 1889, a brand-new yet full-blown public institution. The building itself was stunning, an L-shaped, three-storied edifice of Minnesota sandstone, with generous helpings of marble and featuring an interior open staircase from the basement to the roof. Its location: on a corner of Minneapolis's main thoroughfare, Hennepin Avenue, just beyond the central business district. For the next decades, the Minneapolis Public Library would be the pride of the local citizenry, perhaps the single most unifying institution within an increasingly diverse population.

As a matter of fact, however, the evolution of both the

building and the institution had a history that went back to 1859. That was the year a private citizen created a trust for the Minneapolis Athenaeum, a local subscription library. If much of the early money in Minneapolis came from the rape of the northern forests, it must be said also that the men who gained most from these forests were also the men who founded the Athenaeum, and who year after year stretched its availability to include a wider public. It was lumber baron Thomas Barlow Walker—T. B. Walker—who more than any other individual pursued the goal of a public library, serving all of the citizens of Minneapolis and likewise owned by them. Toward this ideal, the Athenaeum trustees in 1884 hired as librarian Herbert Putnam, a recent graduate of Harvard University.

The breakthrough for a truly public, tax-supported library came in 1879, when the Minnesota legislature passed legislation allowing cities to create libraries and to levy a property tax to support them. Five years later, the Minneapolis city council amended the city charter to create an elected library board and to permit issuing of bonds to build the library, all of which was approved by the Minnesota legislature.

From the beginning, strong organizational and financial ties existed between the Minneapolis Athenaeum and the public library, so it was quite natural that Herbert Putnam's role should be expanded to that of librarian for the public library also. In line with the charter amendment, the public library building included not only a library, but also an art gallery, with space for an art school (the Minneapolis Society of Fine Arts), and a zoological museum (the Minneapolis Academy of Natural Sciences). Eventually the former would find a home of its own. In the years to come, the latter would become a thorn in the side of Gratia Countryman before it disappeared altogether.

In 1886 construction of the library commenced. Concurrently Herbert Putnam went about acquiring a collection of books, respectable in both quantity and quality, in order to have a reputable collection on the shelves by the time the library opened.

By the spring of 1889, the book collection was on schedule and completion of the building was expected to follow within a few months. As yet there was no library staff, so Herbert Putnam turned to University of Minnesota President Cyrus Northrop for advice. Were there any graduates in the June class who might be suitable for library work? He would need to hire several assistants before the library could be opened. President Northrop obligingly furnished Mr. Putnam with two names—Gratia Countryman and Jessie McMillan.

> May 15
>
> Miss Gratia Countryman
> University of Minnesota
>
> My dear Miss Countryman,
>
> I am glad to inform you of your appointment as assistant in the Public Library. The appointment is to take effect from the time when your services will be required and is to be for a trial term of four months.
>
> Your work will not begin until July, at least. But I should be glad to have you come to my office some time next week, to talk it over. Sincerely, Herbert Putnam.

As it turned out, the library building completion was behind schedule, so Gratia did not report for work until October. By then, six library assistants—four women and two men—were energetically preparing for opening day.

Years later, two of the original six would write of these first hectic days that they shared with Gratia Countryman:

> I remember distinctly the first time I saw Miss Countryman. I had heard a great deal about her being so smart (she had just graduated from the University with high honors). What I was prepared to see was a very imposing person with a superior air of whom I would stand in awe. What was my surprise when a slight

little girl in a blue sailor suit and a cap, with a visor perched jauntily on top of her blond curls, very modestly announced herself as "Gratia Countryman." I took to her at once, and we have been the best of friends for forty-seven years.

Our first work together was pasting book pockets and plates in the many volumes which had been dumped into what is now the Technical Room. We worked . . . getting the books ready for the grand opening, December 16, 1889.[7]

Miss Countryman and I received our appointments before graduating from the University of Minnesota in 1889 and were called to begin our work in the library several months before the building was completed.

We started literally on the ground floor, in the present technology room, our main task at the outset being to paste pockets in the heaps of dusty books that were piled on the floor. As I had been assigned to be Miss Cloud's assistant at the issue desk, while Miss Countryman was slated for the post of head cataloger, we saw comparatively little of each other during those first difficult years when both staff and public were learning how to make the most of the library.

As I look over this long stretch of years, . . . there was the great opening evening, December 16, 1889, when [Miss Countryman] paused on her way from the basement to the loft over the librarian's office . . . to join Mr. Putnam and his staff in receiving the multitude of Minneapolis citizens who came thronging in to view the splendors of the new library building and its furnishings. I have a distinct recollection of Miss Countryman that evening, togged out, as we all were, in our Sunday best for the great occasion. She fairly beamed as she tirelessly conducted squads of citizens through the one stackroom, whose shelves were filled with the clean, new books which she had helped to prepare for the grand opening.[8]

1890. While Gratia busied herself developing a catalog system that could encompass the breadth of the library collection, the librarian and the board were already considering expansion possibilities. Within four months of the library opening, two branch libraries were established, one on the north side and one on the south side of the city. The decision involved some risk, given that the branch concept was still very controversial in library circles. The controversy reflected two opposing views as to the role of a public library—should it be a place for scholarly research, to be frequented by serious intellectuals, or should it be a source of education and indeed recreation for the broader public? Herbert Putnam, out of the eastern establishment, stood somewhere in the middle. But T. B. Walker, chairman of the library board, pushed consistently for broadening the library's role to benefit and elevate the common citizenry. No doubt it was such a mindset that first endeared to Gratia this lumber tycoon turned civic philanthropist, with whom she would later align herself.

In June Gratia's sister Lana graduated from the university with a degree in the classics. Graduating with her was Charles Conger, also a classics major and student friend of Gratia. In fact, Charles had once taken a serious fancy to Gratia. Charles and Lana, each committed to the classics and to teaching, entered into a marriage engagement soon after graduation. There had been a time when Gratia might have had Charles for herself, but for Horace Winchell. That time was long past, and as if to remind Gratia of the fact, just a month after Lana's engagement, Horace and Ida Belle were married, following a three-year engagement. The bridal pair set up housekeeping a few blocks from the Countryman home, for Horace was now connected with the geology department of the University of Minnesota.

A Restless Spirit

Miss Gratia Countryman has asked me for a letter of recommendation based upon her work in this Library. I give it with great pleasure, but also with extreme reluctance, for I should consider it a most serious loss to this institution to be deprived of her services. She came to us over two years ago,

> *a graduate of the State University. She had had no special training for library work, but she brought the emphatic assurance from the President of the University that whatever work she took hold of she would master. The prediction has been amply verified. . . .*
>
> Herbert Putnam, Librarian
> December 1, 1891

1891. For all of the library growth, the undiminished civic enthusiasm, and her success in creating the catalog system, Gratia Countryman was not at peace with herself. She was not totally recovered from her broken engagement, and it didn't help that Horace and Ida Belle had taken up residence within a few blocks of the Countryman home. The steady hand in Gratia's young life was still her father, and now he was on the road again, with Gratia de facto head of the busy household in southeast Minneapolis.

In early summer, somewhat overwhelmed by her responsibilities, Gratia made an impulsive decision—to embark on a Lake Superior voyage. Tagging along with a friend whose destination was Buffalo, she traveled east from Duluth on a South Shore Line steamer, then at Sault Sainte Marie left the friend and returned alone via the North Shore Line. By a curious turn of fate, Horace Winchell was traveling alone on the same steamer, returning from a geological investigation into the copper mines of Upper Michigan. For two days, Horace and Gratia were once again the inseparable Hortie and Grace. Late into the night, they walked and sat on deck in each other's arms, both confessing a love that refused to wane. Each admitted to mistakes made in years gone by and both acknowledged that there was no going back.

Afterwards, Gratia shared her feelings with Etta, who alone seemed to provide comfort when it came to Horace. Said Gratia of the leave-taking, "It was a terrible experience."[6]

Late in the year, Herbert Putnam made it known that he would resign as librarian and return to Boston. His resignation would take effect on January 1, 1892. Gratia perceived that her comfortable relationship with Putnam, a relationship that allowed her free reign in implementing a comprehensive yet accessible catalog, was suddenly in jeopardy. Not yet equipped with the confidence that would later be her hallmark, Gratia began making serious inquiries of libraries across the land. She asked Putnam for a letter of recommendation. It was a remarkable recommendation, especially since it gave to Gratia all of the credit in creating the catalog, from which Putnam's own reputation had blossomed.

> December 1
>
> Dear Sir:
>
> . . . At the end of a year [Gratia Countryman] was made the head of the Cataloging Department; and that is the position she now holds. . . . She is one of the best workers I have ever seen: close, conscientious, exact, strenuous. Not content to be a mere worker, she is always a student. She sets herself to study the best methods in cataloguing as exhibited in the Boston Athenaeum and other catalogues; and she has brought to bear upon each new phase of her work whatever she has thus been gaining of critical insight. So that as her work developed, she has developed with it.
>
> In starting the Library, I had thought it would be necessary to import a trained cataloger. As Miss Countryman's fitness has been shown, I have been satisfied to rest the work with her. She is not yet a fully trained cataloger, but with further opportunities for study, she will become so. She will never stand still. And in entrusting to her the responsibility of the most highly technical if not the most important department of a library of 50,000 volumes, growing at the rate of 10,000 a year, I have felt safe. . . . Herbert Putnam, Librarian, Minneapolis Public Library

1892. Putnam was gone from Minneapolis. In fact, he settled in Boston with the intent of practicing law. The career was short-

"The Library Girls," 1892, posing in the art gallery: top row, Gratia Countryman; middle row, Lois Spear, Vera Dunlap, Katherine Patten; bottom row, Louise Lynskey (Mrs. Pierre Baucher), Clara Baldwin, Lina Brown (Mrs. F.W. Reed)
Source: Minneapolis Public Library, the Minneapolis Collection

lived, for in 1895 he would become librarian of the famed Boston Public Library.

Clichés are considered among the worst of literary devices, for they can be so dreadfully overused. Yet this overuse usually reflects the truism involved. In looking over the first quarter century of Gratia's life, a common cliché comes to mind: "Behind every great man there is a woman." For Gratia, the roles were reversed: "Behind this great woman there stands a man." Clearly, in the first twenty-five years of Gratia's life, the statement was eminently true—from Levi Countryman, to Cyrus Northrop, to Herbert Putnam. After that Miss Countryman was able to hold her own!

James Kendall Hosmer, the second librarian of the Minneapolis Public Library, arrived within a few months of Putnam's departure. Like Putnam, Hosmer was a Harvard graduate. Unlike Putnam, he was trained to be a Unitarian minister. Most of all, Hosmer was a scholar. It was said of him at the time and it is still said of him. In fact, during his tenure at the Minneapolis Public Library, he was so busy in scholarly research and writing, one wonders how much attention he gave to running the institution. The best that can be said of James Hosmer here is that he recognized talent and was quick to act. He created the position of assistant librarian and he appointed Gratia to fill it.

Under Hosmer and Countryman, the library began to emphasize fiction, directing more of its resources to purchasing novels. Closed stacks, the traditional hallmark of public libraries, were augmented by open shelves. A place for children's books was set aside and soon expanded into a children's room. The Northside Branch Library moved into a new building of its own, yet in the midst of this all, the library budget was dwindling. These were times of nationwide financial panic and the value of the city's property tax base was falling. Hosmer pleaded with the library board for additional funding, but T. B. Walker, the chairman, responded with lectures on fiscal responsibility, cost cutting, and salary reduction. The standoff persisted. Late in 1894, when Hosmer in frustration left town for an extended absence, Gratia took his place at the library board meetings. Even her winning ways could not resolve the financial crisis in any way favorable to the library administration. This was Gratia's first serious encounter with T. B. Walker—two fighters on opposite sides. Yet here was born their mutual respect, which would eventually evolve into an uncommon friendship.

1893. The Minnesota Library Association, founded two years previously by the librarians of eight major libraries in the state, was slowly developing an agenda. Gratia was secretary of the association, and the office provided a convenient catapult for her second evangelistic venture (if one could call military drill for women students the first such venture). The idea was one of statewide traveling libraries. Individual towns would pool their resources and together obtain sufficient funds to purchase a respectable collection of books. These books would travel in sections from one town to another. Gratia designed a promotional piece, had it circulated statewide, and she prevailed on a state representative to introduce a bill in the legislature. The bill died, but not the idea. Gratia had laid the seeds well.

1895. Early January marked the death of Royal Winchell Winchell, year-old son of Horace Winchell and his first cousin Ida Belle Winchell Winchell. The child had not been well since his birth, and there would never be a second child. When Gratia heard the news, she sat down and wrote her friend Etta: "Horace has lost his only child. To me it is a personal grief."[6]

Unhappy with the decline of morale at the library, demoralized over the lack of legislative support for the State Library Commission bill, and still unable to cast Horace out of her heart, Gratia simply wanted to leave town. But how to do it? Her first thought was to write to her loyal mentor, Herbert Putnam, the new director of the Boston Public Library. And so she did. His reply was as shrewd as it was candid.

24 South Irving St., Cambridge
February 22

Dear Miss Countryman,

If I had intended to dedicate much thought today to the memory to which the day belongs, I should have been frustrated by your note, for its contents have given me sincere concern. At this moment I can write little that would be of value to you in solving your problem, for I know little of the situation here, and what you tell me of the situation in Minneapolis surprises me.

Of course, my first impulse is to say you are indispensably needed where you are. And the safest guide for each one of us in his work is to place himself at the point of greatest effectiveness. That is my first impulse. But I am too ignorant of details to give any advice at all—except this: Contrive to come East as you propose. Contrive it at some sacrifice, if necessary, except the sacrifice of your relations with the Minneapolis Library. From whatever point of view nothing could be better than such a trip. And let the purpose of this trip be bounded by the trip and its training upon your work in Minneapolis. Do not, even to yourself, assume that there is or may be an ulterior purpose.

I would, if I were you, give careful thought to your program. Map out deliberately what you come to search for, and systematize in advance as far as possible. When you get so far in your preparations as to set a definite date for coming, send me word, and I will forward to you any introductions to the New York libraries that you think would be of service as coming from me (though I doubt not that any Dr. Hosmer may think to give you will be equally, if not more, serviceable). If you come to Boston, I will hold here my introductions until we meet.

How much I shall myself be able to see of you will of course depend on the particular pressure that may be on me at the time from my own work. But I hope that it may be much.

At all events you may depend upon a hearty welcome. Cordially yours, Herbert Putnam.

Miss Gratia Countryman: There is one advisor—both sound and kindly—I should think, whom you do not mention. Is not Presi-

> dent Northrop always ready to help? But of course you cannot go to him in matters of detail.

In March, Gratia asked for leave of absence from the library, with expenses, to study cataloging procedures in the New York and Boston libraries. (No doubt she also had a hidden agenda, as suggested earlier by Putnam.) The board denied the request.

1896. Frustrated by this failed effort to achieve a heightened independence, Gratia turned back to her own circle of friendships. The depth and breadth of women's friendships in the late nineteenth century was a phenomenon that had no equal in earlier history and that would fade in the twentieth century, once women were enfranchised. This phenomenon was driven by complex and often contradictory developments.

Beginning with the Civil War, women had indeed come out of the home and into the public sector. Through a growing number of charitable institutions, prosperous married women now devoted time and talent, as volunteers, to bring about social reforms. In addition, twenty percent of American women were in the paid work force, many of them working under impossible conditions in both agriculture and industry. And two-thirds of these women were single, having never married. The well-educated could choose among the uplifting occupations that had evolved earlier as the women's sphere, among them teaching, nursing, social work, and libraries. In all sectors, women earned half of what was paid to men. Single women worked together and they lived together—for economic survival, for emotional support, for intellectual stimulation, for recreation, and for intimacy. In these decades, theirs was indeed a separate sphere.

Well-educated, rebellious by nature, driven by economic need, and spurned by the only man she ever loved, Gratia

Countryman was pursuing this women's sphere with a vengeance.

Clara Baldwin of Delta Gamma days had followed Gratia to the Minneapolis Public Library. She was in all ways Gratia's loyal soldier. Over the next decade, at least four younger Delta Gamma sisters would join Clara and Gratia— Ruth Rosholt, Leonora Mann, Celia Frost, and Florence Livingston. No doubt Gratia recruited them all, knowing well the capabilities of each one. A century later, one might speak of a Delta Gamma "mafia" at the public library, for these women would become the department heads in the twentieth century. But at the time, one was perhaps less critical, for this was a "women's sphere."

As far back as the days of Company Q, Gratia and Clara operated as a team, at work as well as at play. The ultimate test of this friendship presented itself in the spring of 1896, when Gratia was seized by a magnificent vision—forget the library, forget the tug and pull of family responsibilities, escape with Clara for an entire summer! The idea soon evolved into plans for an elaborate adventure—travel by steamer to England, then bicycle through England and Scotland.

Women bicycling through the British Isles! It was a tantalizing idea, for bicycling had become the rage among young women of Gratia's kind. This favorite sport of America's New Woman required either shorter skirts or bloomer pants—both of which raised eyebrows in many circles. But most of all, bicycling meant freedom and an opportunity for exploring one's environment that had never been realized before.

This would be the ultimate in explorations, reasoned Gratia and Clara—to cruise freely through English country roads, each on her own two wheels. They would probe their cultural roots by visiting the shrines of English literature and history. And for dessert they would cross over to the continent—France, Germany, and Bayreuth, in Bavaria, for the most profound experience of all—Wagner's *Ring.*

In one way, this was a bad time to leave. Dr. Hosmer's position was in jeopardy, hence Gratia's own position as well. And Herbert Putnam, the dear, had come up with a probable future opening at the Boston Public Library, though the opportunity still required funding. The dream adventure was too far along to be abandoned in the face of uncertain options, so Gratia and Clara each applied for a summer leave, without pay, and the library board obliged. Wild with enthusiasm, each friend invited a friend. Gratia recruited another Delta Gamma sister, Clara Kellogg, and Clara Baldwin recruited a cousin, Clara Woodman—"The American Women's English Touring and Cycling Company Ltd., Miss Gratia Countryman, Personal Conductor."

But first there was the family in Minneapolis. Sister Lana and Charles Conger were finally married in a lovely family wedding. The bridal pair left immediately for Chicago, where Charles had a teaching position and where Lana hoped to find one. If Gratia regretted for a moment that her own marriage would never be, she rejoiced in the union of her dearest sister to the gentle, romantic classicist from her university days.

From Britain to Bayreuth

How good it did seem to get on our wheels again, and how magnificent the roads were. The drives around Lake Calhoun and the Kenwood Boulevard do not compare to the common country roads which we have been on all the way. You cannot think how beautiful it is to roll along those hard flint roads, with valleys and rolling country all around you; the roads curve around so as to suddenly reveal some beautiful perspective ahead of us. The trees are immense, and the fields and the sides of the roads are edged with the most beautiful hedges. England is just one huge bouquet everywhere we turn, and we get its full beauty riding on our wheels right through the country.

Gratia Countryman
June 28, 1896

1896. On June 15, Gratia Countryman and the three Claras sailed from New York on the German steamer Havel, bound for Southampton, England. The young women traveled second class, sharing a cabin furnished with two lower and two upper bunks. At first the sea was lively. One by one, the passengers succumbed to seasickness and deserted the decks. When the sea quieted, the promenade deck became the liveliest place of all. The little foursome of Anglo-Americans was dwarfed by a crowd of German-Americans on holiday, off to visit the old homeland. "Sunday on board wasn't observed very much. There was no service as is customary on steamers. I think there are too many German turnvereins [organizations of free-thinkers] on board. Last night they had a big dance instead of church, but our little crowd kept up on the promenade deck where the ocean was in sight all around and the moon making a long white track on the waves, and sang hymns."

So began Gratia in the first letter of the series that would cover in detail the three-month adventure. She would write faithfully at least twice a week, often in awe, sometimes in amusement, and always grateful for an education that allowed her to appreciate the historical and cultural significance of every experience. Usually after a hard day's bicycle ride, including detours to all manner of cathedrals, castles, abbeys, and cemeteries, Gratia would set on paper by candlelight at night pages and pages of commentary to "Mama and Papa," in letters to be passed on to the "library girls."

Almost a hundred years later, in 1994, these letters would be published in a single document and perhaps for the first time read together and appreciated as a remarkable chronicle of four "innocents" abroad.[9]

On June 22, Gratia and company arrived in England, in very high spirits.

> Southampton, England
> June 24
>
> ... About nine o'clock we came in sight of the lights of Southampton and were landed at the great Empress Docks. Then you just ought to have seen us get through the Custom House. We sat down to wait until our turn came, but we decided it would not come if we didn't hustle, so Clara B. and Clara K. sat down where we could find them, and Clara W. and I went behind the fence, fished our valises out of hundreds of others, buttonholed an officer, and had them put right through. By that time we couldn't find either of the other girls. They had scattered themselves all over the building. By the time we were collected again, we were so tickled at the way we had performed that we giggled like school girls. Then we hunted for a cabman, who grabbed up our four valises (big ones too) and started. Clara W. started after him, and soon both of them were out of sight and we had another grand scramble finding each other again. Mr. Campbell [the American travel agent] had been with us, and every time we four girls got ourselves together, he would be lost in the crowd. Finally, after a general scramble with Customs officers and cabmen, the five of us after an hour's time found ourselves together in a hack to Radley's Hotel. . . . Mr. Campbell was more rattled than anybody else, and we went into fits of laughter to think how green we were. The English maids tried to keep their faces straight, but they couldn't help smiling at us. To cap the climax, Mr. Campbell produced a coat which he must have either carried off the boat or picked up on the docks thinking it belonged to some of us, whose owner is now probably wondering where on earth his coat is, and at that we just went off and laughed till we cried.

The following morning, having politely shed Mr. Campbell, Gratia and the Claras began serious sightseeing. They visited St. Michael's church, the Norman Palace, and other survivors of the Norman Conquest, all of which Gratia detailed on paper for those back home. Then trunks were shipped ahead, and on a rare sunshiny morning the young ladies set off on their bicycle tour. Over several days, they cycled to Winchester, Salisbury, Glastonbury, Wells, Bath, and Oxford. Having met a young Oxford man enroute, they accepted his offer to show them around Oxford.

Oxford, England
July 5

. . . He . . . took us all over Corpus Christi College, in the dining hall, library, lecture rooms, and all around. Then he took us to some other places where we could not have gone unaccompanied by an Oxford student, and finally he asked us to go back to his room in the college and have some tea. Just think of taking tea in an Oxford student's room; not many American girls have the chance, unless they were previously acquainted. We felt very much honored. . . .

Then continuing north to Banbury, Compton, Stratford, Warwick, Kenilworth, and Coventry, each spot leaving Gratia awestruck, be it by the beauty of the countryside or the magnificence of the architecture. Gratia hadn't yet quite warmed to the people.

. . . I haven't seen a single nice-looking Englishwoman yet. They dress so badly, and their hair looks so untidy, so different from our natty, trim-looking American girls. England is beautiful as a country, and tremendously interesting, and the people are kind and courteous, but I feel very patriotic over here. I like·American best.

On to Chester and Liverpool, then into Wales for a stagecoach trip from Llandudno on the sea into the Welsh mountains, then cycling north to Windermere, Grasmere, and Wordsworth country.

Grasmere, England
July 19

. . . Today we scrambled up a long mountain to a little mountain lake or tarn, which used to be a favorite retreat of

Wordsworth, and there, with the mountains all about us, we sat and read and talked. Easedale tarn, they call it, but it isn't so easy to reach.

North into Scotland—Carlisle and Dumfries, where tens of thousands were gathered to celebrate the centenary of Bobby Burns's death.

Dumfries, Scotland
July 22

... We tried to find lodgings, but every place was full. We had about decided that we would have to go to a crowded hotel when a nice-looking man asked us what we were looking for. I answered that we were hunting for lodgings ... He looked puzzled for a few minutes, then he said, 'Well, we don't take people to board, but if you will come home with me, I think my wife can arrange with you.' ... So we walked along with him, wondering why we were always so fortunate, and why everybody took such especial pains to take care of us. In fact we were almost too astonished to speak, when he took us into a beautiful little house and his wife just trotted around to wait on us. They are nice people from all appearances, and have taken four complete strangers into their little gem of a home out of sheer kindness. ... Just think of Papa finding four bicyclers in short dresses, who were evidently foreigners, and bringing them from the street corners down in town out to our house to stay all night and stay to dinner and breakfast, without consulting Mama, or asking for a guarantee of their respectability. ... I tell you, I never have seen such hospitality as we have had shown us ever since we first stepped foot in England.

On to Old Cumnock, Ayr, Kilmarnock, Fenwick, and Glasgow. It was just a month from the time Gratia and the three Clara's had wheeled away from Southampton.

Glasgow, Scotland
July 25

> . . . These people up here in Scotland find no end of amusement in us. There are not many lady bicyclists up here, and we in our short skirts and high wheels are stared at continually. We find it quite unpleasant to ride through the streets of any town, for the people stop all along the street and look at us, and sometimes they laugh and call out to us. If we happen to dismount, we soon have a big crowd collected all around us. One nice old Scotchman told us that the simple people didn't know any better and that they meant to be civil. I think he is right, they are only very curious about us, and are not well bred enough to hide it. The same people are ready to do anything on earth for us.
>
> We rode on up as far as Kilmarnock—a big manufacturing town of about 28,000. The people were just coming out of the factories as we came to town and they lined up 10 or 12 deep on both sides all the way up the streets. All business and traffic stopped in the city till we had ridden through. We braved it out, however, and rode to the Burns monument and museum, which was what we came to see.

Then by bicycle, steamer and train east to Edinburgh, where the hospitality surpassed all earlier experiences and where history was so alive as to expect John Knox or Mary, Queen of Scots, to come wandering around any corner. Gratia also noted that the United States man-of-war *Minneapolis* was docked at the Firth of Forth bridge.

Time was running short, for the young ladies had tickets for the Wagner Festival in Bayreuth, Germany. Hence on the journey down the east coast of England, the bicycles and the bicyclists traveled by train. Visits to three cathedrals, each a masterpiece of architecture, were a must—Durham, York, and Lincoln. For Gratia, Durham was the queen of them all.

Lincoln, England
August 9

. . . I am afraid I might just as well not try to describe these last three cathedrals. I feel so inadequate to it. When I tell you that Durham is 510 feet long, and that you can see from one end straight down the nave through the choir to the great east window, and that the nave is almost all Norman, just as it was built by William the Conqueror, with great massive piers supporting the roof, beautiful doorways, and the ornamental iron doors, which have swung for eight centuries. When I tell you this and much more, I haven't made you see it. I think Durham made more impression on me than any other [cathedral] . . . so massive, [it] makes one feel that it will endure through all time. As we sat in the back of the nave and saw the choir boys move in slow processional into the choir, and the organ start the echoes resounding back and forth, I think it would have stirred the stoniest heart.

By and by the American cycling tourists arrived in London, spent the night at a boardinghouse at Russell Square and Woburn Place, then on August 12 traveled by train to Harwich on the coast, boarded a steamer, and crossed the English Channel to Antwerp, Belgium. From there they traveled by train through Brussels to Cologne, Germany, for the journey up the Rhine River.

Bayreuth, Bavaria
August 16

. . . You've heard of the "Castled Rhine"—almost every eminence along the banks and almost every jutting crag is crowned with a castle, some in ruins and some in repair. Almost every one is so old that its origin and builder are lost in tradition. We carried with us a book of Rhine legends and read the legends connected with each one as we passed them. You will be familiar with some of them—as the Drachenfels, where Siegfried killed the dragon, and the Lorelei, where the golden-haired Rhine maiden lured the boatmen onto the rocks, and the Mousetower at Bingen. There are just dozens of these castles, any one of which would have excited us terribly when we first came over. We can keep a little more calm than we could at first.

On to Nürnberg and finally Bayreuth for a week of performances that encompassed Richard Wagner's entire *Ring.*

Bayreuth, Bavaria
August 19

. . . The last evening of the festival is over. I hope you've seen good criticisms of it in the paper, for I cannot tell you about it. I have no language to tell you the wonder of such heaven-born music. I cannot even tell you about the magical stage scenery. Everybody I have seen here, from London, New York, or anywhere, says there never has been anything seen like it. Wagner has so successfully combined poetry and music and artistic scenery, and this Bayreuth festival has carried out in every detail the whole of Wagner's bold ideal. . . . The entire story of the *Nibelungen Lied* has been presented, a part each night, so that from day to day we have lived along with the story as it grew. . . . The concerts have lasted from 4 P.M. to 10 P.M. with two short intermissions for lunch. Where but in Germany would it be possible to carry out such a musical festival; but one could sit longer yet for their kind of music and to hear such superb voices and orchestra. But I started to speak of the crowd—every nation in Europe represented, and almost all languages heard. All music-loving people, with animated, intelligent faces. Indeed it was quite a remarkable sea of faces. I never saw just such a crowd before—nothing's common whatever about it.

After all of this, Paris was actually a disappointment to Gratia, except that it was comfortable to hear so much of the American language being spoken on the streets. Back to London, and finally a leisurely week touring the heart of Anglo-Saxon government and culture.

Lincoln, England
August 30

. . . When we touched English shores yesterday, we felt that we had come home again, and the beauty of England struck us almost as forcibly as it did at first. We have been in no country so beautiful as England. When we were in Belgium, the lack of trees was noticeable. . . . In Germany there were great pine forests, beautifully cared for, looking as if they were as carefully cultivated as the hops or grapevines, but no beautiful large shade trees—such as are everywhere in England. When we left Paris, the trees were bare of their leaves, and there was scarcely any greenness anywhere, but the moment we struck England, everything was as luxuriantly green out in the country as it was in the early summer. We just rejoiced at being in England, it is the <u>prettiest</u> country I ever saw.

But now it was time for Gratia to think of family, of home, of the library, and of her future there. Her last letter from London hinted at uncertainties, but along with these an increased sense of her own potential. If things didn't work out in Minneapolis, other avenues were open. Gratia had always known there was the larger world out there. At last she had seen it for herself.

London, England
September 3

My dear ones,

Louise Lynskey has just written me there is a rumor that three of the library directors have gone off to the Library Conference to choose a new librarian. I suspect that it is only a rumor, but Papa would better watch the matter a little if he has a chance. I have told Louise L. to meet me with a letter in New York to tell me if anything happens, but I am not worrying about it at all. If by chance they should take a move so detrimental to Dr. Hosmer and myself, it would affect very much the answer I make to Mr. Putnam this fall. I am sorry you told Emma Maes about Mr. Putnam's offer. I don't want it known, and Mr. Putnam wouldn't want it known that there is a vacancy there [in the Boston Public Library]. Don't say anything to anyone about library matters. It would be better to detach the personal sheets on my letters, for fear they may be read. . . . Yours lovingly, Gratia Countryman.

On September 16, leaving the bicycles behind, Gratia and the three Clara's boarded the North German Lloyd steamer *S.S. Lahn* at Southampton.

On Board *S.S. Lahn*
Tuesday P.M., September 22

My dear ones,

. . . We have had a very rough passage, heavy sea and strong winds. Everybody on board has been sick. Even the sailors and our stewardess couldn't eat. It is needless to say that we were all sick. Clara B., however, crawled out on deck every morning. I kept my berth all day Thursday and Friday, but Saturday I crawled out and sat in the only dry corner there was on deck. All that day and all day Sunday the ship stood first on one end and then on the other, looking as if it fully intended to dive to the bottom.

The waves washed over the deck, even over the promenade deck, in great style, and the ocean stood up like a great wall around us. I tell you, I'm glad I saw the ocean look like that. Nothing could be more magnificent than a stormy ocean, churned into monstrous billows, but we had perfect confidence in this little ship, it is one of the very best on this line. . . .

We girls have been sitting here thinking of the good things we will have to eat when we get home. Baked potatoes just make our mouths water, and scrambled eggs and pancakes and cornbread and groats and pumpkin pie, and all the other good things that Americans know how to cook and no other nation does. Don't you think you can get me up a good meal out of the list? I've got to have baked potatoes anyhow. I'm so hungry I don't know how I'll ever get filled again. I've been fasting, you see, for nearly a week, and my thoughts will run on things to eat.

Hurrah for home; it's a jolly good place, and I'm terribly anxious to hug you both. Will telegraph in New York. Yours, Gratia Countryman.

Clearly the trip abroad had awakened a new confidence in this assistant librarian at the public library. Gratia's vision of traveling libraries had ripened during the months abroad. What was required was a new state institution to be the vehicle for bringing public libraries to every corner of the state. No doubt plans and strategies had been developed by candlelight in quaint English pensions, for when Gratia and Clara Baldwin returned to the library, they were on an evangelistic roll. With the support of the Minnesota Library Association, the two young librarians embarked on an ambitious speaking circuit, reaching out to women's clubs well beyond the metropolitan area. It was heady work at a propitious time when it came to women's political awareness.

It would be another twenty-three years before the U.S. Constitution guaranteed women the right to vote. In 1896, the idea was still considered controversial. But by a quirk of history, the women of Minnesota had since 1876 the right to vote in school board elections and to hold office on school boards. In fact, Horace Winchell's mother had been elected to and served eloquently on the Minneapolis School Board in its infancy. But as yet the privilege did not extend to women when it came to library boards. The Minneapolis Public Library Board consisted of three elected men and three ex officio members—the mayor, the president of the state university, and the president of the Minneapolis School Board. Thus in 1896, Jennie Crays, first woman president of the Minneapolis School Board, became an ex officio member of the library board with full voting rights—the first woman member of a board to which women were not permitted to be elected.

The absurdity of it all had begun to sink in with the public at large, and it strengthened the enthusiasm of women in general for the "little girl with the blond curls." Her upbeat message—seldom castigating but sometimes cajoling, even flattering, and always optimistic—was hard to resist. At this moment, Gratia's mission was the creation of a State Library Commission. (In the twentieth century, it would take other forms: The Library Division, the Office of Public Libraries and Interlibrary Cooperation, and finally the Office of Library Development and Services.) Always the mission would have as its heart the creation and support of libraries throughout the state of Minnesota.

1897. This was the legislative session when passage of the State Library Commission bill seemed assured. The women's organizations of Minnesota rallied, among all parties there was political support, and Gratia virtually camped out in the legislative hallways. But of all the men who had crossed Gratia's path, opposition came from the most unlikely of them all. Ignatius Donnelly, the Sage of Nininger, once a U. S. congressman and always a politician, was now an elected member of the state legislature, and as a populist representative, he wielded great power. This man who forty years earlier had been the inspiration of Levi Countryman turned out to be the nemesis of Levi's daughter Gratia. Almost single-handedly Donnelly engineered the defeat of the State Library Commission bill. Donnelly's Pyrrhic victory would turn out to be his last hurrah, however, for he never again stood for election.

Nevertheless, changes came rapidly. The 1897 legislature proposed an amendment to the state constitution, giving women the right to vote in library board elections, as well as to hold library board office. The amendment was ratified by popular vote in the 1898 general election. And the 1899 state legislature finally enacted the law to create a Minnesota State Library Commission.

What began as "traveling libraries" would eventually evolve into a statewide network of libraries and shared library resources, a legacy that continues to expand and thrive almost a century later, though under other names as the decades march on. Wrote Dr. Hosmer in his 1899 annual report:

Gratia and her siblings, 1901: from left to right,
Lana, Amplius, Gratia, Theophilus
Source: Virginia Buffington Shaw

> As regards this Commission, the establishment of which is a good forward step for our state, it should be said that it has come to pass through the work of the women of the state, and in the forefront of the leaders from the beginning of the effort some years since has stood Miss Gratia Countryman, my chief assistant. By labor with the legislature, by lectures about the state, by interviews with people likely to have influence, by writing for the press, Miss Countryman, more than anyone else, has carried the thing through to a successful issue.

Gratia Countryman was appointed to the first commission and elected secretary. One of the initial commission acts was to appoint Clara Baldwin librarian. Gratia's second great missionary venture had succeeded in all respects!

Family Obligations

> *. . . I am still young and like company, and like to have interests outside of my work, and I have had many a lonely attack in the last five years when I would have bartered my career quick for a home of my own, which I could have to do as I pleased with and filled with friends if I wanted to. Don't you realize why I've worked so hard the last few years and why I've spread my work out beyond this library? Why, because every unmarried woman has to fill the hole some way, and that was my way.*
>
> Gratia Countryman,
> February 27, 1900

1900. These were good times in Gratia's life, perhaps the best times since she had finished the university. Besides the public recognition, there were other events to buoy her spirit. First of all, Horace and Ida Belle were no longer neighbors at home. Horace's growing reputation had landed him a position as geologist for the Anaconda Copper Mining Company, necessitating a move to Butte, Montana. Oddly enough, the Winchell departure had lifted a weight, so to speak. Gratia even found new joy in her old Delta Gamma friendships with Ima and Avis Winchell and even little Louise, who had married one of the Winchell house student boarders, David Draper Dayton. Dayton was now the new young man in Minneapolis affairs, a forward-looking, energetic businessman who was about to build a "department" store on Nicollet Avenue downtown. The venture was to be a family affair—only relatives as investors. But hadn't Gratia come close to being a relative? Dayton invited her to buy stock in the venture. Gratia was flattered, but she declined. (In later years, she would tell the story with relish, for D. Draper Dayton and his descendants became retail store magnates, and the Dayton Company one of the most influential institutions in the community.)

Lana and Charles Conger were now parents of a small daughter, a beautiful child of two years, her name—Constance. With large blue-gray eyes, a perfectly oval face, and dark hair, she was the image of her handsome father. The Congers were living outstate in Minnesota, Charles teaching school and Lana trying to make ends meet on his meager salary. The benefit of the situation was its proximity to Minneapolis and the maintaining of family ties, so important to Levi—and to Gratia. That Constance promptly became "Auntie's" pet came as no surprise to anyone.

On Gratia's urging, Levi had resigned his position with the Pitts Agricultural Company—twenty years of work that he did not really like, while living out of hotels, plagued with recurring asthma, and always longing for home and children. Levi was to receive a modest pension; he intended to supplement it with some sort of independent venture. At sixty-eight years, he was ready to start again, and what could be better for this man of the soil than a fruit farm out west!

Alta Countryman, Gratia's mother, was simply worn out—a lifetime of frugality and immensely hard work. She lacked both the education and the energy to seek out and enjoy a world of the mind—her husband's domain, which he had hammered into his children, especially his daughters. With Levi away, Alta had managed the building of the large Countryman home in Minneapolis, and with the often inconsistent support of her daughters she had managed the home now for twenty years. Over all these years, a constant stream of outsiders had populated the premises—relatives, paying boarders, Gratia's university friends, and other house guests—and for all of his good resolutions to the contrary, Levi was prone to lean hard on Alta—piety and frugality—while quick to forgive his daughters.

Levi and Alta were on the West Coast for the winter, hoping to settle there permanently. Levi's dream now was to be a farmer—a fruit farmer—and never again to have to taste a Minnesota winter. But what about the house in Minneapolis? Through the winter, Gratia was living there alone. But that didn't work for Levi; he needed to lease out the premises for income. This meant Gratia would lease the building from Levi, keep two rooms for herself, and rent out the other rooms to help meet the monthly payment to Father. Thus Levi would have an income and Gratia would have a place to live. Eventually, reasoned Levi, Gratia would find a library position in the West so that at least part of the family could be together again. And since Gratia, too, was dreaming of a country farm, father and daughter would be partners. Intellectually it was a fine idea for the elderly Countrymans, but Gratia simply didn't buy it.

February 27

My dear Father:

. . . To tell the truth, Father, I don't want you to be discouraged out there [in California]. You know well enough that you aren't well here and Mother isn't well, and you both seem to be well and strong out there. There must be good desirable places out there, which you will run across in time. And, my dear father, I wish you wouldn't think of it as a paying investment, out of which you will make money. If you get into a beautiful little place where surroundings are pleasant and which will yield you and Mother enough to live on, not to lay up, and where you can be well and happy the rest of your days, and where we won't need to worry about you, I shall be very happy. . . .

The plan [to lease the family home] doesn't attract me. I have lived long enough in a place where I have to depend on the streetcar and freeze on street corners, and where I am virtually a prisoner after my long day at work, unable to go anywhere because of no one to go with and away off from everything. I am looking forward to living near my work, and near the friends of these later years. . . . Perhaps this may seem like a complaint, but you see, Papa, I am still young and like company, and like to have interests outside of my work, and I have had many a lonely attack in the last five years when I would have bartered my career quick for a home of my own, which I could have to do with as I pleased and filled with friends if I wanted to. Don't you realize why I've worked so hard the last few years and why I've spread my work out beyond this library? Why, because every unmarried woman has to fill the hole some way, and that was my way. Now, I feel the need of seeing people, of touching the live questions of the day, of knowing what people think. I cannot work all day and study or read all the evening. It is making a cranky old maid, an old bookworm, out of me, and I've got to stop it or go into dry rot. . . .

On the other hand, I really hope I may go to California, too, and make a country home for myself, and I am hoping that you and Mother will find a satisfactory place in the course of time.

I want you to do, however, just what seems wise to you. . . . If you and Mother think it best to come back here, I shall be only too glad to have you with me, and I hope to be with you anyway, there or here. . . . Lots of love, Gratia Countryman.

Nevertheless, Gratia did bow to her father's will and agree to stay in southeast Minneapolis, leasing the residence from her father.

April 29

My dear Father:

... I am going to be a financier with you since you called me a poor one.... I do not feel like furnishing up with things that are of permanent value to the house, like fixtures, gas range, etc., without deducting it from the rent. I feel sure that you and Mother will be back here to live by another spring.... The pipes are leaking downstairs, one of the pipes from the furnace is badly rusted. I will see that everything is in good shape and kept up, but as I said before, I think that I shall have to deduct it. Please tell me what you think?

You know I am very different from you in one regard. I like an artistic abiding place. I want my home to be just as much a delight to the eyes as possible—an expression, so far as possible, of the inner life of the inhabitants. In other words, the appearance means a great deal to me, not for what outsiders may think of it, but because I enjoy it and it is a legitimate enjoyment.

You may call it extravagance. I call it living. We will probably never come to the same point of view, and it is useless to do much arguing. It remains my intention, however, to beautify and adorn the place where I must live as far as I am able....

Father, Mr. Babcock is in Berkeley as a professor. He writes me of a $1,200 position in the University Library there. I would enquire into it if you had expressed any desire to stay in California. You can readily imagine that the position (which is head cataloger) could have no attraction for me when I have twice refused the Head Librarianship of Nebraska University at $1,360. I do not care for college work. If you think there is the smallest chance of your staying there, or if your views of California would change if I were coming, and you want me to enquire further into it, I will do it. I some way don't have any idea that you will stay there. I am not sure that you should. You and Mother could go away and spend many a cold winter for what you would pay for a farm.... So good night, Father. Don't get any more homesick than you can help, for you shall come back where you can scold me and call me bad names if you like. Lovingly, your daughter, Gratia Countryman.

July 28
Public Library, Minneapolis

My dear Father:

. . . I have just been out to lunch and it is very warm to go to work. I am taking life very easy just at present. I just think all I can. Dr. Hosmer takes a nap every day and is out at the Lake [Minnetonka] every evening, so I think it is my privilege to save my energy a little also.

You wrote very kindly about the farm, and I think we can make satisfactory arrangements, but my idea is to pay you for it. If I really possess it, even if it takes me some time to do it. And you needn't worry about treating the children unequally, for none of them will ever have occasion to quarrel with me about money matters.

I suppose I really do think a farm is a sort of plaything, or rather a recreation. If I intended to make my living off of it, I would want to buy a good-sized farm and go right on it, but I want to stay in the library and have only a large enough place to pay for itself and yield a comfortable existence every summer. And I do not want you to work it, except for your own pleasure and exercise. I wouldn't have a large farm, for you would want to do everything you could, and if you and Mother don't spend your declining days happily and at your ease, it won't be my fault. . . . Yours lovingly, Gratia Countryman.

Portland, Oregon
October 8

Dear daughter Gratia,

. . . Now Gratia darling. I don't want you to get over that "habit" of writing to me because Mother has got home. You do not write more than enough, although your duties are doubtless very arduous in one way and another.

I note with a good deal of interest your description of the Gideon farm at Excelsior [on Lake Minnetonka, home of the Gideon apple]. Somehow I had got a notion of that as being what we wanted in about every particular. Still I note that you say she has withdrawn the place from the market, which may be just as well for the time being. There is a great deal of land about Minnetonka that is very poor soil, sandy, etc., and so far as that is con-

> cerned, it is altogether undesirable. Poor soil is a poor investment. We will look matters over further when I get back home. . . .
>
> I cut out from the *[Saint Paul] Pioneer Press* a little article on libraries. Is it true that there is serious opposition to the traveling libraries? And is Mr. Hosmer arrayed against it? I see that you are left out of the Secretaryship this year. Is not this the same organization? What is the reason that a wish to discourage traveling libraries is prevalent, and what are the traveling libraries now accomplishing? . . .
>
> Please let me hear from you in full. . . . I remain affectionately your father and friend, L. N. Countryman.

But the sought-after farm would never become a reality, at least not in the lifetime of either Levi or Alta Countryman.

Marie Todd

> *Yes, dear one, such love as has been given us must be kept high and fine. I feel humble before it, like lifting it high, lest it trail in the dust perchance.*
>
> Gratia to Marie Todd
> December 1901

1901. Marie Annette Todd, just twenty-four years old, was the children's librarian at the Minneapolis Public Library, the first one to head a department exclusively devoted to children. She was a beautiful young woman—tall, slim, green-eyed and straight-backed, with long, red hair shaped into bun and softened by natural waves about her face, an elegant presence wherever she went. She had worked her way through the university by substituting nights and Sundays at the library. On her graduation, Dr. Hosmer had appointed Marie to this new permanent position. One cannot imagine that his assistant did not also have a say in the matter.

What a contrast there was between these two women—gentle Marie, floating serenely through the hallways and stacks, while the pugnacious assistant librarian bobbed in and out of the library spaces, spreading wit and wonder in her wake. And yet—

Dear love of mine,

This is the first Christmas we have known each other, though you were here in Minneapolis last year and I could see you every day. It is very different, isn't it? This Christmas I am very near you, though you are miles away. It is strange and hard to comprehend this beautiful relationship between us. I hope it is bringing joy to you, this Christmastide.

Some beautiful thing has been born in us, which grows more beautiful as it grows in vigor and strength. It is not only a deep emotion—a singing heart—but it is a motion power. We call it love—a divine thing.

Into this world, on the anniversary we are celebrating, was born the Incarnation of love, represented in a little child who has become the great motion power through the centuries.

May we, too, as the shepherds who saw the angelic vision, with rejoicing hearts, make our pilgrimage to this divine child and give him our most precious gift.

Beloved, love is the supreme good, and a great love has entered my soul. It has made me face myself and desire to root out unselfishness and all unkindness and impatience. It has made me desire the spirit of this Christ within.

Whether thee has received as much through loving as I have, I do not know. But whether or not, I have had my great joy in giving love.

Thee says in a letter just received that thee is staking everything on the chance of being with me, and I know thee is coming for love's sake. But not staking, dear, there is no gamble in loving, there are only profits even if earthly joy and happiness did not follow.

Yes, dear one, such love as has been given us must be kept high and fine. I feel humble before it, like lifting it high, lest it trail in the dust perchance.

> Oh dear heart, I pray that whatever sacrifices thee may be making, thee will feel rewarded by the love I shall always be giving thee—a love born of the spirit of love. This is my Christmas wish for us, that love may be a transforming power within us, and that our love may be a part of the great fountain of love in God's Universe.

So wrote Gratia Countryman to Marie Todd shortly before Christmas in the year 1901.

1902. Marie Todd and Gratia Countryman took up residence together, in a flat on North Lyndale Avenue rather close to the public library. They would live together as family until Marie's death in 1940.

The Countryman home in southeast Minneapolis was vacated and leased out to others. Levi and Alta were in California, this first year in the city of Ontario. Daughter Lana, with little Constance in tow, had taken up residence there, her marriage to Charles Conger having come to an end. The final denouement occurred in Leadville, Colorado. There Charles was eking out a living by teaching school, while Lana took in boarders to make ends meet. Where Charles was happy-go-lucky, impractical, and generous, Lana was at least as bright, very intense, and prone to a biting tongue. These incompatibilities had doomed the marriage in just five years. Yet Lana would always love Charles. She kept his name and wore his ring the rest of her life.[10]

As a student at Hastings High School, Gratia Countryman once presented an essay on the necessity of a woman to have a profession.[11] Twenty years later, Lana Countryman Conger became a case in point. With her university education, her classics major, and a talent for languages, Lana embarked on a most satisfying career—teacher of high school Latin to two generations of California students. At the same time, she provided daughter Constance not only with a happy childhood, but with one enriched far beyond the norm. What else should one expect from a daughter of Levi Countryman?

About the same time as the Conger divorce, the marriage of Gratia's brother Theophilus—Offie, later Theo—also disintegrated. Theo had worked at Cripple Creek, Colorado, for a decade—almost since the beginning of gold exploration there. He was in the fields most of the year as private consultant and government assayer. It was an exciting, dangerous, and at times extremely lucrative profession, but not conducive to family life. A decade of this was enough for his wife Ada. On her own, she sold the Denver family home and took their three children to Oakland, California. Later, in his memoirs, Theo would write: "I met them in Denver in the latter part of June, said goodbye to all, and did not see them again for nearly a year." Though he would occasionally visit Ada and the children in California, the family ties had been permanently weakened.

All of this is to say that from 1902 forward, Gratia would consider the fates of sister Lana, niece Constance, brother Theo, and Marie her personal responsibility, and she would act accordingly.

In perusing the many surviving papers of Gratia Countryman, one catches glimpses of her private acts of charity—acts not recorded in annual reports, newspaper articles, or support material for the many honors and rewards she would later receive. Glimpses of Gratia's commitment to higher education—a modest stipend to a needy student here and there—come through mention in a thank you letter or listing in an account book. Gratia's friend Etta would later say that these students were at least twenty-five in number, over many years, this in addition to scholarship money that Gratia regularly channeled through her Delta Gamma fraternity.

But nowhere in the material is there a written record of Gratia Countryman as a personal protector of the weak and vulnerable. Yet such acts were legion in the long life of this woman, partly because she was in a position of power. Take for example, Mabel Bartleson.

Late in the year, Mabel Bartleson was hired by Gratia Countryman as a library assistant at the Minneapolis Public Library. Miss Bartleson's resumé read exceedingly well for a woman of that time—native Minneapolitan, elementary public school, a private secondary school in Duluth, and two years at Wellesley College in Massachusetts. Yet, when Miss Bartleson appeared at the Minneapolis Public Library, she might as well have worn a scarlet letter on her blouse, for she was indeed a marked woman, and through no fault of her own. For the next thirty-four years, as long as Gratia Countryman wielded authority, it was forbidden at the Minneapolis Public Library to mention—on pain of dismissal—what every employee knew to be the truth: Back in 1894, Mabel Bartleson had been courted by Harry Hayward![12]

The story went something like this. In 1894, the Minneapolis Public Library stood at the edge of the central city, where a fine old residential neighborhood was giving way to substantial apartment flats. Three blocks beyond, on Hennepin Avenue, were the Ozark Flats, an elegant multiple-family building, and here lived Harry Hayward, twenty-nine-year-old bachelor and man about town. Affable and well spoken, he often lunched at the West Hotel with the city's best lawyers and bankers. Seemingly prosperous and impeccable in dress, on first look Harry appeared to be a fine candidate as husband for the daughters of men such as these.

And such as these included Lawyer Charles Bartleson, Illinois native, Civil War veteran, member of the Minneapolis Club, the Commercial Club, the Minnetonka Yacht Club, and so on. Mr. Bartleson lived with his wife, daughter Mabel, and two younger daughters in an older home across Hennepin Avenue and very near the public library. At 8:00 on the evening of December 3, Harry Hayward knocked on the Bartleson door, to pick up Mabel for a performance at Minneapolis's Grand

Opera House. Harry was well acquainted with Mr. Bartleson and not unknown in the household. One can imagine that all three girls welcomed such a handsome figure. Mabel, then twenty-one years old, was the shiest of the three. She dressed demurely for the event, bid a pleasant good evening to her father, and with Harry proceeded down Hennepin Avenue to the theater. It was to be an 8:30 P.M. performance of the popular musical "A Trip to Chinatown." Harry was in a particularly sociable mood that evening, almost embarrassing his companion during the intermission by introducing her to everyone in sight. At 10:30 the musical was over, and Harry gallantly conducted Mabel back to her home. No doubt Mr. Bartleson had waited up until his daughter was safely under the family roof.

What occurred that night during the performance of "A Trip to Chinatown" was the murder of a young woman, Kitty Ging, while she drove a carriage along Lake Calhoun Boulevard—a carriage rented earlier that day at the West Hotel. The culprit: one Claus Blixt, the alcoholic janitor at the Ozark Flats, where Kitty Ging also lived. But that was not all, for this tragedy turned out to be a murder for hire, with Harry Hayward the perpetrator of the scheme. The Hayward murder trial became the most celebrated trial in nineteenth-century Minneapolis. Harry was convicted and executed by hanging; Claus Blixt went to prison for life; and Mabel Bartleson went into seclusion, vowing never to show her face again on the streets of Minneapolis.

Mabel was sent down to Illinois, to her father's people. There she lived for several years and eventually entered the work force in a Chicago railway agency. But wounds do heal, and by 1902 she dared enter the library in the neighborhood of her tragic past. Thanks to Gratia Countryman, Mabel Bartleson would have a comfortable career at the public library—mostly behind the scenes, for she truly did not wish to meet the public. In later years, she would become liaison to school libraries, working among children who had never heard of Harry Hayward. And when Gratia Countryman, in 1935, put on her own birthday party for the entire library staff, the reclusive Miss Bartleson asked for the privilege of presenting accolades on behalf of the staff. It would be the only public speaking appearance (and hardly public) in her long, sheltered life.

The Scramble for a Chief Librarian

Never mind, Girlie—you'll show them yet . . .
Clara Baldwin to Gratia Countryman
November 10, 1903

1903. It had long been expected, and now it came to pass. Dr. Hosmer submitted his resignation as librarian of the Minneapolis Public Library. He wished to devote full time to his scholarly historical research, especially his two-volume Civil War history, which was already well on the way. As fine a man as Hosmer seems to have been, there was not a great deal of community regret over his leaving. Hosmer's era was marked by stagnation when it came to the growth of the system. In fact, there was an actual drop in circulation, in spite of exploding population growth in Minneapolis. Along the way, the board had seen fit to reduce Hosmer's annual salary from $4,000 to $3,000. Clearly the message had gotten through to the librarian.

On the other side, Hosmer's assistant librarian—Gratia—finally completed the library catalog, almost 150,000 volumes. For this reason alone, the Countryman name could not be ignored in the search for Hosmer's successor. Yet she, too, carried some of Hosmer's stigma. He had turned over to her virtually all of his duties; yet she lacked the authority to pursue them aggressively.

From the moment of Hosmer's announcement, the search —in Gratia's case, the campaign—was on. Promoting her name was an entire circle of women and men in the city and beyond. This plucky young woman, who always looked a decade younger than her years, seemed to attract supporters wherever she went. She was now president of both the Minnesota Library Association and the Minnesota Library Commission. It would not be easy to ignore Gratia Countryman.

Cyrus Northrop, as university president and ex officio member of the library board, was one of the first to pledge his support, though in a thoroughly discreet manner:

> March 12
>
> Miss Gratia Countryman, City
>
> My dear Miss Countryman:
>
> I congratulate you most heartily upon the passage of a bill through the House providing for a $10,000 annual appropriation [for the Minneapolis Library]. You are entitled to all the credit, and I rather think you will get it.
>
> As to the matters referred to especially in your letter, I see no cause for anxiety, and I doubt not in due time everything will work out for the best. I am sure you can afford to let matters take their course without any very great anxiety. Very truly yours, Cyrus Northrop.

The library board had appointed a search committee headed by Jacob Stone, an elected member of the board who made no apology for his conviction that the chief librarian should be a man. His first act as chairman, therefore, was to turn for advice to Minneapolis's first librarian, Herbert Putnam. Putnam now held the supreme library position in the United States, that of Librarian of Congress. In answer to Stone's initial query, Putnam replied:

> April 25
>
> . . . I have your note of the 22nd. I have a very clear opinion as to what your Board ought to do: it is to elect Miss Countryman li-

> brarian. If I am not mistaken (though my knowledge is only hearsay), she has been the actual though not the titular head of the administrative work of the Library for some years past. She has education, energy, system, and plenty of initiative. She keeps in touch with experiments in other libraries for the promotion of their usefulness. She knows Minneapolis and its needs; she knows your Library; she knows every member of the force, his capacities, and his defects.
>
> She is a woman, and if your Board is determined to have a man, she must be excluded; but such a determination seems to me unfair and by no means in the interest of the Library. Unfair, because it is unfair to accept from a woman a man's service and not give her the salary and the title which go with that service. Against the interest of the Library, because I doubt whether for $3,000 you can get a man who will do better than she. You might get a man of wider experience, for she has never lived outside Minneapolis; but against the width of his general experience would be the extent of her practical and local knowledge. . . . Faithfully yours, Herbert Putnam, The Library of Congress, Office of the Librarian, Washington.

The search committee, at least Jacob Stone, pursued the matter further with Putnam, who subsequently put forth the name of George Franklin Bowerman, a graduate of the New York State Library School and a man with extensive library experience. The committee contacted Bowerman, interviewed him, and agreed that he would make an excellent chief librarian. Whatever the merits of George Bowerman, local consensus did not rule out the possibility of a woman as chief librarian.

There were two issues that raged about the community all through the summer. And one of the issues was not whether the chief librarian ought to be a woman. Rather the discussion centered on an appropriate salary for a woman; that is, ought a woman command the princely sum of $3,000 annually, which Hosmer had earned? The other issue was a choice between *two* women, both of whom encouraged their names to be put forward—Gratia Countryman and Letitia Crafts—and each of whom commanded a base of support.

Letitia Crafts had graduated from the university a year earlier than Gratia, with a bachelor of literature degree. Like Gratia, she was a member of Phi Beta Kappa. Following graduation, Miss Crafts went to work for the university library and rose to be assistant librarian. Like Gratia, she was a founding member of the Minnesota Library Association. And unlike Gratia, Miss Crafts had taken special library courses at the University of Wisconsin and at Harvard. In 1900, the first year that women could vote for and hold office on a public library board, Miss Crafts was elected to the Minneapolis board by an overwhelming majority of voters. Letitia Crafts was indeed a viable competitor for the much-coveted position of chief librarian.

The scramble was finally sorted out at a board meeting on November 6, to which the committee brought three names—George Bowerman, Gratia Countryman, and Letitia Crafts. The committee's favored candidate was Mr. Bowerman.

Noting a lack of consensus, board president T. B. Walker proposed going into executive session, with which the board concurred. A straw vote was taken—four votes for Miss Countryman, three for Mr. Bowerman, and two for Miss Crafts. Now it was time for speeches. One of Gratia's supporters spoke eloquently on her behalf. Then Jacob Stone presented the case for Mr. Bowerman; finally T. B. Walker defended his vote for fellow board member Miss Crafts.

The board returned to open session and cast its formal ballot—six votes for Miss Countryman and three for Mr. Bowerman.* The decision was expressed in two resolutions:

*George Bowerman's defeat in Minneapolis became the springboard for his extraordinary career as chief librarian of the Washington, D.C., public library. Appointed in 1904 on Putnam's recommendation, Bowerman headed the library there until 1940, along the way making it one of the preeminent public libraries in the nation.

> . . . that the position of [chief] librarian be tendered to Miss Countryman for the year February 1904 to February 1905, with a salary of $2,000; and that the General Library Committee be requested to report to the board at the next meeting such defects in the management of the library as appear to them most necessary to be remedied.

The vote of confidence in Gratia Countryman was something less than overwhelming, but all of that would change in due time.

Gratia Countryman, ca. 1910
Source: Virginia Buffington Shaw

Part IV. Chief Librarian

The New Chief

I am so happy over Miss Countryman's victory: but so mad about their horrid, snippy, small, mean, stingy, "manly" way of electing her that I cannot write more about it. She will come out alright, though, and will show the world that a woman can add courtesy to the rest of the requirements of a librarian if she cannot add salary.

Mrs. Jacobson, a librarian
November 1903

1903. The final vote caught Clara Baldwin out of town, visiting family in southern Minnesota. Clara had carried much of the burden in the campaign on Gratia's behalf, and she could hardly bear not being in Minneapolis for the celebration.

Saturday noon, November 7
Fairmont, Minnesota

My dear,

. . . Well, well! To think it's really happened and that one thing is settled. I am crazy to hear all details. Miss C. [Letitia Crafts] must have voted for you—I never would have believed it. I suppose she saw she had no possible show and felt she must stand by the woman question. Did the Committee think they must back up their recommendation? And did they vote for Mr. Bowerman? Did he stay until after the meeting? I should hope not. I don't like the salary. It isn't enough, and did they appoint you for only one year?

Sunday afternoon

. . . Some of the above questions are answered in the Saturday evening *[Minneapolis] Journal,* which came this A.M. and which I have just finished reading, that is the various parts about you. I was hoping I would get a letter from you this noon, but I suppose you had to go and have that picture taken yesterday A.M. I don't like it very well, and I don't like it <u>at</u> <u>all</u> in the paper, but it isn't necessary to discuss that. Dear me! How dreadfully you are in the public eye! What I want to know is who was the man who voted for Miss Crafts?

I see a committee is appointed, or rather that the general committee is to make a thorough investigating of everything in the library and branches. Well, dear girl, I'm not sure you don't need our prayers more than ever with the year that is before you. This is a great sort of a congratulatory letter, isn't it? I am somehow oppressed today by the hatefulness of the publicity of it all, and the weight of the responsibility which is coming upon you. Not that I'm not sure that you aren't equal to it, as I know you are, and I'm sure that [the] library will steer a straighter course when you get at the helm than it has since Mr. Putnam left. . . .

Perhaps I won't mail this until tomorrow afternoon, so I'll leave this open. I shall hope for a letter in the morning, as I don't like to get all my news of you out of the newspaper like everybody else. You see I'm jealous of the public.

Monday A.M.

Your letter has just come, and I think you do need my prayers more than ever. If that old board just go and make it as hard for you as they can—how can they be so hateful anyway. I think it was abominable of them anyway. And Prexy [University president Cyrus Northrop] too. I should have supposed he at least would congratulate you after all the things he has said all these years.

Never mind, girlie, you'll show them yet . . . With dearest love, Clara [Baldwin]

My love and congratulations to all the girls. I know they are happy and relieved.

Horace Vaughn Winchell
Economic Geologist
Anaconda Copper Mining Company
Butte, Montana
November 10, 1903

Dear Grace,

It is with keen pleasure that I learn from the *Minneapolis Times* of your merited election to the position of Librarian. Please add my most sincere congratulations to the host of others already tendered you by your friends. Your letter came on Thursday before the day on which the Board was to meet, and too late for me to write to any of them. It was not necessary, however, and might not have done any good, although I feel very well acquainted with Mr. Gale.

I trust you are quite well, and that the new labors and responsibilities will not prove too much for your strength. We are all well and just settled in a good house for winter. Please let me hear from you when you have leisure, and believe me ever yours sincerely, your Hortie.

Wrote Dr. Hosmer in his farewell as head librarian:

As regards my chief assistant, Miss Gratia A. Countryman, I will only say this: At my coming, Herbert Putnam, the most eminent of American librarians, committed her to me with the commendation quite unqualified. To this commendation, I, his successor, after my experience of twelve years, give unqualified endorsement. The Board has shown its sense of Miss Countryman's desserts by committing to her the guidance of the institution. Well endowed by nature, thoroughly equipped by education, specially trained and vouched for by the most skillful master of our profession, minutely familiar with this institution, which in-

> deed her care and counsel have done very much to shape—what can be expected for her but the best success?
>
> Dr. James K. Hosmer
> 1903 Annual Report,
> Minneapolis Public Library

Thus began the thirty-three-year tenure of Gratia Countryman as chief librarian. She was just thirty-seven years old and the only female chief librarian in the country, at least of a major library.

Friends and Colleagues

> *Your encouraging letter made me feel very humble, though very happy. I don't believe there ever was a girl who had more to help and encourage and inspire her than I have had, and as to my work, it was all ready to my hand, and I had only to reap the harvest. . . . If I could feel that your vacation had done you as much good as mine has done me, I should be perfectly happy. You were my first inspiration and should have a large share in any success I may attain. With much love and thankfulness from your own girlie.*
>
> To Gratia from Clara Baldwin,
> Lake George, New York, August 27, 1905

1904. Above all there was Marie. She and Gratia continued to share a flat on North Lyndale Avenue, although both longed for some domesticity in their lives. And at this juncture, domesticity implied a home of one's own, some land, and especially a garden. "Garden" to Gratia meant vegetables, the sort of garden she remembered from her rural childhood—oh, how she longed to work with the soil again. For Marie, the word suggested flowers—a band of color surrounding a garden door and bouquets for the dining table. Dream on, the two friends urged one another—some day!

With her eyes always open for a place to make a real home, Gratia discovered the Lynnhurst neighborhood. This was an area in south Minneapolis, barely within the city limits. The neighborhood bordered on both Minnehaha Creek and Lake Harriet, very near where the lake connected to Minnehaha Creek. Lynnhurst was already an "old" neighborhood by Minneapolis standards, for it had been established as a semiprivate enclave long before the streetcar tracks and sewer lines were laid so far south. Fine homes on broad lots dotted the landscape. In between were groves of virgin trees, remnants of the great forest that had once surrounded Lake Harriet and extended west as far as Lake Minnetonka. Lynnhurst could well be home, mused Gratia, and to check it out she and Marie set up camp for the summer. From a tent, a stove, and two cots perched on an uninhabited hillside, the two young ladies commuted to the library each day on the nearby electric street car line.

And suddenly, there was Horace.

The Strathcona
Nelson, B. C.
June 27, 1904

My dear Grace,

The rather unexpected, and to me quite unwelcome, appearance of Rockwood* in your office at the library the other day caused me to forget to ask you about the Idaho mine in which you seemed to be somewhat interested. If you still care to let me know about it, I will try and get what information I can regarding its merits.

After dinner at Louise's [Dayton] that evening, I started out to your camping place. Draper and Louise drove me about a mile

*C. J. Rockwood was the attorney for the library board.

with their Bucephalus; but I realized that it would be close to morning before I reached you at the rate we were going; so I went for a car. After waiting nearly half an hour for the car, which never came, it was so late that I gave up very sorrowfully the continuation of our very pleasant visit. I tell you this because I want you to know that I highly appreciated your cordial invitation to call, and that I made an effort to do so.

My stay in Butte was short, and I have just been up in the mountains near Kootenay Lake examining a mine in which I am personally interested. When you come west for a vacation, you must not omit a side trip up to this region of beautiful lakes and mountains. It is almost as picturesque as Alaska, and of course you are coming to Montana and Yellowstone Park some day soon.

I do hope that you will let me hear from you occasionally; for I am very greatly interested in your welfare, your work, and plans; and I would so much like to be looked upon as a real friend. Our friends are none too numerous; and so many whom we at first consider genuine turn out the contrary, that it seems a pity to lose a single one, especially such a one as I know you to be.

I am on my way back to Butte now and shall reach there Wednesday. Yours sincerely, Horace V. Winchell.

Horace Winchell was never totally absent from Gratia's consciousness. He would turn up again and again in the years ahead—bringing both joy and sadness—as will be recorded here in good time.

Gratia Countryman was a voracious reader through her entire life, although one begins to wonder wherever she found the time in these busiest of years. During this time of garden dreams, she picked up a little volume just as it was added to the library collection: *Garden of a Commuter's Wife,* by an anonymous author whose pseudonym was "Barbara." Published by Macmillan of New York, its author was soon identified as Mabel Osgood Wright, author of an earlier book on the seasons of a garden. "Barbara's" book became the tonic for Gratia's unformed longings. Barbara had put into words the spiritual qualities that a true gardener might glean from the soil. Never mind that Barbara and her husband, an English aristocrat, lived in New England on a country estate inherited from Barbara's father, with a staff of hired help to run the home, and rustic "peasant" men—Danish, Irish, and Italian—to cultivate the earth. Barbara could yet philosophize on and be immensely satisfied with the harvest of her beloved garden and know herself to be a better person because of it. Such was the gist of *The Garden of a Commuter's Wife.*

And for the moment Gratia bought it all as that which could give new meaning to her own life. She wrote to Barbara in care of Macmillan Publishers. Barbara's response was an unexpected and unwelcome blow.

> Nomansland,
> July 10, 1904
>
> My dear Miss Countryman,
>
> Your letter has interested me greatly, both from its frank confession and its decisive way of expression. I should, if it were not impossible, like to meet you and talk face to face and gain your viewpoint as well as to express mine more clearly. . . .
>
> I have a theory that almost every woman can have a home of some kind and a husband if she allowed her domestic side to develop in due proportion to her other ambitions. That is, I mean that up to twenty-five, if a girl does not meet someone who satisfies some one (if not all) of her romantic requirements, she must be very strangely situated.
>
> But it is just at this period that the "higher education" is the most compelling, and this same Goddess of Wisdom has a fashion of making her votaries so "sot" in their ways, so dogmatic and opinionated, that by the time that this crust has worn off in contact with real life, their youth has gone and with it their adaptability (a necessity in married life) and best hopes for happiness. . . .
>
> The fact that is very evident to me, from observing a varied circle of highly educated women, is that while the ambitions of the woman errant furnish her with motive and a certain exhilarating excitement for the best years of her youth, she begins to long for affection and home just at the point when she is least likely to obtain either.

> You say you long for home and all that it implies. Could you not at some time in your life have had both if something else had not seemed better worth striving for?
>
> This is not a personally impertinent question but one growing out of the desire to prove my theory either in the negative or the affirmative. . . . Write to me again if the spirit moves you, and be assured of my cordial sympathy and of the absolute privacy of the correspondence—Yours very truly, "Barbara." [Mabel Osgood Wright]

Gratia did not answer the letter. She may well have had a good cry from it, but as it turned out, the "Barbara" letter would energize its recipient to mold her life so as to disprove the writer's theory. Gratia may have lost forever the man she loved, but there was no reason she could not have a home, a garden, and even a family, without giving up the Minneapolis Public Library and all the dreams she had for that institution.

The year 1904 marked the beginning of phenomenal growth in the Minneapolis Public Library system. The key turned out to be the unlikely team of two stubborn but immensely farsighted individuals—the library board president T. B. Walker and the chief librarian. Walker believed strongly in growth, for he staked the future of the community on an educated public. In Gratia, he found a perfect ally. And if their views of frugality and generosity did not always mesh, at least they understood each other very well.

Almost since opening day, the beautiful library on Hennepin Avenue had been inadequate in size. Hence, in 1904 construction began on a much-needed addition that turned the L-shaped edifice into a U-shaped building. The expansion added more stacks for books and also better space for the children's room and the reference room.

1905. At the start of the year, Gratia finally received her permanent appointment as chief librarian. With T. B. Walker now thoroughly in her camp, this change of status wasn't even news to Gratia. It was time now for her first annual report, and those who looked to Gratia for a community vision were not disappointed:

> How to reach the busy men and women, how to carry wholesome and enjoyable books to the far-away corners of the city, how to enlist the interest of tired factory girls, how to put the workingman in touch with the art books relating to his craft and so increase the value of his labor and the dignity of his day's work—these are some of the things which I conceive to be my duty to study, if I would help this public library to become what it is for.

1906. Hardly had the annual report come out of the printer's than the words of the new chief librarian became reality. A collection of public library books was set up in two different factory locations—one at the Twin Cities Telephone Company and the other on the Cream of Wheat premises. The year 1906 would see collections of public library books available to firefighters in each of the city's fire stations; by 1911, the factory/business library outlets would grow to twenty, and by 1936, when Gratia retired, the number would reach fifty-three. More than that, thanks to Gratia Countryman, "factory outlets" would become a byword for major libraries throughout the nation.

If this was a time of expansion and change in the library, it was also a time of change and growth in Gratia's ambitious plans for her personal life. For two summers, she and Marie had camped out on a hillside in Lynnhurst, the forested enclave in south Minneapolis. Above them on the plateau stood one of the substantial Lynnhurst homes, and in the summer of 1906, both the home and the hillside lots came on the market for purchase. It wasn't that Gratia really loved the house, it was more the hillside lots behind, where she and Marie had camped and dreamt together. They would build a home there one day, but they were not yet ready. Gratia reasoned that with the large home on the plateau, her homesick parents in California could be in Minneapolis at least part of the year, and there would be space for guests, and possibly household help. Gratia and Marie could have their privacy as well as their individual gardens. Best of all, Gratia could own the back lots, her stake in the future.

And so Gratia went into debt and purchased the house—4726 Fremont—with the hillside lots behind. She and Marie gave up their flat on Lyndale Avenue and moved into the monstrous residence, with its spacious living and dining rooms, four bedrooms, kitchen with pantry, maids' quarters, and more. And for the future, there was the wooded hillside on Girard Avenue behind. For the time being, the Fremont house would be a home to family and friends, as home was in Gratia's childhood.

Levi and Alta Countryman, when they returned from California, were the first to occupy one of the large bedrooms. At seventy-six years of age, Levi hoped to try it once more with The Pitts Agricultural Company!

In late summer, Etta, Esther McBride Brown, also arrived, from Illinois to spend a day and a night with the Countrymans while visiting a dying relative. It was Etta whose education Levi had financed and whom Gratia had shepherded through the university—not all of the way, for Etta had dropped out to marry. Still it would always be Etta to whom Gratia turned when Horace unknowingly invaded her heart, for Etta had been there in the time of heartbreak and Etta understood. In return for Gratia's friendship and trust, Etta had named her first child Gratia Countryman Brown.* Gratia had never seen the child, for ten years had passed since Etta left the city, but the youthful friendship and sisterly love still held firm. It was an emotional reunion, and afterward Etta wrote:

---

*In 1994, the great-granddaughter of Gratia Countryman Brown Fuller lives at Lake Minnetonka, She is five years old and her name is Gratia Countryman Ratzlaff.

Sunday evening,
September 23

Beloved, . . . I am so glad to have seen your dear father and mother and your Marie. What a beautiful woman she is! It is good to have met her and to have the sweet memory to cherish of her gentleness and the peace that enfolds her like a garment. She seems as pure as to be almost passionless—far removed from the tempests that smite the passionate pilgrims in this world.

. . . I am so thankful, dear heart, for my day and night with you. It satisfied a yearning that has been so strong as to be painful, many times in the years of my married life. It is so sweet to think you love me now as ever. I shall never fear again for a moment that time or change will mar our love for each other. . . . Your loving Etta.

Hancock Point

I can feel the hearth fire's cheerful glow
When the deep fog dropped its veil
And we read aloud till the lights burned low
Or thy voice began to fail.

Gratia to Marie Todd, 1907

1907. Having ventured forth as chief librarian to serve an ever broader community, especially those not known for either influence or sophistication, Gratia considered it time to shore up the bases of her library programs, meaning the property owners and others on whose taxes her grand vision depended. On a trip to Chicago, she had come upon a women's club, whose form and goals she found quite appropriate for Minneapolis. She saw the club as a vehicle to raise community awareness among its members and to give them an opportunity to give back something to the community. Gratia reasoned further that such an organization could bring together the wives of the

Marie Todd, ca. 1910
Source: Virginia Buffington Shaw

Minneapolis power structure, giving the women opportunity for socialization, a broader cultural education, and most of all an awareness of the community's needs.

Laying the groundwork, Gratia sent out invitations to sixty women and invited them to her office at the library, to discuss a Woman's Departmental Club, the departments to be three in number: Home and Education; Philanthropy and Civics; and Arts and Literature. By the time the initial meeting was over, the Woman's Club of Minneapolis had come into existence.

A month later, the departments having also had their organizational meetings, a charter membership was defined—93 women, including Mrs. T. B. Walker and Mrs. Horace Winchell. Yes, Horace and Ida Belle Winchell were back in town, for Horace had a new position, that of geologist to the Great Northern Railroad. The Winchells were once again living in the university neighborhood, sufficiently distant from Gratia's Lynnhurst home. Or perhaps the sufficient distance was more a matter of time. It had been twenty years. Especially in the exhausting spring of 1907, there was little time or energy left for regrets.

Gratia had been one of the founders of the Twin Cities Library Club, an organization of local senior librarians initiated a year earlier in Clara Baldwin's Library Commission office. Gratia was now president of the organization, and she prevailed upon the Library Club to host the June meeting of the American Library Association. Gratia extended the invitation—to hold the meeting at the Tonka Bay Hotel on Lake Minnetonka. In the late nineteenth century, Lake Minnetonka had gained a reputation across the country. Especially in the South, it was viewed as a summer resort without equal, and so the Library Association responded affirmatively. With her new Woman's Club* now in tow, Gratia was able to arrange housing at the

*In 1994, the Woman's Club of Minneapolis continues to flourish. With a substantial membership, including a handful of men, it occupies an elegant clubhouse south of the city center and overlooking the Loring Park lake. The club's purpose still includes education, philanthropy, civic outreach, and the arts.

summer homes of Minneapolis's elite as well as a spectacular Minnetonka garden party at Ferndale on the lake, a party that would be talked of for decades in library circles. In subtle ways, it all came to benefit the Minneapolis Public Library, not to mention the reputation of the chief librarian.

But when it was all over, Gratia collapsed in complete exhaustion. Her symptoms were much the same as those of the malaise that plagued her during her university years. She asked for and was granted by the board a two-month paid leave. With Marie as companion for the first month, Gratia went off to Hancock Point near Bar Harbor, Maine, to the summer home of a sister librarian, Katherine Patten. Meanwhile, on Fremont Avenue, Lana Conger arrived for the summer with daughter Constance—companionship for the grandparents at home as well as summer vacation for Lana.

August 1

My dear Father,

This sheet is just for you. . . . Long before I left home, I said to Marie that a renewing of spiritual vigor was what I needed, and that I longed for solitude and quiet in which to gain back the spiritual poise which I need. She agreed with me, and we have both resolved to make our vacation count by a nearer closer coming to Christ. . . .

I do not know how it happened that my strength has so failed me, but I am sure that it will return. Nervous energy does not seem to return so quickly as muscular energy, and I am surprised and a little discouraged that it takes so long, but I suppose I must let things take their natural course. I have a strong body. I am eating well, and sleeping fairly well. We live out of doors as much as we can, and every circumstance is as favorable as possible. I feel better today than I have for a week or more, and hope that I can continually report progress.

Thank you again, Father dear, for your inspiring letter, and the further help it was in the resolve I had already formed.

I probably won't write as much again. It tires me to sit so long in one position. Most lovingly, your daughter, Gratia Countryman.

Saturday, August 17

My dear Father:

Your letter and one written by Lana for Constance came together two days ago. . . . Yes, the house is close to the water, as Mrs. Patten told you, so that all around our point the waves are our front yard. The spray has never reached us, but then we have had no hard storms. . . .

I am so glad to know that you are getting more peas from that second planting of dwarf peas. I am sure they are a good kind, and we will plant more of them next year. Marie and I are delighted always to hear about the garden. We like to hear about the prosperity, and otherwise, of each individual thing in it. I was so glad Constance told us which flowers were in bloom. . . .

Marie is getting dinner. Guess what—lobster. We picked his shell this morning and half of him is being creamed for dinner and the other half for salad. If only Lana could send us some nice mayonnaise. I hope she will teach Freda [the maid] how to make her particular kind, for it is better than most.

Here Marie called me to dinner, and if you want to find anything better than that creamed lobster on toast, you would have to go far to find it. Now we are going to the P.O. through the rain, for we have to have an airing. I wish you could see the rough waves this minute and the low-lying clouds.

I have not been feeling quite so well again this last two days. I go backward a little after every spell of feeling better, but the general progress is surely forward. Perhaps the weather has a little something to do with it, but it seems as if it were my digestive apparatus. I have tried going without breakfast, and without my supper, and have tried reducing all three to a minimum. I have avoided everything that seems to be disagreeing with me, but I almost continually have a sense of weight and oppression, or of flatulency in the intestinal region.

Whether my nerves affect my digestion or my digestion my nervous condition, I cannot say. It seems like the latter, and as I have been doctoring for nearly ten years for intestinal indigestion and constipation, it sometimes seems to me that it has caused this

> failure of nervous force. . . . On the whole, I am much more rested, but it seems very slow, and I am so anxious to start home. I do so want to see Lana before she goes. Maybe I can. Lovingly, Gratia.

The end of August, Marie returned to Minneapolis and Fremont Avenue, while Lana and Constance packed up for California and the fall term of school. Constance would enter the fourth grade, while Lana would meet her fall classes of high school Latin students. Gratia did not see her sister and niece, for she was to stay another month at Hancock Point. Alone in a cottage that was not her own, she wrote to Marie of their August idyll:

> Will you ever forget the golden days
> In the cottage by the sea
> Where we stepped aside from the common ways
> To a haven for thee and me
>
> I can see the fleecy clouds that float
> O'er the distant hills across
> I can see the gleam of a white sail boat
> And the spray its bow doth toss.
>
> I can smell the salty air that blows
> From the seaweed at low tide
> I can smell the sweetest thing that grows
> The spice of the pines, beside.
>
> I can hear the cry of the circling gulls
> And the foghorn's mournful toll
> I can hear the boom and then the lull
> When the heavy breakers roll
>
> I can feel the hearth fire's cheerful glow
> When the deep fog dropped its veil
> And we read aloud till the lights burned low
> Or thy voice began to fail.
>
> But more than the beauty of sea and sky
> And that crowned it all for me

Was thy peaceful face and thy loving eye
And the sweet long days with thee.

To Marie from Gratia, when we spent
the summer on the Maine Coast

During September, Gratia had the company of Katherine Patten, library friend and owner of the Hancock Point property. The summer recuperation continued. Always it was the sea, the rocks, and the forest that medicated, inspired, and healed this child of the prairie. When the aura of autumn lay over the land, Gratia was finally ready to return to home and library.

A Home of Her Own

Last night Marie and I watered our garden, and she got up early this morning and watered some more (I didn't). Yesterday I picked nine dozen ears of corn from the remainder of the peep o'day and the first Golden Bantam . . . I also picked ten big cucumbers. They are not going to bear very prolifically, and neither are the tomatoes. In spite of the fact that there seem to be a good many tomatoes, each plant is much less fruitful than last year—but there's a plenty.

Gratia to Levi Countryman,
August 18, 1908

1908. "Home" in these years was more like a menagerie. To begin with, there were Marie and Gratia, then parents Levi and Alta Countryman, for the summer at least, and then Marie's mother, a widow, who moved in permanently. And beyond that there were the Countryman aunts—Levi's sister and sister-in-law from Hastings, who came for longer or shorter periods, especially if they were ill. Always there was a maid—Freda, Sophie, Anna, Helen, Signe, Agnes—none of whom ever seemed to last very long.

Levi and Alta had become nomads, traveling across country by train twice each year—from Minneapolis to the Washington State farm of Alta's nephew, down to Oakland, California, to Theo's wife and children, then further south to spend the winter with daughter Lana and Constance, then in spring east to Cincinnati, where son Amplius and his wife Adda lived, then back to home in Minneapolis. Levi was not without means—his Pitts pension, rent from the family home in southeast Minneapolis, as well as some investment income—but he still longed for a challenge, especially one that involved the land. Levi went so far as to enter a lottery for government land in Washington State. But in truth it was Gratia who was de facto head of the Levi Countryman family. She was now getting a fairly respectable salary from the library board, $2,750 annually, although it still did not reach the level of Dr. Hosmer's salary five years earlier.

August 8

My dearest Daddy,

Your little note from Chicago arrived this morning. Am glad all was well so far and that your lunch tasted good. I forgot to warn you about automobiles. I hope you will keep an eye on all four sides of you, for they are dangerous things. . . .

I was a little sorry that you were put out about Mother's cloak, for whatever else Mother is, she is very thrifty, buys well, and takes the most excellent care of her clothes. While $144.00 is quite sufficient to clothe her, if she spent it all that way, she loves to give things from her own allowance, as well as you do. Don't you think, Father, that we should take it into consideration, too, that though you have sacrificed much in order to lay aside something for us children, that it would have been impossible for you even with sacrifice to have done so, if Mother hadn't been just that economical thrifty housewife that she was?

Is not the little sum which you possess as much due to her good management through long years as to yours? If she had been like some very good women whom we could name, you wouldn't have had an extra cent. Is it not right to consider that what few little indulgences she may want now are her due, that she really has a part ownership in all you have?

Don't forget that what a woman does as work in a household is as much an economic factor as though she were applying that same energy and labor outside the household. I know that men are very apt to consider that what they earn is theirs—all theirs, to do as they please, even though the wife is working just as hard at home, without wages, to preserve a portion—which in the end she cannot spend without accounting for. You have never had that attitude, and it wouldn't be fair now in Mother's old age to make her feel pinched if she wants, out of this sum she has helped to save, something more than your masculine judgment deems necessary. You know that neither of you need to pinch yourselves for anything to make you comfortable and happy.

Well, I didn't intend to write so much, only I felt a little sorry for Mother in this one little point. Oh, but I must get to work. I am tearing up this building once more and have many things to attend to. I do so hope you are going to enjoy every minute while you are gone. Your loving daughter, Gratia Countryman.

1909. If Gratia was beset at the library by the pressures of growth, she was also subject to strong parental pressure. The former she thrived on; the latter she managed, sometimes sympathetically but more often defensively. Through spring Levi and Alta were at Lana's home in California, where Levi seemed to have little else to do besides write his Minneapolis daughter. Why hadn't his pension check arrived; had Gratia mislaid the papers? The repair bills for plumbing and roof repair on the rented house in southeast Minneapolis seemed outrageous; would Gratia please explain and negotiate? Gratia responded less often than previously, for she had her own home repairs to attend to, not to mention a busy life in every realm.

Countryman Family Group, 1918: standing, Theophilus, Lana, Amplius, Gratia; seated, parents Levi and Alta
Source: Virginia Buffington Shaw

April 24

My dear family,

... Father, I sent your pension papers on some time ago. I hope you have received them by this time. I will go down the first of the week and enquire about your tax receipt.

Mother wrote me such a nice letter and she sympathizes with my cesspool experience. ... I have paid out over $65.00 for repairs on that house this month, fixing the roof, cesspool, pipe from refrigerator to laundry, etc. But it couldn't be helped, and I suppose I won't know it six months from now.

Well it has been another busy week. Some special committees and extra board meetings besides a number of social events which required my best clothes and my most engaging manners.

Miss Woolley, president of Mt. Holyoke College, has been here and we gave her a luncheon at the Plaza, of which I was chairman. ... President Northrop invited Katherine [Patten] and me to dinner at his home tonight, but it has been postponed for a week. I am glad of it, for I should be liable to go to sleep. That is why I'm writing a little note tonight, for I expect Sunday will be a rest day after my church duties are over. ...

A thunderstorm is just coming up, the first of the season, and I am so glad, for the ground in the garden is still frozen hard in spots. This rain will bring the frost out. It is a dreadfully late spring, and I am discouraged about it.

Write me as soon as you get to Oakland. ...

Levi came back to Minneapolis alone in summer, presumably to straighten out the affairs of his income property. He had been unhappy in California, and he continued to be unhappy in Minneapolis, mainly on account of the recurring asthma. In California, Alta had acclimated herself quite well, especially to daughter Lana's home and companionship. The old couple may have quarreled when they were together, but in Minneapolis Levi missed his wife immensely. And Gratia, his daughter and protegé, barely had time for the serious discussions they once enjoyed with each other. From Gratia's point of view, it was time to find a permanent place to live, a place on which the entire family could agree.

Sunday, July 4

My dear Motherkin,

I've been neglecting you dreadfully this summer. Father seems to write every other day or so, and it doesn't seem worthwhile for me to do so. Besides it has been a great relief to me to have him do so. I have had a very busy summer, in fact I have laid out about a year's work to do this summer, and so many are off on vacations that I am pushed to get it halfway done. When I come home, I long to be out of doors and then to go to bed early.

If you can imagine such a growth—the library has grown in circulation 100,000 in the first six weeks of last year. We will reach a total of 750,000 this year, coming up fast toward the million mark. I have $115,000 to spend on it this year. It is a big institution, Mother, it carries heavier and bigger responsibilities than you and Father realize. There are nearly ninety people on the payroll, to be looked after.

If I seem to neglect my proper duties, you mustn't blame me. I've got to get as much rest stowed into the corners here and there, nights and mornings, as I can.

However, I've been pretty well all summer and feel fairly rested too. We [Marie and Gratia] have decided to put off our vacation until the latter part of August, after Ampy's visit. . . .

I am worried about Lana. . . . I would like to get my family settled somewhere where they could enjoy themselves. Father has seemed very depressed ever since he came home. He has had asthma most of the time, and it has discouraged him with Minnesota summers. I think he feels that he must plan a permanent home somewhere. I am asking Offie [brother Theo] to come at the same time Ampy is here, and I hope they will help Father to plan to live somewhere where we can all be, as we gradually give up work. If he could get a piece of land where Lana and he could be well, then Offie and I could come, and perhaps Ampy later, and we could have a family colony. . . .

Our garden is just betwixt and between, peas are coming on and beans, but asparagus and spinach are over. We have had two messes of early peas, and today we are having beet greens and a gooseberry pie, out of our garden. Currants are not bearing at all this year, but raspberries and blackberries are loaded and we are having a fair crop of strawberries. . . . I'll be so glad to see you and I may not write again. . . .

Mother, Ampy, and Offie all came in August. Gratia was determined that they come up with a family solution as to a permanent home. No solution was forthcoming, so in fall Levi and Alta left once again for California to continue their nomadic lifestyle. Hardly were they gone than Gratia's Aunt Lany and Aunt Martha, from Hastings, took their place on Fremont Avenue—frail Aunt Lany to recover from serious illness and deaf Aunt Martha to keep her company. All this in addition to Marie, Marie's mother, and Sophie, the maid. It was December before the household was back to normal.

December 20

My dear Daddy:

I don't know when I wrote you last, but anyway we have sent off a Christmas box, which you will get, and I think Mrs. Todd wrote. I've been in bed for three days with a hard cold or grippe, or something uncomfortable that took my strength, but I'm up again this afternoon and hope to go the the library tomorrow and to take Aunt Martha home on Friday. I think the dear old soul will be miserable if I can't get her home [to Hastings] for Christmas. Aunt Lany keeps her stirred all the time, telling her how she misses her and that she is waiting and watching for her and that she can take care of her perfectly well, until Aunt Martha thinks she must go. I won't try to dissuade them, they are old and childish anyway and don't realize the situation. I shall take her to the station in a closed carriage so that I can wrap her up well, with a warm stone at her feet, and have a closed hack at the other end. But I won't stay in Hastings over Christmas. I shall want to rest, and they will be company enough for each other. . . .

I'm so glad you approved of my not selling the [Fremont Avenue] house. I saw through Judge Jamieson's letter at once, and didn't lose one mail telling him I would accept nothing less then

$9000.00 cash down. Now since he hasn't taken me up, it isn't for sale at all. It is mine and I am going to keep it, and fix it up and furnish it, and live in it as long as I am Librarian, and we won't need to be worried about it.

Well, Sophie went home this morning, and Mrs. Todd has temporarily taken the reins. I don't know what will come next. A Merry Christmas to every one of you. . . .

December 27

My dear Mother:

I've got to write so many letters that I'll just write you a short one now to tell you about our Christmas. . . . We received a good many nice things, but . . . it would take too long to list the little gifts. One of them was a surprise to me, a very exquisite embroidered handkerchief with my initials worked daintily in, from Horace Winchell. After [so many] years it seemed strange to receive a gift from him.

Sophie has gone home, Mrs. Todd is doing the work for awhile, and we are very comfy. A Happy New Year to you all. Lovingly, Gratia.

The Furnace and Jack Ryan

. . . Have you, in time before a freeze-up, shut off the garden standpipe, and cleaned all the water out of the pipe from the little pipe in the lowest point in the back lawn—and also have you turned off the water from the south side water cock? If you have forgotten these, they will be frozen beyond repair. And that reminds me: have you finished up all the garden truck? And did Marie get all her flower garden work done that she had planned to have Mr. Ryan do this fall? . . .

Levi Countryman to daughter Gratia
November 1909

1910. The year began with a flourish: the library board granted the chief librarian a twenty-five percent pay raise, to an annual salary of $3,500. At last, Gratia's salary surpassed that of her predecessor in his last year. While Levi and Alta were on their winter wanderings—from Washington State to California—Gratia kept them well informed on home news, reminding them always that Minneapolis was home. Home now included not only Marie and her mother, but also Mrs. Todd's sister, and an ever-changing sequence of household maids, all dutifully recorded for the absent senior Countrymans:

Sunday, January 9

My dear family,

. . . We don't let the furnace go down very much at night. I fix it up pretty well just as I go to bed, and Mrs. Todd gets up at 5:30 and turns on all the drafts and goes back to bed. Sometimes she throws on a little coal, but the house has been plenty warm for breakfast. After breakfast I fix it up for the day, and Mrs. Todd only has to throw on more coal about 5 P.M. until I come home to fix it for the evening. I can keep a fine even fire all the time, and I have used almost all pea coal.

We have had zero weather for nearly a month, with only one or two warm days, almost every night is 10°–20° below. I think we have had nothing below 20°. But there has been no wind, nor storms, not a single unpleasant day for us to come and go.

January 12

My dear Father,

. . . Perhaps you will be interested to know that Judge Jamieson walked casually into my office last night, and in the course of incidental conversation said he would be glad to turn his offer into an all-cash offer and make it $8,750. I told him the house was not for sale now. But he may offer me my price before he stops. . . .

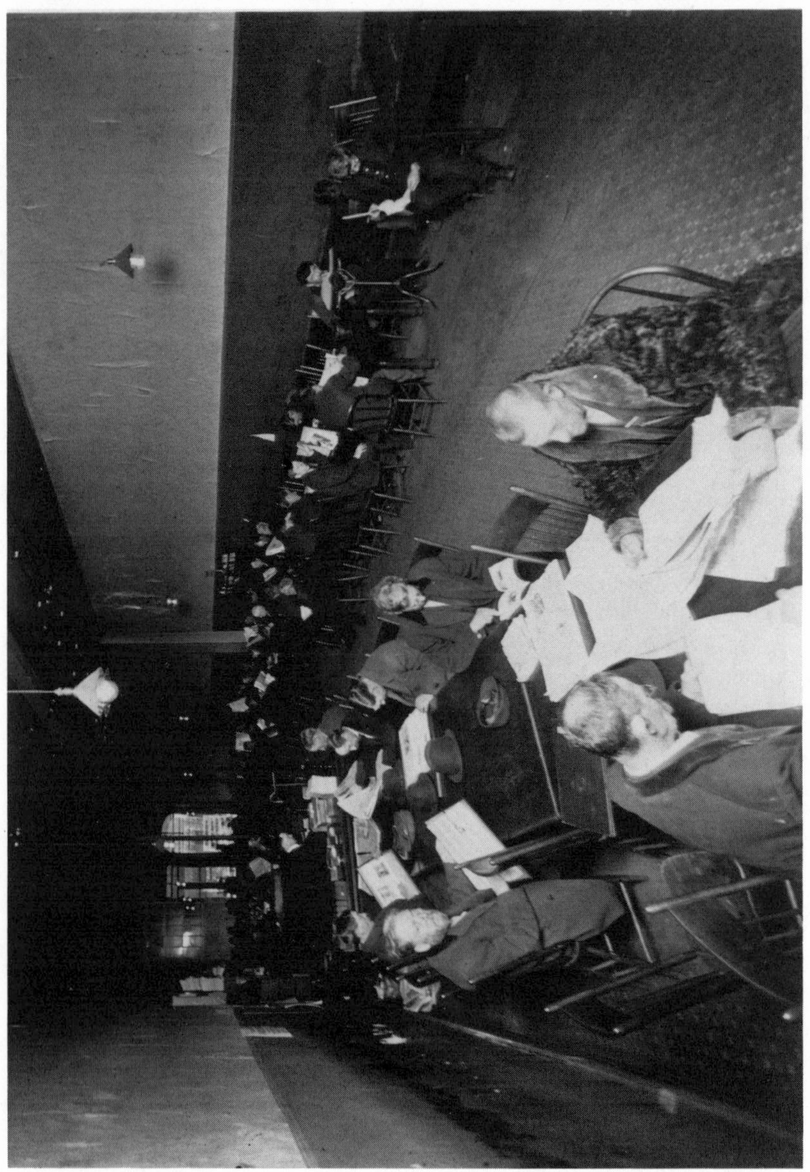

The Reading Room at Bridge Square, 1910
Source: Minneapolis Public Library, the Minneapolis Collection

Sunday evening, January 29

My dear Mother:

. . . I take your last letter and pick out the questions—here goes: What sent Sophie off? Well, I don't know, except that she . . . decided to go home for Christmas and said [she would not] work again until spring. . . . I haven't heard anything from Sophie. She was exceedingly kind to Aunt Martha and took great pains to make nice dishes for her and to serve them on time. Indeed she was kind to all of us and I have missed her greatly, even though I did not always trust what she said.

The present girl has been here a week. Her name is Anna Sanford . . . She seems to be a fine girl. She is very clean and loves to do housework, wants to sew for us whenever she finishes her other work, and takes great interest in what she is doing—not at all like a Scandinavian.

Makes good bread, is a pretty good cook and a good laundress. As far as I can tell, we have a treasure. She hasn't had a fair show at the furnace yet, for the pipes that heat the water tank filled up this week just as they did last winter. The men have had to dump the fire to fix them, and now they have put them in so that they stand vertically instead of horizontally, and we can't throw coal in or get the poker in at the back without much effort, and they will be obliged to come and change them. It is a great nuisance and an expense which I hope will not be repeated next winter. . . .

Sunday evening, February 6

My dear Father:

. . . Speaking of the underdog, I had about a half day of it yesterday and it most made me sick. In the morning I went down to a new reading room we have just established in the Center Block,*

*Center Block was the site of Minneapolis's original City Hall, a trapezoidal building set upon a trapezoidal block, just across from the principal railway station. Here the city's two main thoroughfares—Nicollet and Hennepin Avenues—merged, just short of the major bridge that spanned the Mississippi River. By 1910, the City Hall and County Courthouse were housed together in a magnificent sandstone edifice several blocks away. The abandoned City Hall and its surroundings gradually deteriorated. Center Block had become home to transients, especially those down on their luck. The Center Block reading room was short-lived, for the Park Board soon demolished the building, displaced the inhabitants, and constructed Gateway Park—a more respectable facade for visitors to the city.

which the Park Board now owns. We have one of the stores which reach from Hennepin to Nicollet with entrances from both streets. It is in the lodging house district and catches the unemployed and tramps. I made preparation for about 150 at a time, and it is practically full from 8:30 A.M. to 10 P.M., and I believe it will do lots of good.

After leaving there I went to the Newsboys' Club, where I have placed books, and spent an hour there with the homeless little urchins and the splendid young fellow who is in charge of the club. I no sooner had gotten back to my office than I was confronted by poor old Jack Ryan, looking so haggard and thin, no overcoat and apparently breakfastless. He wanted me to give him work, and then he asked if I didn't have some place he could stay and do any work for me he could. I told him I hadn't and sent him with a letter to the Gas Co., who are doing considerable construction work this winter, with a request that they give him work. I believe that Jack is as honest as the day is long, if he only weren't cursed with a taste for drink.

Well, his face just haunted me and I began to think of the Good Samaritan, who asked no questions about the past character of the poor fellow, or who or what he was, but he took him home and clothed him and fed him and cured him and gave him money for his journey, and I thought it was a great idea for me to give sums for charity and refuse the first individual case that was thrust upon me.

Well, I telephoned out to Mrs. Todd, and we thought we could put up a cot in the basement and he could take care of the furnace and probably get more or less work nearby. So then I went down to the Gas Co., got an order for him to go to work, and then tried to find him.

He gave me his address in one of the lodging houses and I sent a boy down twice to find him, but I haven't found him yet. I will try again tomorrow, for I'm worried about him. If I find him, you may miss any clothes you have left lying around, for he looks half clad and cold. It is all very well to think it is his fault that he can't take care of himself. But I'm inclined to think it is society's fault that the weak are made weaker by the presence of continual licensed temptation, and I'm mighty sorry for the underdog. . . .

People are still enquiring for our lots. I imagine there will be something of a boom out here. . . . You and Mother will surely plan to come back this spring now. . . .

Monday A.M., February 14

My dear family:

. . . Well, our household has undergone some changes since I last wrote. Our Scotch girl [Anna] felt too good for her place and was pretty impertinent to Mrs. Todd, and I just told her she might go. She left Thursday afternoon, and that very night Mr. Ryan turned up. We have made him a bed in the basement and he is happy as a clam. He takes care of the furnace splendidly, goes after water, cleans the porches and walks, shakes the rugs, and I guess he would do everything if we would let him. He is as handy as can be. I can't get him to leave the premises to look for work, even among the neighbors. He says he doesn't want to go downtown, and I verily think he doesn't want to earn anything, for fear he will go down and get drunk. I told him I wouldn't have him here if he drank. So he sticks right to the basement, except when we call him up for meals or send him on errands. Poor fellow, he seems just a grateful Newfoundland dog. He is anxious for spring to come, so he can make the garden for me. . . .

Sunday P.M., February 20

My dear family:

. . . We have been having a spell of 20° below for a week or so ourselves and, my, how the coal does fly. Jack Ryan keeps us so beautifully warm, and he keeps the cellar so clean as a parlor. He has done splendidly so far. But this week Mrs. Randall had him wax the floors of her house, which he does very well, and on Friday night she paid him $1.75. I thought he would want to go off, so sure enough on Saturday morning he asked me if he could go to get some of his clothes. I told him, "Yes, but come back in time to fix the furnace for the night." I had to stay for my library lecture last night, so I telephoned home about 6:30, and he hadn't come. I felt badly about it. When Marie and I got in about 10:30 he hadn't come yet, and I just expected he had gone on a $1.75 spree.

But this morning I heard him at the furnace before I was up. The girl had let him in, and he told me that he had come out about 11:00 last night and had left his bundle of clothes on the side porch, and not being able to get in, had gone back to a lodging house. But there wasn't a sign of liquor about him, not a sniff of it. And I felt that he had gained a victory over himself. I'm not sure that it wasn't because there was somebody relying upon him and his sense of being needed held him. I can't expect him to reform, but every week of good feeding and physical rest will strengthen him against an attack and I think he will try hard.

Our Scotch girl [Anna] left the very day Mr. Ryan came. I never liked her. She kept telling us that she was brought up a lady, etc., and I wanted to tell her that a real lady didn't need to proclaim herself. But we now have a little German girl [Helen], who is quiet and cooks well and seems to be clean and neat. We have liked her very much so far.

(I just now went down to the kitchen since dinner, and Jack Ryan was wiping dishes for the girl so she could get off early and because he gets so lonesome staying down cellar all the time and likes to keep doing something, and bless you he was wiping them as deftly and nice as any girl you ever saw.)

I tell you, Father, I'm going to keep a home for unfortunates some day. I'd a heap rather do my charity for the individual than for the mass. "I was hungry and ye took me in," suits me better than a subscription list, even though the latter will get my help too. . . .

Friday, March 4

My dear Father:

. . . We are having a warm spell and the snow has gone down rapidly, making a nasty walk from here to the [electric street] cars. Jack Ryan nearly melts us. He can scarcely keep the fire low enough and keep it alive. He has been pounding rugs for the Pattens all morning, and painting our refrigerator this afternoon. I keep him busy with such jobs all the time, to keep him out of mischief. . . .

March 20

My dear family:

. . . Mr. Ryan had his backslide this week. He went off St. Patrick's Day and stayed all day, coming home the worse for wear and bringing two bottles in his pockets. I gave him a piece of my mind and told him the whiskey would leave or he would. He settled down and worked hard all day Saturday, but he didn't come home last night and I don't know as he will tonight. Well, he stood it about a month and I imagine he will be terribly ashamed when he gets over this bout. When you see splendid intelligent men go down under the grip of drink, you can't blame poor Jack Ryan too much. I won't have him here drunk and he knows it, but I'll take him back when he sobers up. . . .

March 30

My dear Father,

. . . I never saw so beautiful a spring. Yes, I got the red lettuce seed and was glad to have it. I don't know whether to plow the garden or not. Mr. Ryan is pretty irregular. He hasn't been here now for several days and I suppose he is on a spree. . . .

April 3

Dear Father and Mother:

. . . Mr. Ryan has braced up again and is working regularly by the month for Harry Baker. In the evening he does what I need about the house. If this weather keeps up we will have to take off the double windows. Haven't had any furnace fire for two weeks, or more, except an occasional wood fire in the morning.

I see Mr. Ryan now over at the Waller's uncovering some of the plants. It has worried him that no one was taking care of her garden, so I guess he is doing a little to satisfy himself. He has carried off the leaves and raked up everything. Today he has given the back yard a good wetting for we haven't had any rain. I think we will begin spading up some garden tomorrow. . . .

April 13

My dear Father:

. . . I have dismissed Jack Ryan, couldn't depend upon him . . . Your loving daughter, Gratia Countryman.

In spite of Levi's protests regarding his asthma and the detrimental effect of Minnesota's climate on it, both he and

Alta did return to Minneapolis the end of May, taking up residence in the already well-populated Fremont Avenue home. There they would stay until Gratia sold the home a year hence.

Gratia considered her greatest achievement for the year 1910 to be the Gateway Park Station—a distribution place for library books down where the likes of Jack Ryan spent their days and nights. In her annual report to the library board, Gratia devoted the last two pages to this pioneer enterprise:

> [Gateway Park] Station formerly occupied a large store building in the old Center Block, which has been recently demolished by the Park Board. The station closed in May, and for several months it seemed impossible to find suitable quarters in that locality. Finally, a large room, splendidly located, was found on the second floor facing the Gateway Park, and just a block away from the new Great Northern Depot. This place was secured and the station was re-opened October 25th.
>
> It was first thought that perhaps it would not be as well patronized as it was in the old quarters, since it was on the second floor, but any fears on that score have been dispelled. . . . The average daily attendance is about 500, and the Sunday attendance about 600. . . . The writing tables are constantly in use, as also are the game tables. Regular checker tournaments go on here every evening. The circulation of books is very small, smaller than ever. As a rule, the men who come in here do not care to take books away on a card; they prefer to read in the room. A good many have no place to take books to; or, if they have, it is a poorly lighted room in a cheap hotel. The service to these homeless men is the comfortable, decent, well-lighted room in which they can pass their leisure time pleasantly and perhaps profitably. The service to the city is large; these men would, in many cases, be considered vagrants and sent to the workhouse; many of them would be drinking and doing themselves and perhaps others damage if they were not spending the evening in a warm and comfortable reading room. This room is an excellent place to study human nature and some of the large social problems.
>
> Respectfully submitted,
> Gratia A. Countryman, Librarian

An Aborted Candidacy

Gruss aus Bad Nauheim, H. V. Winchell
Postcard to Gratia, 1909

1911. The star of Horace Winchell continued to rise. He was now in private practice as an international geology consultant, his clients being the owners of mineral rights. Horace and Ida Belle continued to live in Minneapolis. Still, Gratia could expect to receive a picture postcard, at her office, several times each year. The postmarks varied—Colorado, Alaska, Germany, Mexico, China, and Russia—for when assessing mineral reserves anywhere in the world, Horace Winchell of Minneapolis was the man to call.

In these years, membership on the Minneapolis Public Library Board was considered the most prestigious public service responsibility in the community. Though six of the nine members were elected by popular vote, the prestige generated was so substantial that members served on and on. A case in point was, of course, T. B. Walker, board member and board president since 1885. But Letitia Crafts's board longevity was also of some note. She had served since 1901, the first election in which women were permitted to participate. Lettie would have liked to have become chief librarian, but it had turned out otherwise. Now, at the age of fifty, she took early retirement from the university library, announced that she would not run for re-election to the Minneapolis Public Library Board, and further that she was about to be married and would leave Minnesota permanently.

Responding to this sudden board opening, the remaining board members conferred and sought out as a candidate a man who in every way was one of their own—Horace V. Winchell.

But when the news reached Gratia Countryman, she was at first shocked, then saddened, and ultimately moved to action.

Gratia composed a handwritten letter to Horace, to the effect that if he allowed his name to be placed on the ballot, she would resign her position at the library. Horace's response to this ultimatum was prompt and indeed generous.

Imperial Hotel, Portland, Oregon
September 5

My dear Grace:

I hasten to reply to your letter of August 29, just received. It comes as a surprise to me, for it had not occurred to me that there could possibly be any disadvantage to you or to your good name if we should be more or less thrown together in library work. It is the only branch of civic work in which I take personal interest and almost the only position of public service which I would accept.

Desirous of learning your views, I called upon you at the Library on three different occasions, the last time being the day I left home, but was never fortunate enough to find you there.

It is probably unnecessary for me to say that I shall at once write to Mr. Walker and Mr. Gale withdrawing my candidacy.

Wishing for you the most abundant and long continued success, and for the city the benefit of your services as Public Librarian as long as it shall suit you to retain that position, I beg to assure you of my profoundest esteem and friendship, and remain Yours sincerely, Horace V. Winchell.

Part V. Single Mother

The Branch Explosion

> *Librarians are above all else social workers, and as such are most interested in anything which helps them to a fuller understanding of the needs and wishes of the community which they are serving.*
>
> Gratia Countryman,
> December 1913[13]

1912. If there ever was a time of synergy in the life of the Minneapolis Public Library, it was in the year 1912. Gratia herself couldn't have designed a more supportive library board—T. B. Walker, first of all, then Edward Gale, son of Samuel Gale, who had earlier served and cast his vote in Gratia's favor without hesitation, and now the newest board member, David Draper Dayton. Dayton was married to the youngest Winchell daughter, Louise, hence the brother-in-law of Horace Winchell. In fact, Horace had suggested Dayton's name to Walker when he withdrew his own as a board candidate. For the moment, Cyrus Northrop, Gratia's longest standing public fan, was not on the board. He had just retired as university president, giving up his ex officio seat on the board, but he would return in another year, as a duly elected board member.

This was also the year that Lettie Crafts resigned from the library board. Although Lettie and Gratia traveled in the same professional circles, there was always a certain diffidence between them, for Lettie had once coveted and almost won Gratia's position. But now Lettie was gone, and so too was Jacob Stone, who never wanted a woman as chief librarian.

Into this new and comfortable environment came the Carnegie Endowment Fund offer—a nationwide opportunity to build new libraries, including branch libraries, all thanks to the munificent philanthropy of Andrew Carnegie. Carnegie was from the generation of T. B. Walker, once a poor boy, later turned steel magnate, and in the last two decades of his life an extraordinary philanthropist. Gratia was prepared to take full advantage of the Carnegie Endowment opportunity. Well supported by Walker and the board, she applied for funds to build not one but four new branch libraries in Minneapolis, each one to be an architectural gem and a beacon in the community. Indeed before the year was out, the Carnegie funds were promised and the libraries were on the drawing board, each a distinct model for enlightened twentieth-century learning.

The first of these libraries opened the same year, in the neighborhood of the newest and the poorest of the immigrants—the Slovaks on the Mississippi River.* It would be followed in 1914 by a branch located on land given by Sumner T. McKnight, a wealthy landowner in Minneapolis. This library, the Franklin Branch, would be well stocked with books and periodicals in Norwegian and Swedish, a haven in this neighborhood of Scandinavian immigrants.** But McKnight was by no

*The Seven Corners Branch was closed in 1964, then demolished to make way for a new highway.

**In 1994 the Franklin Branch serves a diverse neighborhood that boasts the largest concentration of Native Americans in Minneapolis.

means the first to donate land for a library. T. B. Walker, a year earlier, had donated land for the branch library that still bears his name,* and a decade before that former Governor Pillsbury had donated land near the university and provided the funds for the branch that took his name.** The other two branches out of this 1912 grant would open in 1915, each designed with its neighborhood in mind. How much credit goes to Gratia Countryman for this virtual explosion of branch libraries is difficult to measure, but she was indeed the catalyst that moved it along at an incredible pace.

By all measurable standards, 1912 was a great year in Gratia's long life. The previous summer, the wily Judge Jamieson had finally offered Gratia her price, in cash, for the home on Fremont Avenue—not the lots behind, however, for Gratia intended to design and build a home that would fit her to a tee. First of all, it would stand precisely on the hillside spot where she and Marie had pitched their tent a decade earlier. It would have sleeping porches to accommodate every inhabitant of the residence, for Gratia believed strongly in sleeping outdoors—in any season. It would have five bedrooms, plus a maid's room on the first floor, with its own sleeping porch, for Gratia was truly an evangelist when it came to the health benefits of fresh air.

Gratia essentially designed the house herself and acted as her own contractor. Had she not a quarter century earlier done

---

*In 1981 the library system abandoned the original Walker Branch building, a neoclassical edifice that was said to be Gratia's favorite. Walker Branch was moved across the street into a new innovative underground library building. The old Walker building still survives, though extensively altered on the exterior. In 1994 it is home to the Junior League "Clothes Line."

**The Pillsbury Branch disappeared altogether in 1967, replaced by the Southeast Branch a few blocks away. Yet the elegant building donated by Governor Pillsbury still graces the east bluff of the Mississippi River. It has been fully restored by Dolly Fiterman and in 1994 is home to her Fine Arts gallery.

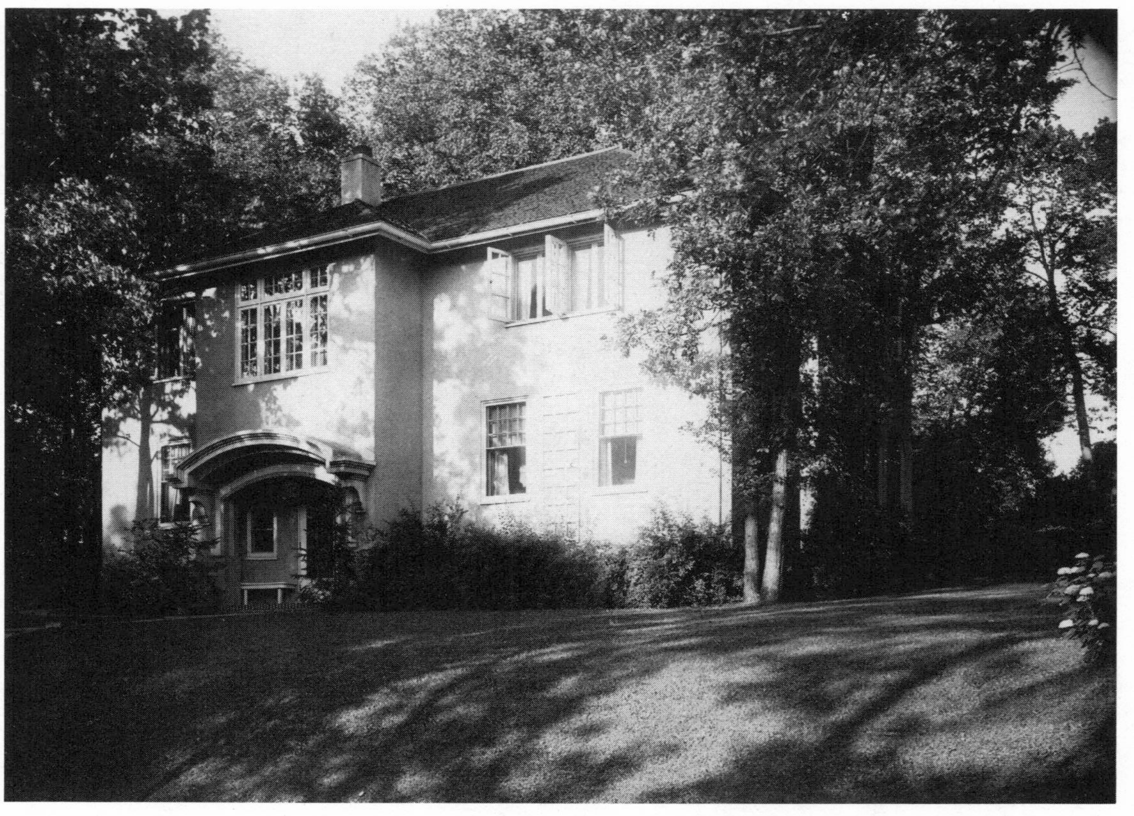

Gratia's home at 4721 Girard Avenue South, Minneapolis, ca. 1922
Source: Virginia Buffington Shaw

better than the contractor in supervising the building of her parental home? So reasoned the chief librarian, who was no less diligent in overseeing the construction of four branch libraries than she was in supervising the building of her own home.

Having to vacate the Fremont house months before her new home was finished, Gratia stored the furniture and moved into a hotel near the library, while Marie found a boarding-house nearby and Marie's mother went out to California.

By winter, the home on Girard was finished. Gratia and Marie moved in—their first time alone with each other for almost a decade. There would be no elderly Countrymans with them this year. Levi and Alta were ensconced at Long Beach, while daughter Lana and granddaughter Constance were traveling in Europe. This was Lana's "sabbatical"—a year away from teaching to study the classics, or whatever one studied in those days, while on an extended tour of the Continent. With Lana was the wide-eyed Constance, so at home with adults and so open to whatever of knowledge and beauty was offered her. Auntie Gratia, who was financing the entire adventure, had watched closely the development of this remarkable child. As much as Gratia recognized the profound influence of a father on her own life journey, she respected the rich education offered to this niece by a divorced mother, who virtually raised the child alone while working at a full-time profession. One might surmise that in observing Lana and Constance, Gratia first contemplated the possibility of raising a child herself, without a father in the home.

1913. It had taken several years to find a qualified assistant librarian—interviews, trips to library meetings, letters to college presidents—but Gratia had been eminently successful. She had found a young man in whom she had complete confidence, and one who commanded total respect from the growing library staff—one Richard Lavell. He was all that Gratia might have hoped for, and more, rising to every occasion as work mounted in the wake of a rapidly expanding institution. Sadly, his tenure would be short-lived.

December 7

Dear Father and Mother,

. . . The uppermost thing in my mind now and for several weeks has been Mr. Lavell. He was taken sick last August with jaundice, and he didn't respond to treatment very well. His wife was expecting a little one, and we all thought it was caused partly by worry over her, for he was extremely sympathetic. He wasn't able to leave the house when she was taken to the hospital for childbirth. She and the baby, however, were soon home again in fine shape and able to look after him again. Sometime in October he came back to the library and worked part time, although he was a golden green color. He was finally taken down with an attack of sharp pains, which the doctor diagnosed as gallstones, and which they decided had been at the root of his trouble all fall.

He recovered from that attack and came back to work, but the doctor persuaded him to operate for gallstones much against the judgment of the rest of us. . . . So he had the operation, and for five days grew steadily stronger. We thought he was making a wonderful recovery. . . . He was quite suddenly stricken down with hemorrhages in the wound . . . The wound had to be opened up again and clots of blood washed out. But he never recovered from it . . . and sank away in three days.

We cannot yet realize it. I was so accustomed to talking everything over with him, to making my plans and leaving them with him to carry out. I do not seem able to come to the realization and to reorganize my staff to meet the situation. There is no one who can take his place. . . . Everybody on the staff loved him and worked shoulder to shoulder with him.

His poor wife with two little children, one a baby only six weeks old, is in a sad situation. Their income stopped with his salary: there had been heavy expenses all fall and very heavy at the last. He had no life insurance because he had always had a touch of Bright's Disease. He had put what he could into a little home, but it is mortgaged still about $1,800. We are trying to raise the mortgage among the library staff and his classmates. There are so many of us that we hope we can raise it all. I do not know what the poor little woman can do until the baby is old enough to leave. It has all been so sad that we couldn't think of much else, though goodness knows I have been forced to think of more things than usual and am setting right to work to find people to do the work, for the library booms right along. . . .

December 14

My dear Father and all,

. . . Just as I arrived home, Marie was starting to her grandmother's and will return by way of the church. She and I don't hit our happy home together very much of the time. We just keep on the go all of the time. I cannot think of anything that would be such fun as to have quiet evenings at home once more, she doing some sewing and I reading aloud as we used to. No such idyllic quiet and leisure as that any more. Don't you tell me that I don't want to move out on a nice quiet farm and raise pigs or any other old thing that will grow easy, because I do. . . .

January 11

My dear Father,

I had a very pleasant trip to Chicago, got on the track of two or three young men who I think could fill Mr. Lavell's place, but haven't engaged anyone. I have been promoting people to fill most of the vacancies and getting new subordinates. I like to promote whenever I can, for it gives the staff a much more loyal feeling and gives the young members ambition if they know that good work is rewarded. There is no one to promote to Mr. Lavell's place, and I really dread to train in a new person to so important a place.

We have raised about $800 in the staff for a memorial to Mr. Lavell. I wish it could have been the whole $1,800 which he owed on his mortgage.

. . . Love to Mother and Mrs. Todd. . . . Lovingly, Gratia.

1914. To commemorate the twenty-fifth anniversary of the Minneapolis Public Library, the *Minneapolis Morning Tribune* featured a series of thirteen "Criticisms of the Library" by prominent citizens and a final rebuttal by the chief librarian herself. As it turned out, the articles were less criticisms than suggestions for future outreach. In her customary fashion, Gratia turned each suggestion to her own purpose—praising most of the ideas as ones the library had already considered but were unable as yet to pursue for lack of sufficient funds. The message came out loud and clear—an appeal to the public to support a raise in the library tax mill rate. Wrote board member Dayton afterward:

> The Dayton Company, Minneapolis
> December 1
>
> My dear Miss Countryman:
>
> The articles appearing daily in the *Tribune* have interested me very much, and I cannot help complimenting you on the very masterful way in which you have replied to the various criticisms. When I first saw the announcement of these articles, I felt that yellow journalism, or rather "yellow Tribunism" was going out of its way to smirch a well-conducted public institution, but I now feel that the series may be of benefit both to the public and to the library. Sincerely yours, D. D. Dayton.

Shortly before Christmas, the first library automobile was purchased by the board—an Oakland, for $1,000. It was to be used for library purposes during the day and by the chief librarian evenings and weekends. Thus began Gratia's love affair with the automobile. The Oakland would be but the first in a long series of sedans. During weekdays, the library handyman doubled as chauffeur and deliverer of books throughout the system, but otherwise Gratia Countryman was behind the wheel, as she would be for another thirty-five years.

Love's Bondage

Oh love, oh love, so wounded, why don't you speak and tell him how you feel?

Gratia Countryman, 1916

1916. It is difficult these many years later, even with Gratia's surviving papers, to understand just what prompted her to write the tragic lament that she later dated "1916." Though Europe was fully involved in a bloody war and the prospect of United States entry was highly likely, Gratia's career and her personal life appeared to be in good balance—Marie, family, home, and friendships, all in abundance. Yet, some impulse motivated Gratia to set down on the pages of a simple tablet a lament of lost love, and later to preserve it for posterity.

Love's Bondage

Each day they played and worked together. Each day they smiled a bit more joyously and clasped each other's hands more gladly.

"How sweet a friend he is," thought she, "working and playing are all the same to me when I can walk beside him." And so they sang, and picked gay flowers and tossed them at each other, running in mock chases, hiding in the misty grasses, peeping into little brooklets at their shining faces. Dream lives they were living, scarcely conscious of a future, because today was so entrancing.

One day some golden words fell from his lips like scattered dewdrops. He scarcely noticed, but she reached out and caught one in her palm. There it lay, a tiny golden key. Wondering, she clasped it: All the long night through she thought of it, till her heart began to dance with joy of knowing what it would unlock. Sincere and friendly had been all these thoughts together. So gently and unfearing in the morning she unclasped and showed him what had fallen from his lips. But he [responded] half knowing and more solemn than was usual,

"I had missed it, it will open every corner of my heart, glad am I that thou hast found it. Wilt thou use it just as freely as thou wilt enter in if thou desire. There is not a single entrance I would wish to close against thee. There is not a thought I have, not a dream that comes at night, not a hope that draws me upward that I would not share with thee. Try the key, oh lovely one."

Oh so tenderly she entered, gazing all about her, thinking

"How much better than I dreamed." But it was her radiant presence, lighting up her whole surroundings, it was just her soul's reflection turning back its beauty on her. Each day she found a new door, used her key and entered farther, till she came upon the fortress and the sound tones of his heart. Then they turned and clasped each other, she so gentle, trusting, heavenly sweet, he so wondering and so adoring.

"Thou hast followed thy heart's guidance to the very center of my heart, which is closed against all others. Beloved, wilt thou stay?" And she answered,

"Nothing could dislodge me, except thou bid me go. If we ever leave each other, thou wilt be the one that goes."

So dwelling in each other's hearts, reaching back to tell each other even childhood thoughts, they learned to know each other wholly, and to feel a reverent faith each in the other.

Days and days of sweet content and happiness came and went and the little golden key was never thought of. One day she touched the bolt of her fortress and it did not yield. But it didn't matter, she would get her key if she wanted it. Just occasionally she wondered where it was, and once in a while with just a shade [of unhappiness] she looked for it. She wanted to live in his heart, but she didn't want to be locked in; that began to feel like a prison and love could not hold love a prisoner.

With loyalty she endeavored to hide the little shade of unhappiness, but with love's delicate sense he felt it without mentioning it. Just a little more each day she looked askance at him and said,

"I didn't know him as I thought," and her gentle face was hidden from him more and more by a little mask unfathomable. Joy seldom now came glorying in her face, for she was now a prisoner.

No longer did their thoughts commune with each other without words—an air of aloofness became more noticeable—now no more glad rushes into his arms—no little comforting, soothing whisperings into his bowed ear. Oh love, oh love, so wounded, why don't you speak and tell him how you feel?

But he watches her unhappily, he speaks unwisely, he occasionally upbraids her, what does it mean? Why is she so distant? Does she not love him? Did she not come into his heart of hearts of her own free will? Did he not give her the key to do as she wished? What has he done? He is growing irritable, he has a right to feel annoyed and pained. Why should she hurt him so? He could stamp his foot at her. She is not so gentle as he thought, nor so tender. She is growing hard lines about her lovely lips, and unrelenting lights in eyes that once would look so long and satisfyingly into his.

Oh love, so long you did endure the unhappiness and pain, often you let them glimpse again—the love once felt, and catch a song so faint. But finally, no faintest song could reach her ears, no faintest breath of love could touch her heart. She could not be love's prisoner any longer. She must leave, she could not bear one moment longer. In her gentle but firm and unmoved voice, she turned on him whose heart she held:

"Can you not see that through these many months my love has failed and now no longer lives? I beg you give me freedom."

Like one struck dumb, he looks at her, his loved one and then,

"I cannot understand"—

"My words were clear. I wish this bolted door to open, no longer do I wish to stay."

"You say you do not love me; you cannot mean it. My soul is knit to yours, we could not part, oh love, be kind—We've been so happy."

"Please let me go"

"You have the key, I'll turn away while you depart."

"I have not had the key since first I came, you've locked me in, you've kept me selfishly in your fortress for fear I'd go away. At first I did not notice, nor did I mind, but now the room is stifling, I must breathe freely."

Amazed, he glanced about, the room had smaller grown it seemed, no large and roomy spaces, he hadn't noticed that before. The door looked heavy, the bolts had grown so large and clumsy; he fumbled for a key, yes here in the lining of his pocket it was caught. He just dimly remembered now that in some yielding embrace it had dropped from her hand, and he had not given it back. Did she think he had meant to lock her in?—Oh dear heart, had she thought it for so many years that now she couldn't be persuaded?

But what was the drip, drip, drip he could hear, just little drops where his words had stabbed, he would turn the key and let her go before he bandaged the hurt. Where is the keyhole?

"I cannot find it, dear, perhaps you see it."

"Here is the key, I'll turn the heavy lock if you can fit the key"—

"Alas, the keyhole too has gone, grown up with selfishness and pride."

Then ran great shivers of remorse
deep, bitter rivers of remorse,
dense black clouds of remorse,
an icy avalanche of remorse,
remorse, remorse, relentless black remorse.

Why oh why hadn't he seen the room of his heart contracting, why hadn't he seen the bolts enlarging—why had he not seen the door closing forever on her happiness—and now it was too late to give her what she craved.

So they must stay, he bitter with remorse and pain, she listless and indifferent, enduring to sit beside him and occasionally in her gentle way trying to ease his pain, while bearing hers—counting the drip drip of the life's drops, until the eternal angel of life bursts earthly fetters and takes them where repentance and forgiveness bring a baptism of new life and love finds perfect liberty.

Whatever torment, whatever remorse still remained with Gratia, all would soon be overwhelmed by a new life force, her love for a small boy—Wellington.

Wellington Greenway

We have taken a homeless little boy to live with us. He is nearly eight years old and bright and affectionate. We have grown very fond of him in the four weeks we have had him. . . . if he turns out to be as nice a child as he seems, I may possibly adopt him.

Gratia Countryman, 1917[14]

1917. In early January, when the library was used as much for protection against the elements as it was for reading, a small boy sat quietly reading books in the library children's room. He was there every Saturday and often during the week when he should have been in school. It was the children's librarian, Ruth Rosholt, who first took notice. She called in Marie Todd, and together they inquired of him: His name? Wellington Wilson. Where did he live? A few blocks that way, across from where they were building the new store [Dayton's]. Where were his parents? He lived with his mother and she was busy during the day. She told him to go to the library.

While Ruth Rosholt worried about the child, Marie Todd was already spinning dreams about this boy with the trusting, open countenance, the dark, curly hair, and such a genuine interest in the books. Yet the child was only in second grade. One day Marie took Wellington's hand and led him to Gratia's office. He soon became a regular visitor there. At first Gratia held back, for she was indeed the chief librarian. But then she watched as the child responded to Marie's gentle ways, and she was deeply moved by his insatiable need for affection. When Gratia finally took him into her arms, it was plain to see he had found his way into her heart.

Ruth Rosholt made the initial inquiries, at Wellington's school, for Ruth's sister turned out to be his teacher. She learned that the school was as concerned about Wellington as

Wellington Wilson on Hennepin Avenue, early spring, 1917
Source: Wellington Countryman

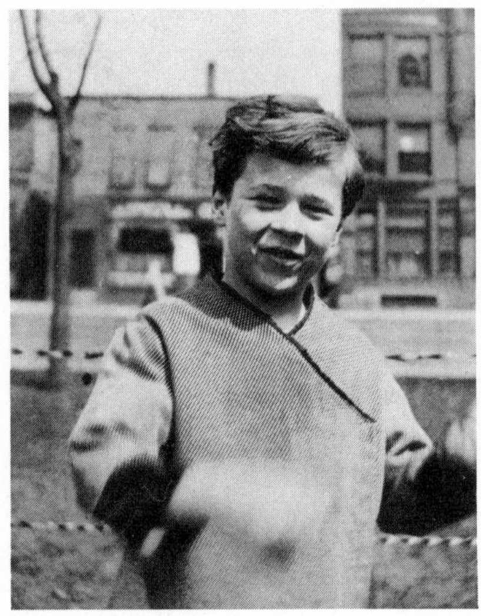

Miss Wilson I
see that you
my mother not
can not so you
any harm do me
because Just
I'm little
you

Wellington's jottings on paper at church, Mothers' Day, 1917
Source: Wellington Countryman

the three librarians. But it was Gratia who took the step that would change Wellington's life and her life forever. She phoned the child protection office, which mounted an investigation. Satisfied with its findings, the state began proceedings to take the boy away from his mother and to deport the mother from the United States back to her native Canada.

As the story unraveled, it became known that Wellington's mother, Agnes Wilson, was not his natural mother, although she claimed to be and was indeed the only mother Wellington had ever known. It seems Wellington's mother was a young woman in the Province of Manitoba, unmarried, working as a maid and unable to care for her newborn child. When Wellington was two years old, she gave him away to a childless couple, Agnes Wilson and her husband, from Brandon, Manitoba. Two years later, Agnes Wilson left her husband and, taking Wellington with her, went to the United States with another man. They settled in Sioux Falls for a while, but the man was cruel to both mother and son. So Mrs. Wilson took the boy and fled to Minneapolis. They were newcomers, living in a one-room apartment downtown while Mrs. Wilson made ends meet in the most demeaning of all professions. She became a prostitute. Each day she went out on the street after sending Wellington to the library.

In short order, Wellington Wilson was removed from Agnes Wilson's care and placed in the hands of the State Board of Control. When Mrs. Wilson could not produce Wellington's birth certificate to prove that she was his mother, the state temporarily terminated her rights. Gratia was appointed Guardian ad litem, and Wellington moved into the house on Girard with Gratia, Marie, and Signe the maid. For four months it was a love feast all around—new clothes, school days at Margaret Fuller School, neighborhood children, swimming, picnics, and most of all attention, attention, and more attention. It was as if the boy were recouping in a few months a lifelong dearth of affection, for he gave every bit as much as he received.

Wellington on his birthday, June 10, 1917
Source: Wellington Countryman

On Mother's Day, Wellington attended church with his new Aunt Gratia and Aunt Marie. As the preacher droned on and on about the beauty of mothers and motherhood, the boy made pencil notes on a scrap of paper. After the service, Gratia picked up the paper. On it he had written in beginning script:

> Miss Wilson I see that your not my mother so you can not do me any harm just because Im little

All that summer Gratia's household was in motion, preparing for the marriage of niece Constance—Lana's daughter. She had just completed her freshman year at the University of Minnesota and was about to marry a classmate, Gilbert Buffington. On September 6, in the presence of Lana, Gratia, Marie, Wellington, Mrs. Todd, the Buffington family, and assorted friends, Constance and Gilbert were married. Years later the occasion would be remembered almost as much for Wellington and his white Lord Fauntleroy suit as it would be for the bride and the groom.

Gilbert had expected to enter the army as soon as he was married, but he was rejected as being underweight. Hence the honeymoon was to be a few months on a working farm in Wisconsin, so that Gilbert could join the army and go off to war [the First World War] with the other young men. As the couple prepared to leave on this wedding trip, Gratia took Gilbert aside. Would it be possible to take Wellington along with them? Why? Then Gratia confided the reason: Wellington was about to be removed from her care; it was possible that she could lose him forever. These weeks were critical, and she simply didn't want Wellington in school, or in any other public place.

Wellington did go on the honeymoon. Later he would remember with fondness the weeks at the farm with Constance and Gilbert, especially the chickens and the children across the road.

Earlier in the summer Agnes Wilson had returned to

Canada under a deportation order that specifically exempted Wellington, noting that there was on file a petition for adoption by Gratia Countryman.

Agnes Wilson returned to Brandon, Manitoba, but she was not about to give up Wellington without a fight. She appealed to Canadian authorities for help, insisting now that she was his *adoptive* mother. Subsequently the British Vice Consul in Minnesota, representing the Canadian government, protested the cavalier handling of Wellington's case and reminded the State Control Board that the boy was indeed a Canadian citizen. The Vice Consul procured from Agnes Wilson's mother—one Amelia Parks of Toronto—a document stating that *she* wished to adopt the boy.

By September, the international implications of Wellington's future had thoroughly intimidated the State Board of Control. The board decided to take a neutral ground: terminate Miss Countryman's guardianship rights and take custody of the boy. The deportation that Gratia so feared did not take place, but as a ward of the state Wellington could not stay in her care.

So Gratia did comply, grudgingly. She fetched Wellington from Wisconsin and allowed him to be picked up by the authorities for delivery to the state orphanage at Owatonna, sixty miles south from Minneapolis. In the meantime, she intended to move heaven and earth in order to adopt him.

Wellington's birth mother, Annie Magee now Moore, had been informed of Agnes Wilson's claim and of her deportation. The young woman appealed to the authorities on her son's behalf:

> The Superintendent of the Humane Society
> Minneapolis, Minnesota
>
> Dear Sir:
>
> You have in your custody a child named Wellington Wilson. Mrs. Wilson adopted him 5 years ago in Brandon [Manitoba],

> from a Miss Magee. I am Wellington's mother. At that time I was a poor girl working for a living and work was hard to get. Mrs. Wilson was then living with her husband.
>
> My husband is at the front [in France]. I have two other children now. . . . My husband would not let me have him if I wanted to, for he does not like him. But I love my boy and my heart often yearns for him. And I would like you to do the best by him you can. Is this Miss Countryman all right? . . .
>
> [Wellington] was born in Winnipeg General Hospital the 10th of May 1909. I went there from the Home of the Friendless in Winnipeg. I was at the home 3 months before the baby was born. I came there from Oak River, Manitoba, Canada. [I] worked there when I got in trouble. I went back there to work when the baby was 9 months old. . . . I worked for a Mrs. Jackson and boarded the baby in the little town. I used to walk 3 miles to see him nearly every night. I got weary. I met Mr. Moore. He wanted to marry me and rest looked sweet, but he would not have me unless I gave up the baby. We fixed papers up . . . to keep it secret from his family, and I adopted the baby to Mrs. Wilson. Those papers were not signed in the presence of any lawyer. We signed them at home. She sent me the copy. I put my name to it. That was all. . . . This is the whole truth of my tragic life. The father of the child is a farmer in the Oak River District. My uncle wanted me to sue him for money, but I loved him too much. I was 18 years old. The father was 32 years. He is still at Oak River. I can get letters from friends to prove I am Wellington's mother. So please do not do anything with the child without first consulting me. I am willing to suffer for anything if only the boy will be saved. If you send him to me, I will do the best I can for him. I could have him now that my husband is away. . . . Annie Magee (Mrs. E. V. Moore) . . . Brandon, Canada.

Annie Magee's letter notwithstanding, the British government was not about to lose one of its young Canadian citizens that easily. Accepting the fact that Agnes Wilson was not fit to adopt the boy, her mother, Amelia Parks, certainly was fit.

The battle was on in Minneapolis, but down at the Owatonna orphanage, Wellington was adapting well.

Owatonna, Minnesota
November 5

Dear Aunt Marie,

I received your letter and also the funny things. I was glad to get them. Miss Ross said I could put them on the plates for the boys. We had a lot of fun at our Hallowe'en party. Each child got a bag of popcorn, a cookie, and a banana. I will learn the 23rd Psalm soon, for most of the children here can say it, and they will help me.

I'll send you one of my school papers soon. I like school very much. At night we go to bed at 7 o'clock. Give my love to James and David. I often think of them, but am pretty happy here too. Please send me my bathing suit for we go swimming every Friday.

Thank you again for the box of presents and please write when you have time. Lovingly, Wellington.

1918. Wellington wrote again after New Year's.

Owatonna Minnesota
January 18

Dear Aunt Gratia,

Our school started last week Wednesday. We had two weeks vacation and I played all the time. I hope you had a merry Christmas. Thank you for the raisins and also for the nice book. We have a library and can draw out books. I like to read them. . . . I have learned the 23rd Psalm as you asked me to do. . . .

I also want to thank you for the box of candy. I have written this letter in school. It is now time to close. Please write to me soon. Lovingly, Wellington.

P.S. Give my love to Aunt Marie. I think of her often.

In February, Gratia Countryman's adoption petition came before the Juvenile Court of Hennepin County, in Minneapolis. It was during the reign of Judge Edward Waite, perhaps the greatest of all judges when it came to reforming Minnesota's juvenile justice system. Wellington, now eight years old, was brought up from Owatonna for the proceedings. It was for him a pleasant adventure, for he spent most of his time in the Court House outer hall, reading and playing with Aunt Marie. Inside the court room, the attorney for the British Vice Consul along with Mrs. Parks from Toronto faced Gratia Countryman with her attorney, while a representative of the State Board of Control proclaimed his office to be strictly impartial in the matter.

The proceedings took on Old Testament proportions as each of the would-be mothers, under interrogation, staked her all for the life of the child. The high point in the drama came when Gratia's attorney presented a signed petition from Annie Magee Moore of Canada, consenting to her child's adoption by Gratia Countryman. But even this seemed insufficient as the Vice Consul's attorney pointed out the risks involved in adoption by an unmarried woman. When Judge Waite had had enough, he ordered a recess. The judge summoned Wellington from the outer hall and took the boy into his private chambers alone. With the door closed, he invited Wellington to sit down on a large leather hassock; then he looked the boy straight in the eye and posed the question: "Wellington, would you rather live with Mrs. Parks or with Miss Countryman?"

"I would rather live with Miss Countryman," Wellington replied.

In a decree issued March 4, 1918, the court ruled

> . . . that from and after the date thereof the said child be deemed and taken to be the child and heir of the petitioner, Gratia A. Countryman, the same as though born to her in lawful wedlock, and that the name of said child be changed from Wellington Wilson to Wellington Greenway.

Years later, when Wellington was old enough to wonder about such things, he asked Gratia why his second name was Greenway.

"I chose it for you, Wellington, because long ago I fell in

love with the greenways of England, just as later I fell in love with you."

That may have been just part of the truth. Gratia probably withheld the Countryman name from the adoption to mollify her father, for Levi Countryman had strongly opposed his daughter's decision to adopt a child. From the beginning, Gratia always gave her son's full name as Wellington Greenway Countryman. After Levi's death some years later, she had Wellington's name legally changed to Wellington Greenway Countryman.

The War

> *Up to the time of actual declaration of war, it seemed to us absolutely necessary to be impartial . . . to give as much weight to German material as to the Allied. We have confined our activities since the American participation to such subjects as could alienate no loyal American.*
>
> Gratia Countryman, May 1917

The First World War had began in August of 1914, following the assassination of the heir to the Austrian imperial throne by a Serbian nationalist. Through a complex arrangement of alliances, the war pitted Germany and Austria-Hungary against England, France, Italy, and Russia. At the beginning, public opinion in America had been divided—from wholehearted support for "our English cousins" to strict neutrality. In communities such as Minneapolis, where the population was increasingly mixed—the established families generally of Yankee English stock and the new immigrants from continental Europe—there had been an early polarization of opinion. As months turned into years and the human cost of the war mounted, public opinion generally had gravitated to support for the alliance dominated by England.

For almost three years, the public library had been in a peculiar position. American librarians in the nineteenth and early twentieth centuries were daughters of the Anglo-Saxon tradition, and library materials reflected this historic bias more than most librarians realized. Gratia Countryman, however, was keenly aware of both this bias in her realm and also of the neutral, if not pro-German, tendencies within a large segment of the immigrant population. These tendencies existed not only among German immigrants, but also among Scandinavians, and even among those from eastern Europe, where people had had enough of fighting and dying for others' imperial ambitions. Gratia had developed a policy of promoting materials that held a German/Austrian bias as well as those of the traditional British bias.

In April 1917, the United States entered the war on the side of the English–French alliance. President Woodrow Wilson proclaimed a courageous postwar peace philosophy—fourteen points that would end all war in Europe. Public opinion was caught up in the idealism of Wilson's plan, and American soldiers went off to Europe to fight and sometimes to die.

The Minneapolis Public Library and its chief librarian became instant leaders in the national effort to win the war and bring peace to the world, for that was the gist of the president's call to arms. Gratia's old friend and mentor Herbert Putnam, as Librarian of Congress, was appointed to organize a library War Services Committee, and within a month he was querying librarians across the country. Gratia was quick to report to her old friend that books on appropriate subjects were fully on display: Military science, history of countries engaged in the war, maps, battle lines, submarine zones, all continually updated, gardening and farming, patriotism, Americanism, nursing and first aid, compulsory training, and more. Furthermore, the library was about to furnish a librarian along with 5,000 books to

Thomas Barlow Walker, president of the Library Board, ca. 1920
Source: Minneapolis Public Library, the Minneapolis Collection

the Fort Snelling army recruiting and training grounds just outside Minneapolis. Gratia's report to Putnam concluded with a twist all her own.

> . . . Since vice and disorder are accompaniments of army life, the library should help to combat the vicious influence on the adjacent community. Recreation should be encouraged by the library. Labor conditions and especially child labor conditions should be kept before the people by books, leaflets, lists, etc.[15]

Soon after submitting this report, Gratia Countryman was appointed to the select War Services Committee of the American Library Association. By Western Union telegraph, Gratia contacted the man she knew would not disappoint her when it came to public philanthropy. T. B. Walker's support would smooth the way to other givers. So reasoned the chief librarian.

> T B WALKER 650 HIGHLAND AVE OAKLAND CAL
> CAMPAIGN BEGINS NEXT WEEK FOR ONE MILLION DOLLARS TO PROVIDE LIBRARIES IN ALL ARMY CANTONMENTS LIBRARY BOARD HAS CHARGE OF CAMPAIGN IN MINNEAPOLIS OUR QUOTA IS TWENTY THOUSAND MAY WE HAVE YOUR SUBSCRIPTION BY WIRE
> GRATIA A COUNTRYMAN SEPT 18 1917

Nor did Walker disappoint her.

> September 28
>
> My dear Miss Countryman:
>
> I received your two telegrams, one asking for a subscription, and the other acknowledging receipt of my answer to your inquiry.
>
> If you find that the amount I noted will be less than my proportional obligation as compared to other subscribers, or if you are coming out short, let me know and I will increase the amount. . . . Very sincerely yours, T. B. Walker

Gratia Countryman

T. B. Walker

> *WHEREAS, Mr. Thomas B. Walker has crowned a lifelong devotion to the City of Minneapolis and to its material and intellectual welfare by the gift to the city in his life-time of his entire art and scientific collections, and has added for good measure the gift of a site for a proposed new Public Library Building to house the collections now given to the city, as well as the Public Library proper, a site than which none could be more appropriate or better fitted for the purpose desired; and . . .*
>
> Library Board Resolution
> November 14, 1918

1918: Thomas Barlow Walker had for decades been among Minneapolis's most influential citizens. Like others of his kind, he had emigrated from the east in his youth, at a time when opportunities were there for the taking. And take he did. Known in most circles as "T. B.," Walker had been eminently successful in the lumbering industry and later in real estate development. At one time or another, T. B. Walker had a financial interest in most of Minneapolis's business areas and in the Lake District. And like many successful men of his generation, Walker in his later years sought ways to give back to the community from which he had so greatly benefited. In 1918 T. B. Walker was seventy-eight years old. He had been president of the Minneapolis Public Library Board for more than thirty years—its entire lifetime—and that was but one of his many philanthropic endeavors.

T. B.'s wife had died a year earlier. The death of a loved one, especially of a lifelong companion, often causes one to contemplate his or her own mortality, also to seek out new meaning for the time yet remaining in one's own life. The intensity with which T. B. Walker pursued his philanthropic goals after his wife's death gives strong evidence of such a mindset. Furthermore, his deep involvement with the library and its chief librarian added an interest that surely filled a personal void in the old man's heart. These were the conditions that nurtured the growing friendship between T. B. Walker and Gratia Countryman, who was twenty-six years his junior.

From its beginnings, the library building had been a joint enterprise, home to the Minneapolis Society of Fine Arts, the Academy of Natural Sciences, and the Minneapolis Public Library. T. B. Walker was the historic link, for he had always been a trustee or board member of all three institutions. However, as early as 1889 when the library opened, it was clear that the space could not comfortably hold three such diverse institutions. As the years marched on, the competition for space and for attention only increased.

The Society of Fine Arts was the first to escape the triangle. In 1915 it built its own home, a magnificent classic Greek edifice that became known as the Minneapolis Art Institute. That jealous guardian of the public library, Gratia Countryman, welcomed the separation with undisguised pleasure. In fact, she had been quietly building the library's own art collection, reprints, books, and folios, which could be borrowed on a library card. Now without the Society of Fine Arts, the public library was free to have its own art department, which promptly came into being with Marie Todd in charge. Marie added music to her realm, by making available to borrowers the newest sound technology—cylindrical phonograph records. Once again the Minneapolis Public Library was way out front in the services it could offer the community.

And still Gratia was dreaming of more.

By 1918 victory was imminent in the World War abroad, the war that was to end all wars. In every sector of American life, plans were being made for the post-war time, and most of these plans had to do with expansion. In Gratia's case, the end of the war suggested an opportunity to build a new public library—a twentieth-century edifice that would adapt more easily to the widening role of the institution as well as to its expanding collection.

The dynamics, however, turned out to be otherwise, for the departure of the Society of Fine Arts from the library building had created a situation that was far beyond Gratia's control. And it all had to do with her employer-turned-friend, T. B. Walker, who was a serious collector of art—European paintings as well as Asian treasures.

Back in 1914, when plans were first made for the new Minneapolis Art Institute, Walker had suggested that one wing be devoted to his art collection, a wing for which he would provide the funds. But the younger trustees, the molders of taste in Minneapolis, deemed Walker's collection inferior and outdated, in other words, not suitable for contemporary society. Walker's proposal was summarily rejected.

T. B. Walker did not accept this cultural snub with equanimity. He may not have had the vast financial resources of some of his peers, but he did have an ace in the hole when it came to assets. In 1918 the Walker family home on Minneapolis's Lowry Hill was perhaps the largest home in the city. For certain it was located on the most prestigious piece of property—an entire double city block at the edge of the city's best neighborhood and bordered on two sides by park board property. Directly across Hennepin Avenue was Loring Park, the city's central park and lake, beyond which lay the central business district. With two major streetcar lines converging at the spot, the location was considered prime in all respects. More than three-quarters of a century later, it is still considered one of the prime locations in Minneapolis.

T. B. Walker had an idea—he would propose a gift to the City of Minneapolis that the city simply could not refuse. He would offer his Lowry Hill property, excluding only his homestead, for the purpose of erecting a new public library. In addition, he would give to the public library his entire collection of European and Asian art, and he would see to it that there was gallery space in the library for the art collection. T. B. drew Gratia into his confidence. She took up the proposal with unbridled enthusiasm, suppressing any doubts she might have had about taking on another art collection.

With Gratia fully behind him, T. B. Walker executed a deed dated August 5, 1918, giving to the City of Minneapolis most of his Lowry Hill block and conveying to the city his entire art collection. The deed contained a major contingency, however: a library must be built and the library building must house the art collection described in the deed. Most of the library board members were delighted with the proposal; Gratia was ecstatic.

> August 17
>
> My dear Mr. Walker:
>
> I hope you will not think that the [library board] committee is slow in preparing the report of acceptance. It is our idea to prepare a statement which will include some general summary of your gallery, its value, and beauty, and the munificence of the gift. . . .
>
> The report ought to be so well put together and worded that it could be given out to the papers as the best statement that can be made. . . . It may take a little more time than you might feel was necessary if you did not know of the kind of a report we were trying to compose. . . . Sincerely, Gratia Countryman, Librarian.

And so Gratia went about preparing a statement by the library board that not only would be appreciated by the benefactor, but also that could quiet the grumblings among politicians and others not on the board.

> . . . NOW THEREFORE, BE IT RESOLVED, that this Board . . . hereby in behalf of the City of Minneapolis and all its citizens accepts the gift under the conveyances this day tendered, subject to all the terms and conditions thereof, and pledges its most earnest efforts to carry out the wishes and high intent of the donor . . .

This resolution, so carefully worded by the chief librarian, was passed by the library board on November 14, 1918, three days after the armistice that ended the First World War.

1919. In the spring of the year, one great responsibility was lifted from Gratia's shoulders—that of managing the Countryman family home in southeast Minneapolis. It had been almost twenty years since she moved out and her parents gave up permanent residence in Minneapolis. For all those years, the house had been leased out, with Gratia as rent collector and manager of plumbing, roofing, and all the other maintenance tasks. The postwar real estate market provided the motivation for Levi, in California, to allow Gratia to sell the property. Her own property interests had already expanded beyond the city, for a year earlier she had purchased property on the south shore of Lake Mille Lacs, Minnesota's largest inland lake. Located a hundred miles north of the city, Mille Lacs was still substantially a wilderness—scrub forest, marginal farmland, with much of the area inhabited by native Ojibway Americans. Somehow it all fitted with Gratia's dream of life in the country, no doubt supported by the expectation of raising a child, that he too might have roots in the land.

It was just a year now since Wellington came home to stay. If Gratia did not give him as much attention as she would have liked, Aunt Marie and Signe, the maid, did so in abundance. What Gratia tried to instill in Wellington was the kind of responsibility demanded of her by her father. For instance, she went about teaching the ten-year-old boy carpentry tools and tasks, having hired a carpenter to build a workbench in the basement. Wellington's first task was to build a snow pusher, since Gratia had assigned to him snow removal tasks. As it turned out, Gratia built the snow pusher while Wellington watched. Afterward she considered the snow pusher experience a failed effort on her part and began to realize that Wellington's childhood world was eons away from her own. It was Marie who understood the boy best and to whom he responded most easily. Yet it was a happy household, and Gratia could enjoy, praise, and be proud when in this first full year of school her son brought home mostly A's and nothing below a B. To a colleague and friend, Gratia wrote:

> March 15
>
> My dear Miss Abbott,
>
> . . . You should see my small boy by now. He is growing very fast, and is very much established in my home. Miss Todd and I would not know what to do without him. He frequently comes down to the Library on Saturdays, where he either plays in the carpenter shop or binds books in the bindery. This morning he has been collecting stamps in the Order Department. He is dear, and I know we are going to get lots of comfort out of him.
>
> The new building for the library is not a certainty yet. The Legislature is dallying over it, but I think they will certainly authorize the bond issue for it. No legislature would quite want to take the responsibility of losing the Walker gift by not authorizing the bond for the building. . . . Gratia Countryman.

The legislature did authorize a bond issue, $250,000 to build a new public library, leading to discussions of design and architects between the chief librarian and the donor. The spring of 1919 was one of those glorious seasons in Gratia's life when personal and public life blended and blossomed together. Walker would have taken up her entire spare time, had she allowed it, for he was designing libraries in his head and sounding out architects across the country. Gratia was loathe to limit his enthusiasm, which was running well ahead of reasonable expectations, but she could limit the discussions—to once a week, on Sunday afternoon.

After church and dinner, the great Pierce Arrow sedan would pull up at 4721 Girard. Gratia and Wellington, in their Sunday finery, would descend the steps. The chauffeur would hold open the rear passenger door. Inside would be sitting the diminutive, bearded T. B. Walker, who would make space for the diminutive chief librarian next to him. After Gratia was seated, the chauffeur would settle Wellington next to the driver's seat, and off they would go for a Sunday afternoon drive.

In Wellington's case, Sunday afternoon drives in the Pierce Arrow were the epitome of childhood adventure—around the lakes, along the parkways, inevitably around the great block where the new library would be built, followed by dining out. The understanding was that there be no talking in the front seat, either by the driver or by the chaperon. If Wellington was sometimes forgetful in his duties at home, he was quite clear about his responsibility in the Pierce Arrow. On drives with Mr. Walker, he—Wellington—was his mother's chaperon. *That* she had made clear.

Probably Wellington did not understand the meaning of the word chaperon. His mother, however, was dead serious. There was talk at the library, and among colleagues elsewhere, that T. B. Walker had a "case" on Miss Countryman.[16]

From the outside, it certainly looked as much, for the widowed Mr. Walker was plying both mother and son with such gifts as could not be refused. To the mother T. B. presented an ancient copper and gold vase from the time of the earliest Chinese dynasty and retrieved from the mud of the Yangtze River, also a Ming dynasty porcelain rose petal bowl. For the son there were ancient Egyptian glass coins and a tiny box of colored stones taken from a mosaic floor in the ancient city of Pompeii. There may have been other gifts also; these gifts are still in the possession of Wellington Countryman, kindling fond memories of Sunday afternoon drives in Mr. Walker's Pierce Arrow automobile.

Years later, when one could speak more casually about such things, Gratia acknowledged that T. B. Walker might have been rather fond of her but that she "would have none of it."*

*Alice Brunat, the head of the library children's room under Gratia Countryman, has this to say on the subject: "We librarians believed that Mr. Walker was in love with Miss Countryman, but she was very discreet."

June was a great time in this year 1919. The national conference of the American Library Association was meeting in Asbury Park, New Jersey, not far from New York City. Gratia was attending with her long-time friend Clara Baldwin, still director of the State Library Commission. Such excitement there was at this conference, where the women were at least as visible as the men. The United States Congress had finally passed an amendment to the Constitution giving women the right to vote. Before it could take effect, however, the amendment still had to be ratified by thirty-six state legislatures. Everyone at the library conference, of course, knew it was Congress that had delayed the amendment too long; it would be clear sailing among the states. (And so it would be, for in August of 1920, the thirty-sixth state ratification put into effect the amendment, in time for the 1920 presidential elections.) Among the participants at Asbury Park, this was indeed a month for rejoicing.

Meanwhile T. B. Walker was in New York City, looking over the public library and the Metropolitan Museum of Art. The purpose was to see what could be learned from these monumental buildings in the way of ideas that could be transferred to the proposed library in Minneapolis. Between Asbury Park and Manhattan there was a frenetic exchange of letters and telegrams. Gratia wanted to visit both institutions in New York. Walker insisted that neither had anything to offer the Minneapolis Public Library, but if she wanted to come to New York, he would make a reservation at the Seville Hotel, where he was residing, and indeed would be delighted to see her. Gratia demurred, saying rather that she would return to Minneapolis via Cleveland and Detroit. Again Walker could not understand why this was necessary, for plans of both libraries were available in Minneapolis, and anyway it was too hot. He intended to go immediately back to Minneapolis, and he thought Gratia ought to do the same!

In September, at a special meeting, the library board voted to "authorize a competition of invited architects to submit floor plans and sketches of elevation, the successful contestant to receive a prize of $1,000.00; his plans to be the property of the Library Board; the Board to be under no obligation, however, to appoint such a successful competitor as the architect of the building. For such a competition, the librarian is to furnish the necessary data."

1920. The prospect of a new library dimmed, for influential segments of the public increasingly perceived the whole project as T. B. Walker's scheme to take over the library with his art collection. At least that is how the city council majority viewed it. The council and the city bonding authority simply would not issue the bonds that had already been authorized by the state legislature. This was bitter medicine for the old man.

For Gratia it was simply a challenge—a challenge to be overcome. She sat down with her friend, and together they worked out a proposal that would defy any naysayer and in addition would remove the museum of the Society of Natural History from the library premises. From the beginning, this museum was a thorn in Gratia's side, just as it was a symbol of pride for Walker, its founder and president. In the proposed new agreement, T. B. Walker would increase the size of his real estate gift to include virtually the entire Lowry block, reserving just the residence for himself as long as he chose to live there. Then this land, too, would become part of his gift to the city. With the added parcel of land, as proposed, the city would build two compatible buildings—one to house Walker's art collection and the natural history museum, the other to be the new public library. The library board agreed, and on November 16 the agreement was signed.

But it still wasn't enough for the public, and as the months marched on, opposition solidified even more. Walker modified his offer again, changing the time by which the library and gallery should be completed in order to complete the agreement, but the response continued to be negative. The new library simply was not to be.

Eventually Walker withdrew the offer entirely and began plans to build his own gallery on the Lowry Hill land. The city's $250,000 authorized bonding power was used to issue bonds for the construction of a fourth wing on the public library, completing the square and enclosing the center court. The natural history museum continued to be housed at the public library, at least for another decade. T. B. Walker was reelected to the library board and continued to serve as its president, but his days as civic leader and major philanthropist were past.

Rules of Conduct

> *In those years, my mother was the disciplinarian while Aunt Marie was the arbitrator. One might say my mother performed the masculine role and Aunt Marie the feminine. The maids also had much to do with my bringing up. I liked them all, especially Signe and later the one who brought along a small daughter to play with me. When I think of my mother and of all the people who lived with us, I realize she opened her heart and her home to people who were unlucky in love or had suffered some other emotional loss.*
>
> Wellington Countryman,
> July 25, 1992

1922. Alta Countryman, Gratia's mother, was dead after a long and useful life. The last two decades she had lived in California, never quite adjusting to the nomadic existence foisted on her by the restless Levi. To his credit, Levi had nursed Alta most lovingly in her last months. Yet after her death, he was moved to write, ". . . I wish candidly to show to the world that I have not used my wife as I should have done. Though I loved her, I would sometimes get sour, morose, and peevish and remain so for hours. Her kindness, her tenderness and unchanging affections—those healing remedies have cured me. LNC." Levi insisted on having Alta's body cremated and the ashes buried in Oakwood Cemetery at Hastings, next to her two small children, Minnie and Jason.

Quite aware of her father's loss, Gratia was determined to arrange a permanent home for him. She invited him back to Minneapolis, to a home that now included Gratia, Marie, and Wellington, along with a maid and her child. Beyond this core family, there were a series of extended visits by entire families. For awhile it was the library's crippled elevator operator with a wife and two children, followed by a refugee family from Europe with three children, and after that a minister's family between church assignments. For Wellington, home was a revolving circle of children with parents, presumably brought in as playmates for him.

But for the adults, it really wasn't working out that well. To begin with, Marie Todd, whose hand had gently guided Wellington in these years, was not well. She had always suffered occasional migraine headaches, and now, at forty-five, she was stricken with recurring and excruciating pain in her face—*tic doloureux* was the diagnosis. Various medical treatments were tried—injections of alcohol or phenol. These provided only temporary relief at best. As loving as the relationship between Gratia and Marie was all these years, Marie was now one more family member to be looked after.

There had been times in Gratia's life when she deferred completely to the judgment of her father. Had he not been the all-important mentor of her early life? In recent years, however, it was Gratia who advised, even chastised, her father, but always within the bounds of immense love and respect. In this year 1922, Levi once again spent the summer months in the hostel on Girard Avenue. One can only surmise how he—and Gratia—dealt with the dynamics of a family, including an ailing family member, sharing its home with strangers, no matter how ample the spaces.

In the late twentieth century, it is not difficult to imagine how Wellington might have dealt with the obvious tensions and confusion. At thirteen he was into adolescence, no longer the dear little fellow that Marie had brought into Gratia's office five years earlier. Enter the elderly Levi Countryman, who was never at a loss for words. He observed a growing lad somewhat out of control; he chastised him as he had chastised his own sons fifty years earlier; and he no doubt chastised daughter Gratia also, for allowing it all to have gotten out of hand. If Levi had entertained thoughts of making his home with daughter Gratia, the summer of 1922 cured him of such fantasies. In October, he made plans to return to California, but not before drawing up rules of conduct for a child he deemed totally lacking in discipline. And Gratia, quite involved with library and community affairs,* concurred:

4721 Girard Avenue South
October 18, 1922

To All Whom It May Concern:

Appreciating the fact that I have good and loyal friends in Miss Gratia Countryman, my foster [sic] mother, in Miss Marie Todd, and Grandpa Countryman, who by their treatment of me, and bearing with my faults, show that they love me, and have an earnest and abiding desire for my future well-being:

Therefore I gladly subscribe to the following Rules of Conduct which I shall honestly endeavor to follow and ask you, and others who may be interested in my welfare, to bear with me from time to time until I shall have surmounted the difficulties inherent in my nature.

Therefore, by your aid and the help of God:

---

*In 1922, Gratia was elected to the American Library Association Board of Directors. Also in this year, she organized the Hennepin County Library System and became its first librarian, in addition to retaining her role in the Minneapolis system.

1st I will be truthful on all occasions, and under all circumstances.

2nd I will be honest in all my dealings with everyone.

3rd I will use no profane or vile language anywhere or at anytime, either privately or publicly.

4th I will endeavor to copy the manner and customs of the gentleman, especially those of good men or boys known to be good.

5th I will study the Ten Commandments and endeavor to follow the very highest concept of their teachings, for they are foundation principles.

6th I will treat everybody with due respect, whether I am so treated or not.

7th I will endeavor by every power in me to correct all bad habits such as heedlessness or thoughtlessness, or forgetfulness, or selfishness.

8th I will do what I am set to do without delay, and without argument, when asked to do such work at a proper time. I will learn, therefore, to comprehend my daily duties, either of labor or study, without being constantly reminded of them, thus learning to be dependable in all ways expected of me.

9th I will never indulge in the use of intoxicating liquors of any kind, I will not ever engage in the vile practice of using tobacco in any form— smoking or chewing, nor in the very offensive and evil practice of the use of opium in any form, all of which habits are filthy and often lead to gross immorality, sickness, poverty, and death.

In following out these set rules for daily conduct, I shall learn to respect myself and to deserve the respect of all who know me, and especially of those who love me most, and desire my highest good, and thus to feel that in doing good service and living an upright life, I shall be of some good to the world, and best of all establish a character that shall stand the test of time and eternity.

(signed) Wellington Greenway Countryman

Witnesses
L. N. Countryman
Gratia A. Countryman

Grandpa Countryman and the rules of conduct made a deep and abiding impression on young Wellington, not because he succeeded in adhering to all of them but because the summer of 1922 was his farewell to childhood and it had not been a happy leave-taking.

1923. After Christmas, it was agreed by the adults that Wellington should finish out the school year in Duluth. He would live with Constance and Gilbert Buffington, whose honeymoon he had shared some six years earlier, only now there was a third member of the family—three-year-old Edwin. Wellington would finish out the eighth grade in a Duluth public school. Just one more change in the life of a boy whose roots were fragile at best.

Gratia Countryman had decided to sell her house. In fact, she hardly consulted the two who shared it with her—neither Marie nor Wellington. In Gratia's mind, it was simply time. From the day the house was built, Gratia had received offers to buy it, for the Lynnhurst neighborhood had evolved just as she imagined it would. With city parkways and parkland fully developed, ever grander homes were being built along Minnehaha Creek and on Lake Harriet. The home on Girard had well served its diverse and often transient inhabitants. But managing such a large, welcoming home was simply not compatible with Gratia's overwhelming responsibilities downtown. She intended to sell the property and use the money from the sale to finally build her home on Lake Mille Lacs. Eventually she would retire there. That was the ultimate plan, for with Marie ill, Wellington in his most obstreperous years, and the library so demanding, Gratia did not envision that she could hold on much longer.

Then summer arrived and Wellington came home. The unhappy autumn months—when Grandpa Countryman was in charge—were but a dim memory. If Wellington had once been Gratia's chaperon, in the summer of 1923 he was her companion and helper. Every weekday they drove in the Buick sedan downtown to the library. Wellington's tasks were in the bindery, the men's place at the public library. The bindery was run by a master book binder, Oscar Berg, who was an absolute favorite of Gratia's. She went so far as to boast of being matchmaker in his marriage.

It had happened this way: Years earlier Gratia had hired a young girl, Anna, to be a library page. Anna was bright, but she had completed only an eighth-grade education. Oscar and Anna laid eyes on each other very early. Gratia observed and Gratia decided: Oscar's wife must have some education. Gratia encouraged Anna, in fact, virtually ordered her to attend business school, presumably to upgrade her skills for a better position, but in fact also to broaden Anna's general world perspective, which it did. Later Anna would recall in gratitude the impact of Miss Countryman on her life journey with Oscar.

Over the summer, Oscar plied all of his paternal instincts on the fatherless Wellington. Each evening the chief librarian checked into the bindery and fetched her son—into the Buick and home to Lynnhurst. For Wellington the best part was "King's Highway," named not for King George but rather for Colonel King, whose farm had once graced all of Lynnhurst and more. King's Highway was a long stretch downhill, then uphill, with no cross streets. With Wellington in the automobile, Gratia would speed up before the decline, then coast downhill uninhibited and uphill as far as possible. It was a game that mother and son played, as much for the pleasure of the mother as for the son.

On a Monday evening at the beginning of August, when Gratia and Wellington reached King's Highway, Gratia did not speed up in preparation for the long hill. What, asked Wellington, was the matter. Gratia replied: "Wellington, I don't feel like playing today. I am very sad right now because the man I was supposed to marry died. His funeral is tomorrow and I shall not be there." Wellington said nothing, but he noticed his mother was wearing a gold filigree ring with a diamond in it. He had never seen this ring before and he would never see it again.

Indeed Horace V. Winchell, internationally known mining geologist, had died the previous Saturday. So reported the *Minneapolis Tribune.* Winchell was just fifty-eight years old and living in Los Angeles, having recently moved there from Minneapolis. The death was sudden and unexpected. The funeral was to be a private affair, in the Minneapolis home of his brother-in-law, library board member D. Draper Dayton. The list of pallbearers read like a who's who of Minneapolis men.

Gratia had read the notice in the paper on Sunday. She had phoned Etta McBride Brown, now living in Minneapolis, to come immediately to her home. Decades earlier, it was Etta to whom Gratia had poured out her heart when Horace became engaged to Ida Belle while Gratia was wearing his ring. Now it was Etta to whom Gratia turned again, this time with a quiet heart: "Etta, what do you think I have been doing since Horace died? Reading and burning letters. When he was another woman's husband, I tried not to think of him. Now that he is dead, he is mine."[6]

In August, Gratia and Marie and Wellington spent two weeks at Lake Mille Lacs, leasing a grand stone house along the shoreline adjacent to Gratia's property.* It was a month of recovery, not only an emotional rebirth for Gratia, but also a physical recovery for Marie. She had been to the Mayo Clinic, where her *tic doloureux* was corrected with surgery. It was a radical correction, cutting an important facial nerve. For the rest of her life, Marie would be paralyzed on one side of her face. The surgery had diminished the beauty of Marie's counte-

*This stone house would eventually become the lodge for Izaty's Camp, later Izaty's Lodge, and finally, Izaty's Golf and Yacht Club, where in 1994 it is used for small gatherings.

nance, but it had also brought comfort and new energy to her body and spirit.

It was in the stone house at Lake Mille Lacs that the trio coined its joint name—the name that would define their future lake home and farm—Wetoco, for Wellington, Todd, and Countryman. The month in the stone house was a rebuilding of relationships all around. Wellington would enter high school in September, at Pillsbury Academy in Owatonna. And one day, if all went well, Wetoco would be his, for Gratia understood the boy well enough to know that he was truly meant for the out of doors.

In fall, the Lynnhurst home was sold and vacated, with the recouped investment banked until time to build Wetoco. Wellington was delivered to school at Owatonna, while Gratia and Marie moved into a leased flat in southeast Minneapolis, near where Gratia had lived during her university years. The flat had just two bedrooms.

1924. Levi Countryman had advanced cancer. What began the previous summer as an ugly mole on his back had been left unattended. It was now a serious cancer, spread to the spine and elsewhere. Levi had gone east to Cincinnati from California to spend the winter with his doctor son Amplius. Amplius had seen the mole and urged his father to attend to it, but Levi had ignored his son's pleas until it was too late. As Levi's health deteriorated, Amplius also took sick. Gratia began insistent pleas to her father. Never mind that she was now living in a two-bedroom flat; Father must come home to Minneapolis where she could take care of him!

February 5

My dear Father,

. . . I have been thinking that it might be wise for me to come down and bring you up here. Or if it would be unwise for you to come up until warmer weather, then I believe that Dr. Tee could find a nice rest home where you could be well taken care of until Ampy is better.

I do not know what is best to do. I wish I were there to talk it over with you, but I know you will do what is best for the others as well as for yourself. For I'm afraid Adda [Ampy's wife] would not be able to give you care just now, if you should need attention. . . .

Daddy dear, I feel that you, too, must have the very best of care, and I would like to think that you are in a good warm rest hospital with good care while Ampy is still so critically ill.

I will come for you if the doctor advises it. Poor Adda, I am so sorry for her distress. I can only pray for God's loving kindness to take care of us all. Lovingly, Gratia.

On February 8, Gratia marked her twentieth year as chief librarian with the opening of a new library—the East Lake Branch. This opening was *her* party and the guests were *her* librarians, the entire professional staff, each of whom received an engraved invitation.

In the following week, Gratia went down to Cincinnati and brought back her ninety-two-year-old father. He was far sicker than she had ever imagined. She set up a bed in the living room of the flat, hired a daytime nurse, picked up Wellington from school, and sent for her long-absent brother Offie—Theophilus—who was still in the gold fields of Colorado.

Levi lived just a few weeks longer, but he died at home as he had wished. Afterward, Gratia wrote to her absent sister, Lana:

March 29

My dear Lana,

This is a lonesome house tonight with Father gone. I have cared for him so constantly for the past month that I expect to hear him call any moment.

He was so patient all the time, so Spartan-like when he suffered and so considerate of making us trouble, that I loved him more than I ever had and realized the deep piety of the man's soul and his wonderful spiritual insight. If ever a man had a right to enter his mansion in heaven, our dear old father deserved it.

He was up until a week ago. Then he was too weak to get up. . . . All day Thursday and Friday he was sleeping because of the morphia hypodermics, but we reduced these last night and he became conscious. We knew that he tried hard to talk to us, but he made no sounds, only moved his lips, and we couldn't understand. We thought he was dying but that he might live a day or so. So Offie went to bed at 10 o'clock last night. Wellington and I sat up until 12 o'clock, and he seemed to be breathing easier and was unconscious, so we went to bed. At 1:30 I got up again and he was still breathing easily, so I thought I needn't sit up. At 4:30 I got up to give him another hypodermic and he was gone. I so deeply regret that I didn't stay beside him until the last, and I shall probably always regret it. But I had been up so much and was so sleepy that I didn't realize. I think that he never returned to consciousness. I hope not.

We took him over to the undertaker early this morning, and the services are to be at Lakewood [Cemetery] Monday at 12:45. . . . At Father's request, we are cremating him, and later I will take his ashes down by Mother's [at Oakwood Cemetery in Hastings].

It is such a comfort to have Offie here. He has taken so much care of Father and has been just as tender as a woman. Father enjoyed him, too, as long as he was able. And he thoroughly enjoyed being here in our little flat, where the distances were so short.

Oh, I feel as if I had lost the best friend I ever had in this world. He loved us all so deeply and would have done anything for us. . . . I wish you and Ampy could have been here, but I know that was impractical. Affectionately, Gratia.

Part VI. Benevolent Autocrat

A House for Marie

Gratia Countryman was a great organizer. She had the knack of finding the best people for all the jobs. She was pretty much a dictator, but she was always nice about it. When she asked that something be done, it was always for the library, not for her.

University of Minnesota
Professor Emeritus Rodney Loehr
October 5, 1992[17]

1925. In the earliest years of the Minneapolis Public Library, when the first branch library was established and initially housed in an elementary school, the relationship between libraries and schools raised issues not easily resolved. For example, after the First World War the Minneapolis Public Library established libraries in most city schools, expanding as funds permitted. Gratia liked it that way, but now the Board of Education sought to take over these libraries. Gratia recognized that in the school environment, librarians were becoming second-class staff, and she set about to correct the situation before she lost control.

"Marie's" House on France Avenue in Robbinsdale, ca. 1930
Source: Virginia Buffington Shaw

During the 1925 state legislative session, Gratia organized her troops statewide and camped in the state legislative halls. In a way this was a replay of Company Q, for once again Gratia was the lieutenant while her lifelong ally Clara Baldwin played the role of on-site sergeant. Their goal was to obtain for certified school librarians the benefits to which certified teachers were entitled, namely: participation in the State Teachers' Retirement Fund. Like most of Gratia's campaigns, the lobbying effort succeeded in spite of opposition from educational circles. The pressure and hours had taken their toll, however. She longed for an early retirement and quietly prepared to build her home in the country.

Thus in the summer of 1925, "Wetoco Lodge" became a reality. The grand cottage was constructed on Gratia's Lake Mille Lacs property, and it was designed to her detailed specifications. It was a two-story home that lacked both plumbing and electricity, but what a place it was! The kitchen was outfitted as for a country lodge, where grand-scale cooking might be the norm. All of Gratia's protestations to the contrary, she really couldn't stand to be alone for any length of time. She expected to entertain weekend guests in large numbers, and the kitchen centerpiece—a giant wood stove—fitted well to her expectations. The ample kitchen cupboards held glassware and china for twenty-four persons, accessible through double doors both from the kitchen and the living room. A massive field stone fireplace, floor-to-ceiling bookcases, and casement windows made up the four walls of this spacious living area. A guest room lay off to the rear, and to the side were French doors leading to the lakeside dining porch along with a stairway to the second floor. True to Gratia's belief in fresh air, two of the upstairs bedrooms were corner spaces with screens along two sides, yet protected by great overhanging eaves and wooden shutters. The other two bedrooms, including the master bedroom, looked out onto Lake Mille Lacs. These two rooms were enclosed with proper windows, although the ceilings were unfinished beneath the rafters. All together one had the impression of a very civilized existence, even while roughing it in northern Minnesota.

In the decades to follow, Wetoco would offer hospitality to upwards of two hundred different visitors, mostly weekend and week-long guests—family, friends, and most of all library colleagues in abundance. Probably the entire professional staff of the Minneapolis Public Library spent time at Wetoco at some time or other. Always Gratia was the gracious hostess who preferred to do the cooking herself while parceling out to her guests the many menial tasks that needed constant attention.

With the lodge under construction most of the summer, the Wetoco trio spent August in a cabin at Lake Itasca, the source of the Mississippi River. This was to be an interlude especially for Wellington, who suffered greatly from summer allergies. It didn't turn out that way, however, for afterward each of the three, in his or her own way, would remember Lake Itasca as the place of the terrible quarrel!

The issue was *space,* not at Wetoco, but back in Minneapolis. Gratia was conserving her funds so as to have everything she had dreamed of in the new cottage. This meant not only curtailing living expenses, but also giving up Wellington's boarding school. The two-bedroom flat in southeast Minneapolis was sufficient for the three, since Gratia and Marie had always shared one bedroom. And Wellington's room remained Wellington's room, even when he was away at school. Now in the fall he would inhabit it continuously, for he was to start his junior year at Marshall High School in Minneapolis.

The quarrel involved Marie's niece, Marian Jones, who was about to enter the university. She was from Greeley, Colorado, and Marie wanted the young lady to come and live under her protection and under her roof. Probably what Marie really wanted was a home that resembled the Lynnhurst home where she and Gratia had earlier lived so happily. But with Gratia's funds invested at Mille Lacs, this possibility no longer existed. Still, Marie pressed for an arrangement by which Marian could join the family, and Gratia resisted. The quarrel took on such a dimension that Marie actually picked up and left Lake Itasca, claiming that she would find a place of her own.

Gratia was devastated, and for the remainder of the time at Lake Itasca she was completely out of sorts. Wellington had difficulty coping with the presumed loss of his Aunt Marie; yet he did not dare to share these feelings with the brooding Gratia. Instead he turned back to his earliest years. He constructed a daybook of memories, a journal of his lost childhood, complete with illustrations of the homes as he remembered them—both in Brandon, Canada, and in Sioux Falls.

> Mr. Wilson was my first foster father. Mrs. Wilson was my first foster mother. Frank was Mrs. Wilson's suitor and her betrayer. His last name I do not know.
>
> [The Wilson home in Brandon:] On the left side from the sidewalk were sweet peas which grew against the side of the wall and lattice work about half way back, connected to the house.... In back of the lattice there was a garden. Back of the garden was a fence, and I distinctly remember Mrs. Wilson talking to a neighbor. Over beyond this fence was an alley road and then a big yellow brick house.... I also remember the location of some sheep and horses.
>
> The first thing I ever remembered was the time Mr. Wilson woke me at midnight and gave me bread, butter and brown sugar. I estimate that was in the year 1914 when I was four years old.... I remember trying to ride a streetcar for a penny. Evidently the conductor was kindhearted, for I rode the whole distance. I remember the car turning the corner and I got off. I walked a little ways. I believe I was headed for a person's house called Aunt. There had been a litter of setter pups. These I believe were dead and were to be buried. I don't know how I got home.... I remember having a can of green paint, and I painted the end of a beer case and placed my hands on the paint. I remember the green paint all over the inside of my hands, which I thought was exceedingly wonderful. The house I lived in was not a big house. It was a white bungalow having a porch in front and a porch at the side, on the whole very low....

> I seemed to be living happily there, but Agnes Wilson wasn't. I presume Frank and she were enamored of each other at this time. Although I think she liked him, she didn't love him. I remember distinctly her saying that he had begged her to let him come along. She consented. The next few days I remember traveling on the train. I had just learned the word Winnipeg, as I remember jumping up and down in the seat saying Winnipeg! . . . I presume we passed through that city and continued on to Sioux Falls. I remember asking where Daddy was. I don't think I got any answer. . . . We arrived at Sioux Falls where I think we stayed for about a year. I was then five years old. I also remember the house and location. Our house was low down while the others were on a bank . . . I went to a party. I remember trying to catch swinging doughnuts and bobbing for apples. . . . I remember playing with a girl, and she had a great many toys and was evidently very rich. I remember her because she was always saying "don't." . . .

Wellington did not lose his Aunt Marie after all. In fall the two women were together again. Gratia had capitulated and leased a three-bedroom flat. Wellington entered Marshall High School and Marie's niece Marian Jones moved in.

1926. The first decades of the century spawned an incredible number of women's organizations, each dedicated to the betterment of the community in one way or another. Gratia Countryman was a founder of several of these organizations; she was a member of most of them.

These were heady times for American women. Expectations ran high, for had not victories both in war and in women's rights spawned a new world order? Working women—especially the women "downtown"—determined to cement their common achievements and interests with an organization they could call their own. Thus in 1919, the Business Women's Club of Minneapolis came into being, with its first president none other than Gratia Countryman. Occupying rented rooms in the business district, the organization grew and flourished. Its membership soon number close to 2,000, including a newly elected state legislator, an architect, several doctors, nurses, lawyers, teachers, social workers, store clerks, office secretaries, librarians, beauticians, shop owners, and other business entrepreneurs. In fact the principal founder and major underwriter of the organization was Elizabeth Quinlan, owner of Minneapolis's largest and most exclusive women's fashion store.

Inspired by Gratia's leadership and her commitment to the twentieth-century's New Woman, the Business Women's Club rooms soon encompassed an exercise room, dining facilities, a lounge, and a library. In fine weather the members engaged in intramural tournaments on the city's golf courses and tennis courts, and at all times of the year they organized theatricals and parties. In Gratia's view, this women's club should offer nothing less than the elite men's clubs offered, except the elitism. Unlike both major downtown men's clubs, the Business Women's Club membership included all manner of white-collar women. The single club exclusion was men. They were not allowed "in the lounge back of the first rug, except on Saturday nights."

In the flush of 1920s prosperity, members deemed it prudent for the club to construct its own building. With surplus funds and members' gifts, the club quietly purchased a piece of prime downtown property. It lay directly across the avenue from the Minneapolis Club, an exclusive men's domain where women guests entered through a rear door. Then in 1922 the members incorporated as a holding company and mounted a major financial campaign. It was a full military organization with a colonel, a lieutenant colonel (Gratia Countryman), an adjutant, three majors, and ten captains. The war cry: $250,000 and 2,500 members." Neither goal was ever reached. Yet the project went forward, and in March of 1926 the new Business Women's Club of Minneapolis opened its doors on Second Avenue. The attractive building, somewhere between italianate and art-nouveau in style, was a two-story edifice with the most modern of facilities inside. "Facilities" meant offices, a full four-lane bowling alley, spacious lounge, card room, auditorium, tea room, kitchen, library, a dormitory rest room, and two well-lit regulation pool tables. It was the ultimate in a women's downtown club.*

Clearly Minneapolis women were on the move, and Gratia Countryman was out in front. The library too was prospering in these years, for it was a time of prosperity everywhere. Real estate was inflated, and the library was reaping the fruits, for virtually its entire sustenance derived from taxes levied on real estate property.

It was a time to celebrate and a time to escape!

And escape they did. Gratia and Marie each took a two-month leave from the library, beginning in June, along with Gratia's secretary and another library friend. The four women went off to Europe together, Gratia having first delivered Wellington to a farm in Wisconsin. The plan was that Wellington would work for his board and room, with the assurance that if his work did not pay the farmer sufficiently, Gratia would remit the difference at the end of the summer. But Gratia had miscalculated. Within a week of Wellington's arrival,

*The Business Women's Club of Minneapolis prospered briefly, then began a steady decline. The stock market crash in 1929 and the Great Depression that followed proved disastrous for the organization. Declining membership eventually forced the club to sell its building and move to leased quarters in the West Hotel, also in decline. Years later, the Business Women's Club disappeared entirely from the community. But it was probably more than money that sealed the fate of this last vestige of the women's sphere. The political victory won by women in 1920 had essentially destroyed the sisterhood that brought it about. Fewer and fewer women viewed a business *women's* club as the route to economic and political power. It was the men's organizations that counted, though it would still be decades before these male bastions were made accessible to the business women of Minneapolis.

In 1935 the Business Women's Club building was purchased by a Jewish men's fraternity—Gymal Doled (Gamma Delta), later renamed the Standard Club. Its location became a symbol of anti-Semitism in Minneapolis. Daily, Jewish doctors, lawyers, and businessmen walked up Second Avenue for lunch at the Standard Club while their non-Jewish peers took lunch at the Minneapolis Club directly across the street. As mainstream clubs gradually abandoned their discriminatory policies, the Standard Club too was destined for oblivion.

the farmer let him go, sending him back to Minneapolis. Wellington spent the rest of the summer with a school friend. He vindicated himself and paid his way by mailing out hardware catalogues, dismantling an old house, and learning to drive an automobile. When Gratia returned and learned the whole story, her initial anger turned into a grudging respect as she realized that her boy had finally come into his own.

1927. Wellington completed his senior year at Marshall High School and graduated in spring. In fall he enrolled in business school, but the classroom environment was not for him. He wanted to get out into the world and be on his own. In the summer of 1926 he had tasted freedom, and now it was time for real adventure. In this, he was not much different from his uncle Theophilus Countryman—Offie— who was still out in Colorado, not in good health, but unwilling to abandon his adventures in the gold fields of the Rockies. With Gratia's blessing and her good connections, Wellington went west to build tunnels for the Great Northern Railroad.

Down at the library, the Staff Association was deep into a project, the legacy of which would outlast all of the staff—*Library Ann's Cook Book.* Well organized and well bound, the cookbook contained a mountain of good recipes, especially for those who liked to entertain. And the library women did indeed like to entertain. There were luncheons, dinner parties, afternoon teas, and dessert bridge evenings. The library women of Minneapolis were a large and active social circle, which Gratia carefully nurtured through her own participation. Year after year, her daybooks attest to these lively events. Gratia's own contributions to the cook book include "Halibut Mousse," "Rainbow Meat Loaf," "Italian Ravioli," "Macaroni and Cheese Loaf," "Apple Roll," "Florida Delight," and "Simple Tortes."*

1928. T. B. Walker was dead at eighty-eight. He lived just long enough to see his art collection mounted in the new Walker Art

*See page 325 for Gratia's recipes.

Gallery on Lowry Hill. Still, he was never reconciled to the betrayal of his library dream by forces that he did not understand. Until the end Walker held onto the presidency of the Minneapolis Public Library Board and enjoyed a respect bordering on affection from his chief librarian. His passing thus marked the end of an era in Gratia's life, a time when she turned to men as her models and her mentors—first and foremost, her father, Levi Countryman, then Cyrus Northrop and Herbert Putnam, and last of all, dear old T. B. Walker.

Gratia was sixty-one years old when Walker died, hardly an unformed individual ripe to be molded. Yet it was only after Walker's death that she came to view herself as others had viewed her over many years—a model for and mentor of women and of men, especially of the young.

1929. It was a surprise event, organized by the staff of the public library, on February 1 in the auditorium of the Business Women's Club. The occasion: the twenty-fifth anniversary of Gratia Countryman's ascension to the position of chief librarian. The program drew on the myriad talents of the diverse library staff—musical selections, a picture show with photos of staff members as infants, and the dramatization of an afternoon in a junior high library. Reportedly, Gratia was surprised beyond words. The climax was a presentation by Augusta Starr on behalf of the entire staff:

> Hail, Gracious Lady! Chieftain of our band!
> To thee we bring our homage as thy due.
> Famed through length and breadth of all this land,
> Yet to each one of us a friend most true. . . .
>
> Thou hast been ever the Leader, keen and strong,
> While we, thy flock, come slowly, stumbling past;
> Ever the Captain spurring the sluggish throng,
> While we trail far behind among the last. . . .

Grant to us now a boon, we pray of thee,
A gift long since desired by all thy crew—
Sit for thy portrait that thy friends may see
A picture fine, and boldly drawn, and true;

Painted in everlasting colors fair
Such as only a skillful artist can,
The vision and force, the eyes, the face, the hair,
The soul of Gratia Alta Countryman.

Gratia did agree to sit for the portrait. It was completed a year later by a local artist—a somber portrait of a seemingly sober woman—and presented by the staff to the library board. Though Gratia was immensely moved by this act of staff devotion, she never really liked the completed portrait.*

Gratia commemorated these twenty-five years in her own way. She had persuaded the library board to establish a permanent endowment fund, the proceeds of which would be used solely for the acquisition of new books. Upstaging the staff party by a day, she went public with her campaign to raise the endowment funds.

In the spring of 1929, Marie Todd came into a small inheritance. It was Marie's turn now to have a house of her own, with significant help from Gratia. Marie purchased parts of three lots out on France Avenue in Robbinsdale, a developing suburb adjacent to the city. Gratia selected the architect, old friend Hiram Livingston, and together with Marie commissioned a Dutch colonial home that included two baths, plenty of bedrooms, and the inevitable screened sleeping porch. It may have been Marie's home, but Gratia carried the mortgage and probably made most of the decisions. In late summer the house was completed; the two women moved in, and Gratia's sister Lana arrived from California for a year-long sabbatical.

*In 1994, it hangs on the third floor of the library in the office of the Minneapolis Collection.

Early in autumn there was a kind of euphoria in the area. Gratia and Marie were living once again with the trappings of a propertied class; the library was completing the most dynamic year in its forty-year history; and the city was absolutely giddy with prosperity.

There had been danger signals all summer long, a slump in the real estate market and a decline in capital investment. Yet the stock market was inflating so rapidly that even the most novice of investors couldn't help but make money. Already in September the stock market had begun an uncomfortable decline, but it was not until October 24 that the bottom fell out of the market. With virtually the entire investment community buying on margin, the crash precipitated a massive demand for loan repayments, leading to a virtual collapse of the financial community. In Minneapolis, as elsewhere, the real estate market plummeted, businesses failed, and those firms that survived laid off employees to the bare bones. It all happened in a relatively short time, and when things seemed to have hit bottom, in time they got even worse.

This mood of apprehension notwithstanding, the library board and staff observed its fortieth anniversary in December, at a dinner in the Art Department of the downtown library. Four decades of success were joyfully celebrated in song and skit, beginning with the opening of the library—a staff of eight, 13,502 books on the shelves, and a circulation of 200,000 books in the first year. This compared to the year 1928, when the library employed a staff of 300, with 500,000 books on the shelves, an annual circulation of more than 3,000,000 books, and an outreach that included Hennepin County farms, city factories and firehouses, hotels, hospitals, and schools. It was time to be proud, as Gratia boasted that more than one out of three Minneapolis residents owned a library card and used it regularly.

It was also time for caution. Anxious times were ahead, in the nation, in the community, and at the library. Gratia was giving up any thought of retirement. Her library was headed for trouble and her personal life at a crossroad, the latter having to do with one Genevieve Macdonald.

Genevieve Macdonald

Never says anything unkind about anyone. Thinks the best of everyone. Quietly does many thoughtful things and feels sympathy toward anyone in trouble. . . . A woman with a fine spiritual nature which is always felt in her presence. The kind of character to which one looks up. Most conscientious in her work, and in all of the personal relationships. Makes no stir, works quietly but forcefully.

From the Public Library Performance Review
of Miss Macdonald by her Supervisor,
Miss Countryman, June 14, 1931

In 1928 Gratia had hired Miss Genevieve Macdonald, a Canadian librarian, as a temporary replacement on the Bibliographic Committee. Miss Macdonald came well recommended by the chief librarian at Calgary. He wrote, "Miss Macdonald has been with us for some ten years and our reference librarian for the bulk of that time. She is a woman of most unusual gifts and most attractive personality. We value her more than I can tell you. She is unusually well read, has great charm, and an unusually strong personality. I cannot recommend her too highly in every respect."[18]

Genevieve was on leave from the Calgary Public Library and had not intended to stay beyond the year, nor had she anticipated what would happen during that year. She completed her temporary assignment in June, left Minneapolis, and returned home to Calgary. Gratia's letter was not far behind.

Wednesday, July 26, 1929

Beloved, my beloved, when I think that thou wast in the world a year ago and I had no knowledge of thee! Now as I send birthday greetings to thee, I can only express the deepest gratitude that thou was born to bless all of us who have come to know thee. . . . Do you remember quoting to me out under the trees on the Lake of the Isles Boulevard, "And I who looked for only God found thee."

May I quote back from the sonnets, "I love thee with the breath, smiles, tears of all my life! And if God chooses, I shall but love thee better after death."

May birthday after birthday, year in and out, find us closer and closer, more understanding and more sympathetic not only of each other, but through each other, of all the human family. My love has always stood more erect in thy presence, and if I should never see thy face again or hear thy voice except in dreams, I should still always stand more erect and aspiring for having had these last five weeks. . . .

I couldn't have dreamed of thee, and I was not looking for thee or anyone. Thee was just God's gift, and I can only give thee one real birthday gift, my appreciation of this gift and my heartfelt desire to be worthy of it.

What was it that drew these two women so close to one another in such a short time? One might speculate, for both had once loved and lost. In Gratia's case it was Horace Winchell. For Genevieve it was the young man to whom she became engaged in 1914. He went off to war with the elite Scottish Black Watch Highlanders and he never came back.

Later, under the signature of Miss Countryman, chief librarian, a formal position offer went off from Minneapolis to Genevieve Macdonald at the Calgary Public Library.

October 19

Dear Miss Macdonald:

Will you accept a position in our Readers' Advisory Service at $1800.00 per year, beginning January 1st?

> I think you already know fairly well the nature of the work. Last year was a trial year. Mr. Lewis reports a much increased work this fall, and we are sending out considerable publicity among people who should know about this service for Adult Education. (I prefer to call it Continued Education.)
>
> I shall be glad to know as soon as convenient whether you want to consider it. Very truly yours, (signed) Gratia A. Countryman.

On the last day of December, Genevieve Macdonald came to Minneapolis and moved into Marie's house, to share the rest of her life with Gratia Countryman.

1930. This was the beginning year of the trying times, a peaking of library circulation—3.7 million books in a single year—even as the library's financial base shrank and withered. Library usage mushroomed in direct proportion to growing unemployment. Gratia may have created the new Readers' Advisory Service with Genevieve in mind, but the timing was perfect. In the vocabulary of the 1990s, the public library had created an adult education format closely resembling a "university without walls." Explained Gratia:

> The Readers' Advisory Service . . . is designed to help the adult whose business or domestic responsibilities prevent him from taking formal courses, whether by correspondence or in day or night classes. He may not have completed a grade school education or he may have attended school irregularly . . .
>
> The [personalized] typewritten course may consist of a few books or of several. It may progress from a simple book to a difficult one, as in grammar, or from one period of time to another, as in a historical subject. Sometimes a course may touch the different aspects of a subject, as in psychology or sociology. Perhaps it is the study of poetry or of some one author. . . .
>
> Reading and study become alive and vital if we know someone who is interested in what we are. We need someone who will discuss that puzzling passage, listen to a particularly lucid explanation, appreciate that graphic description, or exchange opinions

In the Library Technical Room, 1920
Source: Minneapolis Public Library, the Minneapolis Collection

> with us. The readers' advisor may be regarded as a sympathetic tutor, ready to help the reader with his difficulties and to share his enthusiasm. . . .[19]

Other innovations followed—lectures in the library, radio listening at the library, followed by audience discussions, weekly book reviews broadcast on radio—all to fill the time and improve the morale and minds of a large population afflicted by unemployment.

Armed with new ideas and a natural optimism when it came to the human potential, Gratia Countryman was becoming the most sought after speaker in the city. She made the entire circuit of men's luncheon clubs, promoting new programs and reminding listeners of the library's historic outreach.

> The library is serving as a relief institution, for in these times, not only must physical relief be given, but harassed minds and spirits need rest. Many cases every day show we are reaching new persons. A typical example is that of a mechanic, out of a job, who came to us and said now he would have time to realize a life-long ambition. He wanted to read [Horatio] Alger books. Hundreds of persons who find they have time for reading are served each month by our Readers' Advisory Service.
>
> Every bedside in the 15 Minneapolis hospitals is reached twice a week by someone from the library to offer them good reading. The shorter working day and week are inevitable in the future. More leisure time will result, and the library is preparing to serve these persons with reading offering a chance for self-development. . . .[20]

If this was a time when the public library's influence on the community was at an all-time high, it also was a time when the chief librarian herself was offered accolades of every sort from an adoring public. In 1931, the first of these was awarded by the Interracial Service Council of Minneapolis—the Civil Service Honor Medal because her "unselfish devotion to the cause of constructive help for all classes of people has made her influence felt in many movements that make for enlightenment and better understanding and because her many years of service to Minneapolis as chief librarian have been a blessing to our community."[21]

In December, on personal invitation from President Herbert Hoover, Gratia went to Washington and participated in the President's Conference on Home Building and Home Ownership. And six months later, in June of 1932, she was awarded an honorary master of arts degree from her alma mater, the University of Minnesota:

> To devote a life to unselfish public service, to be an evangel of education for all ages, to use books to unlock the hidden resources of youth, to use them to instruct maturity, and to provide companionship for old age, thus bringing honor and distinction upon the commonwealth and enlightenment to its citizens, and with no thought of personal gain—for these reasons, Gratia Countryman, the University of Minnesota, by action of the entire Administration and of the Board of Regents, confers upon you the degree of Master of Arts, with all of the rights, duties, and privileges which pertain to that degree here and elsewhere.[22]

This was the fourth honorary degree awarded in the history of the university, the previous recipients having been former university presidents Folwell and Vincent and former United States Secretary of State Frank B. Kellogg. When Gratia was asked afterward how she felt, she replied, "Happy of course! I am more pleased, more appreciative, and more humble about this recognition than about anything that has ever come to me because it is the first time there has been such direct acceptance of my efforts toward education."[23]

1933. This was indeed a pinnacle for the chief librarian, seemingly universal acknowledgement of her lifetime mission. In this period of short money supply, the Northwestern National Bank featured Miss Gratia Countryman in an invited lecture series designed for women. Gratia's topic: "The Household Budget." To replenish the supply of loanable library books, Gratia literally took to the streets. With Kiwanis, Rotary, and a host of women's organizations participating, the drive for books exceeded Gratia's expectations both in quantity and in quality. Beyond and above all this was the success of the Readers' Advisory Service, under its director Genevieve Macdonald.

But what about Marie Todd? Was it not she who created an art collection that library patrons could literally carry home with them? Was it not she who first made phonograph records a loanable item, beginning with the Edison cylinders and moving on to whatever technology came along for providing music to the masses? Over the years, Marie's art and music rooms had been emulated by the best known libraries of the nation. In Minneapolis they commanded fierce loyalty from a circle that spanned all ages. Wrote one of Marie's youthful patrons almost sixty years later:

> Along the Library south wall, centered in a stretch of the alley, was an access door quite unlike those awaiting the visitor at the main entrance. This modest opening was most suitable for a lad escaping from the church next door and its midweek prayer meeting, moving from darkness to light as it did. Then just a quick walk down the corridor to the stair and up to the first floor back right lay the entrance to the world of musical recordings. Here in this spacious room, for a brief moment, he was able to suspend time out there and immerse himself in the sound flow found nowhere else in his world. Listening rooms with clear glass walls were there waiting, mostly unoccupied at night. Kind women who knew everything were also waiting and were not dismayed to hand out, for perhaps the 20th time to that same young person, those precious 78's of Sibelius's 2nd Symphony or the pizzicato movement of Tchaikovsky's Fourth. . . .
>
> The Fine Arts Room was on the third floor, available by winding up the lofty, marble and wrought iron main staircase with its huge curved windows overlooking the street scene. Only the young or the serious researcher was likely to climb to those

> heights. Among the discoveries to be made in the Fine Arts Room was a remarkable collection of postcard reproductions of the world's finest cultural offerings, done in color and in black-and-white: paintings, drawings, architectural renderings, photographs. I hesitate to think how woefully undeveloped would be my appreciation for the female form were it not for that eclectic collection. "What a diligent child!" or "What a remarkable attention span!" must have been the musings of the librarians as they witnessed my lingering eye on card after card through tray after tray. The world's definition of beauty housed in a two- by three-foot filing cabinet![24]

This was the world created over many years by Marie Todd —once Gratia's beloved "thee" and always Wellington's gentle "Aunt Marie." In the unsettled world of Depression America, that which defined Marie's character—art and music of the ages—had lost its luster, for her health was beginning to fail. Call it a premature aging (Marie was now fifty-six years old), perhaps the result of high blood pressure, or a remnant of the old *tic doloureux*. No definition could really explain Marie's gradual deterioration. At the time one dared not say the word, but in all probability Marie Todd had fallen into a deepening depression, and quite likely it was triggered by the arrival of Genevieve Macdonald, Gratia's "Vieve."

In the spring of 1933, Gratia's brother Offie, now Theo—elderly, somewhat broken, and with very little funds—accepted her invitation to come home to Minneapolis. Theo's children were long grown and somewhat estranged from him. Their mother had raised them in California while Offie led a bachelor existence in the Colorado mining fields.

Thus, on France Avenue, Theophilus Countryman became the fifth member of a household that already included the three library women and a full-time maid. It was a difficult fit at best. Gratia would say later that this was the worst spring of her life, not only because of the dynamics at home, but also because of the deteriorating financial situation at the library. With a household overflowing, Gratia was seized by an overwhelming weariness—a combination of physical and mental exhaustion. She arranged a two-month unpaid leave from the library and spent the time at Wetoco Lodge with Theo. Occasionally Wellington joined them, a week at a time between job assignments, for in these years he was involved in large-scale construction, from Minnesota's Iron Range to Mississippi's levees.

Genevieve also took unpaid leave from the library and from France Avenue. She went off to Vancouver for the summer. Marie stayed at home, to tend her garden and presumably keep her corner of the library afloat.

At Wetoco Lodge

> *These August days have been glorious, cool, sunshiny, delicious. Our woods are not magnificent but very domestic and intimate, and I've especially loved them this summer when the trees have been my quiet companions, lifting "their leafy arms to pray,"*
>
> Gratia to Genevieve, August 1933

1933. Gratia's summer sojourn at Wetoco was planned as a retreat, a time and a place for remembrance and for revival. Thus she later considered it providential that Constance's letter should have reached her just there.

Constance Buffington was Gratia's niece in Duluth and was truly closer to Gratia than an ordinary niece. She had lived in Gratia's home while attending the university some seventeen years earlier. She and her husband, Gilbert, had taken Wellington on their honeymoon at a time when Gratia feared authorities would snatch the boy from her and return him to Canada. Later, in Wellington's obstreperous adolescent years, he had spent a semester in Duluth with Constance and Gilbert. Above all, Constance was the daughter of Lana, for whom Gratia felt a lifelong responsibility.

> Dear Aunt Gratia,
>
> I almost called you up last night until I remembered I couldn't, for you had no phone. At one o'clock we got a telegram from Florence Conger [Charles Conger's second wife] saying my father had died at 7:30 that evening. Nothing more. He looked so strong and well when I saw him this spring that I can't imagine a sudden illness. I am asking Florence to write me more about it. An auto wreck, perhaps.
>
> Of course, Auntie, this is no heartbreaking blow. I think I saw him once in the last ten years and he was not as good to me as Uncle Theo. But the breaks in the immediate circle of our family are crowding in so fast.* I do dread the shock for Mother. She is so repressive, and none of us can know what it will mean to her—the very end of her connection with romance and young life. She is so lonely there by herself in Ontario as it is. Oh, I do wish you were here to talk with me. Everything is so confused. I can't feel the grief of a proper daughter and yet I can't feel impersonal either. Love to you, Constance.

What memories this letter called forth in the reader! Charles Conger, the gentle poet and classicist from Gratia's university days. Friend Charles, who but for Horace Winchell could have been Gratia's. But Gratia never loved Charles. She loved only Horace. In time Charles loved and married her sister Lana.

Two sisters, each of whom was once betrothed—the older one in a love that was never consummated yet never denied by either side—the younger one in a love that was fully consummated yet later shattered through disappointment and rejection. Questions arise: Which sister was more blessed and which sister suffered the greater loss? To such questions there are no answers.

---

*Gratia's brother Amplius had died in Cincinnati some months earlier.

In the forest at Wetoco, Gratia pondered this long-suppressed corner of her heart. Yet her feelings were beyond sharing, even with Genevieve, to whom she would turn for comfort.

Wetoco Lodge
Wednesday, July 19

My precious friend [Genevieve],

I'm writing by candlelight so mustn't write long. I've been thinking of you having such a happy reunion with old friends, but tonight you have been having a reunion with me, as I sat in the quiet twilight with the gold beams just lingering on the tree trunks. . . . I'm trying to rest and do pretty well. But I think I'll try to get Agnes to come up. I like to be abed in the morning and not think of meals. The men are so good, but they have to eat and so do I. Well[ington] and I are driving over to Wahkon this evening to telephone Marie. If she will come up Friday evening, Well will drive down tomorrow for her. . . .

Wednesday

My dear one,

. . . Yes, I'm staying right in bed. On the porch in your bed—night and day. Elizabeth [Bray, daughter of an old friend] is doing splendidly. She baked bread, such good bread, yesterday. Today she made a cake and she does everything so well and so fast. I'm so sorry I didn't bring her at the very start.

My program is to have my breakfast in bed, then get up sometime in the forenoon and walk around and stay up for dinner, and then back to bed for the rest of the day. I sit up between while in bed to rest my back and knit or play solitaire or read awhile, though I haven't read much. . . .

Wellington and Theo drove to Duluth yesterday and brought Lana down.* She will be with me for a week. . . . The cows were in

*After Charles's death, Constance sent for her mother to finish out her summer vacation in Duluth. Lana returned to California in time for school opening. Worried about her mother, Constance sent her son Edwin back with Lana. He lived with his grandmother for three years, attending the high school where she taught Latin. He never fully understood the reason for the arrangement. In his adult years, Edwin Buffington harbored a great regret that his adolescence was spent away from his Duluth family, especially from his father.

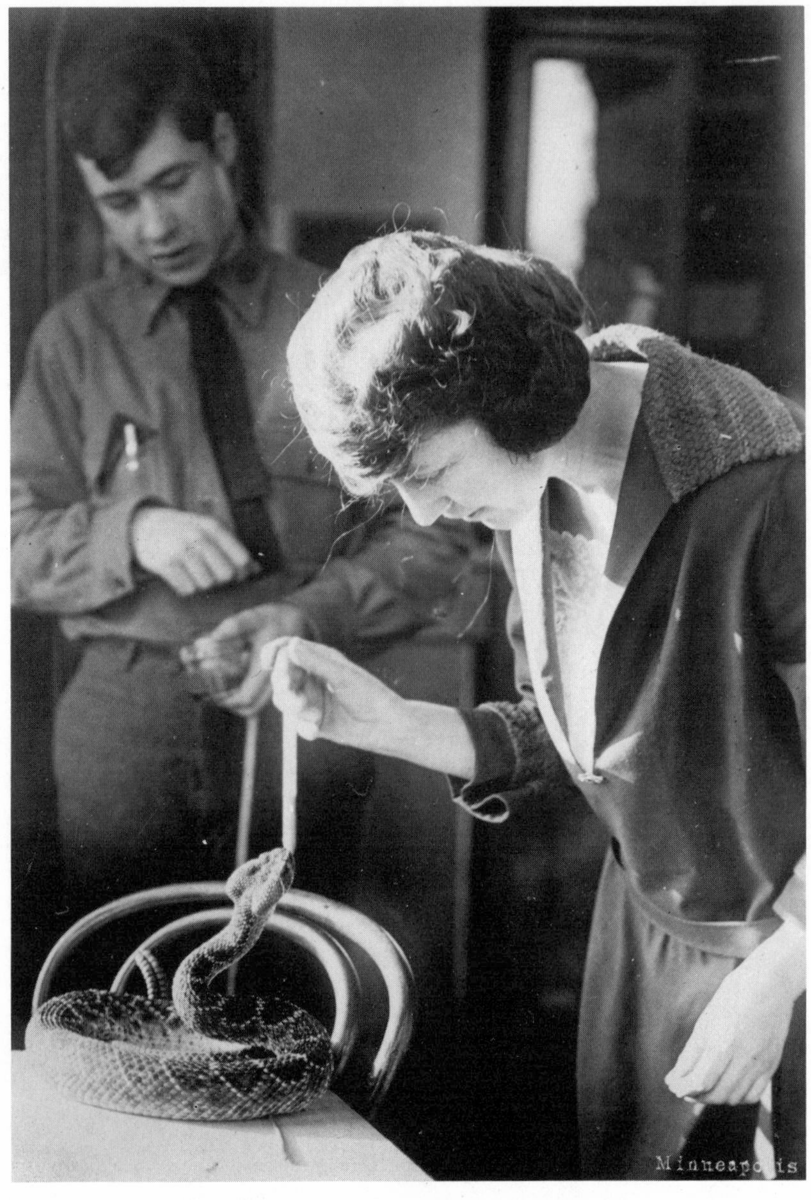

Grace Wiley, with one of her snakes, and Wellington, ca. 1927
Source: Wellington Countryman

the corn last night, the whole family; they made a mess of things. So Theo has picked several dozen ears which Lana will salt down, except what we can eat. . . . It isn't easy to write sitting up in bed, dear heart, but Wellington is going over to Wahkon presently and I want to send this. . . .

Dear heart of mine, thee dwells in the very corner of my being and I am happy just thinking of thee. Now good-bye, with love, GAC.

Sunday

Dear one,

I've just been helping Elizabeth [Bray] to get a very good dinner, all in the pressure cooker, after staying in bed until 11:30. Wellington had three big helpings and pronounced his mother a good cook. He has been so sweet and kind to me and has been working very hard getting those giant trees cut down. I shall miss him in spite of that fact that I wanted to be alone. As I grow better, I like better and better his cheerful whistle and banging ways, for I think I am less nervous and sleep better, especially with the help of luminal. . . .

Poor Wellington has hay fever so badly. I'm sorry for him, but he keeps right at his work. I think he likes it. The splitting up of two great trees has given him something regular to do. Marie will be up, I hope, the last of the week, and I'm looking forward to that. Now, perhaps only postals from now on, best so, *nicht wahr*? Yours, GAC.

The Snake Lady

. . . Why should Minneapolis not have a good zoological garden? It is the live part of this museum that attracts the children; yes, and the grownups, too. Whenever the alligators are fed, everybody, old and young, gathers around the tank to enjoy the sight; the children love the turtles and

> *even the snakes, and listen with breathless interest to talks about their habits and usefulness. . . .*
>
> Gratia Countryman, "Shall we have a Museum," *Minneapolis Parent Teacher Broadcaster* Fall 1929

1933. Ah, the museum! From the beginning it had been a thorn in Gratia's side, but Gratia understood politics at least as well as she understood human beings. Without the museum there might never have been the great Minneapolis Public Library. The museum belonged to the Minnesota Academy of Natural Sciences, an organization that dated back to 1873. Among its distinguished founders had been Professor Newton Winchell (Horace's father) and T. B. Walker. Walker was president of the academy for most of its life. The academy offices and museum had occupied the top floor of the public library from the time of its opening, and much of the museum collection consisted of specimens contributed by Walker. The pundits had called it a "dead" museum to which nothing was ever added and from which nothing was taken away, that is, until the arrival of Grace Wiley as curator, in 1922. By that time the once ample academy finances had dwindled to nothing. The library board determined that Mrs. Wiley's salary should be paid from library funds. As long as T. B. Walker ruled, Gratia Countryman was in no position to challenge the arrangement. But that was not the principal issue.

Grace Wiley was the issue. By education she was an entomologist. By nature, she was absolutely attuned to some of nature's most curious creatures. Under her care, the museum had become anything but dead. Grace Wiley's world included turtles, lizards, chameleons, alligators, toads, and above all else, snakes. It was the snakes that established Grace Wiley's reputation and eventually caused her demise. Children flocked to the library, not only to see the live creatures, but even more to watch Mrs. Wiley handle her pet snakes. She was a tiny woman, and her fine fingers moved in snakelike ways that only increased the children's fascination. Grace Wiley and her snakes were in demand in schools throughout the city. In a time when automobiles were the exception, she carried the most poisonous of specimens in a satchel as she rode the streetcars to her school destinations. She encouraged children to pet her snakes, after first taming them with her limber fingers. When it came to snakes and children, Grace Wiley—the snake lady—was in her element.

After the death of T. B. Walker, members of the Academy of Natural Sciences proposed turning over to the library all of its property. But the library board really didn't want the property—not the mummy, not the pickled octopus, not the geological dioramas, not the crustaceans, nor the plaster model of a paleolithic homo erectus. And for Grace Wiley, *living* creatures were all that counted.

Encouraged by the library board, Gratia Countryman went to the public with her own proposal, to find a new home for Mrs. Wiley and the museum:

> Almost all cities the size of Minneapolis have their zoo. Even towns like Minot, North Dakota, or Virginia, Minnesota, have good zoos. It seems to us who have watched the interest in this small museum that the time is ripe for a movement to establish a zoological garden or a municipal museum or a combination, even if it begins in a small way, as it is just beginning in St. Paul. We would like to suggest a way by which a movement may be started and encouraged. Nothing is ever done unless the people themselves show an interest and make a persistent and sometimes long-continued effort to accomplish it. There surely must be hundreds of people in Minneapolis who are interested in some form of nature study and would willingly get behind a movement for a real municipal museum or zoological garden. . . . Such an interested group could be a nucleus around which interest . . . could crystallize. There may be even now some public-spirited persons

> ready to help such an enterprise with benefactions if they once see evidence of interest. . . .
>
> *Minneapolis Parent Teacher Broadcaster,* Fall 1929

Gratia's plea drew little response. After the stock market crash, the idea of a municipal zoo was beyond ordinary comprehension. The museum and Grace Wiley were not to be unloaded, for the Academy of Natural Sciences went ahead and dissolved the organization, leaving all of its collection to the public library.

Mrs. Wiley's snakes may have been a delight to the city's children and a favorite subject of the city newspapers, but they were a constant worry to the chief librarian. The library maintenance men refused to clean the museum premises, for often as not they would discover one of the snake cages open and one or more poisonous snakes slithering across the floor. Grace Wiley herself would often be in the museum alone late at night, feeding, petting, and talking to her snakes, especially her favorite rattlesnake—Huckleberry Finn. One night the inevitable happened and Mrs. Wiley was bitten by a snake that was shedding its skin. She calmly called a cab and went to General Hospital for treatment, just in time. The experience did little to increase her caution, but it did much to increase the chief librarian's consternation.

In December of 1933, Grace Wiley and her snakes finally left Minneapolis. Mrs. Wiley was offered a position in the reptile wing of the new Chicago Zoological Park at Brookfield, Illinois. The other live creatures in the library museum found new homes, and the space once again became the "dead" museum where nothing was ever added or taken away.

National Prexy: The ALA

Ignorance has always been a menace to civilization. The world has progressed by ideas, by thinking, and we are going to work out a new world society, not with arms but with brains. Men and women who are studying and thinking are fitting themselves for the new conditions they must live in. As I have watched the throngs in our reading rooms, I have thought not so much of the leisure time they were trying to fill as the habits of reading and thinking which were fitting them, whether they realized it or not, to adjust themselves to new situations.

Gratia Countryman, in her American Library Association presidential address, as quoted by the *New York Times,* July 9, 1934

1934. In October 1933, at Chicago, Gratia Countryman had been elected president of the American Library Association (ALA). It was the worst of times for libraries. As the depression deepened nationwide, budgets were being cut to the bone. Yet Gratia was on a new high. The snakes were gone, and her name was abroad in the community as never before. Wrote a major city newspaper:

> Minneapolis loves and honors Gratia Countryman most because she traveled and tramped its street in the early days to study the reading needs of each of its little outlying districts; because she has had thought for the bedbound, the povertybound, the troublebound, and has offered them her greatest solace, books; because she has believed and still believes that taking books to people who need them is her job; because she does that job with the sympathetic understanding which makes a book a benediction.[25]

Energized by this demonstrated confidence, Gratia mounted an ambitious library campaign for increased financial support from Minneapolis and Hennepin County. Her strategies

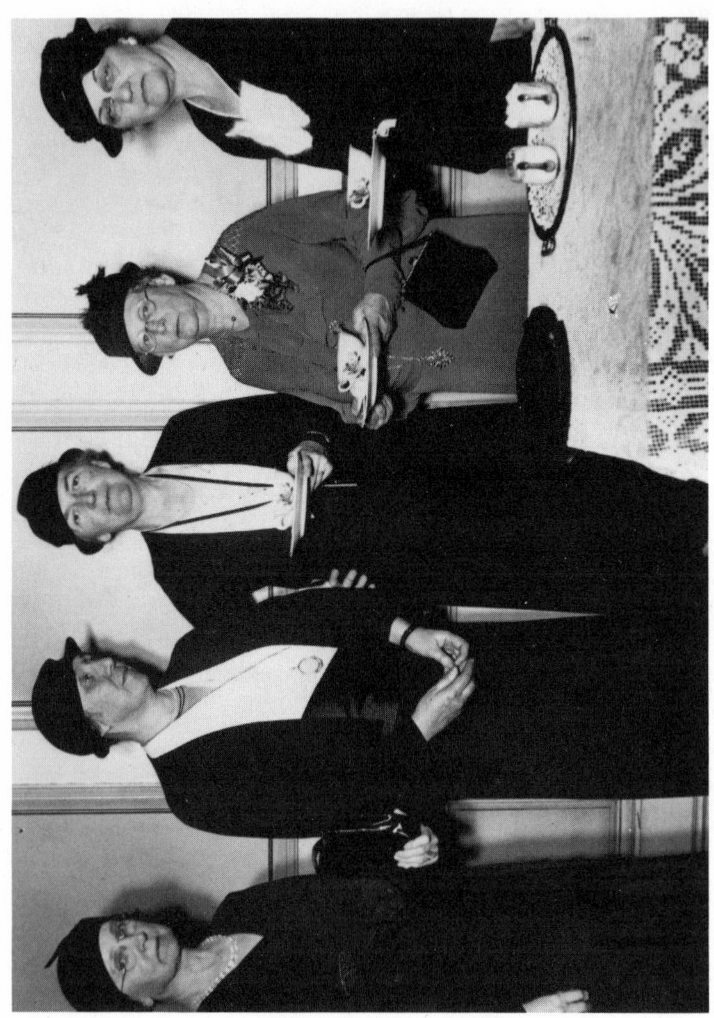

Woman's Club Tea for Gratia, newly elected president of the American Library Association, 1933: Gratia, second from right; on Gratia's right the club president, Mrs. Wilbur F. Decker

Source: Minneapolis Public Library, the Minneapolis Collection

WHAT CAN YOU DO TO HELP THE LIBRARY?

20% added cut in the Library appropriation

Stops the buying of books.

Closes the Library and all its Branches for 3 months.

YOU CAN

See your alderman and ask his help in getting support for the Library

Urge any organization to which you belong to send resolutions to the City Council and Board of Estimate and Taxation asking adequate support for the Library.

Write letters to the Board of Estimate and Taxation and to the newspapers telling them what the Library is worth to you and to the community.

Talk to your friends and neighbors and enlist their support.

YOU CAN SAVE THE LIBRARY

would become the model in a national arena—to create a lobby group of the city's 200,000 library patrons. The centerpiece of the campaign was the leaflet Gratia created—printed by the tens of thousands and distributed not only through the public library system but also through every organization in town over which the chief librarian had any influence.

By midyear Gratia's reputation and her message were alive and well across the land. In June the *New York Times* featured her efforts in a lengthy article, under the headline "A Missionary Library." The article began, "In Minneapolis the public libraries are as unacademic as Miss Gratia Countryman can make them. The very sound of her name intimates her ardor in getting books to people who want them and in bringing those who care little for reading to want books. . . ."

The library system limped along through the year, thanks to a one-time loan from the Board of Estimate and Taxation. In fall Gratia pleaded for more funds in 1935, but the prognosis was even worse. As it turned out, the saving of the library system would come from a new source—the federal government, through a subsidized work program called the WPA [Work Projects Administration]. This was the brain child of President Franklin D. Roosevelt and his "New Deal" program.

1935. In May, with the blessing and support of the Minneapolis Public Library Board, Gratia was off to Europe again. This time it was to attend the Second International Library and Bibliographical Congress in Madrid. Gratia was no longer president of the ALA, having served out her year. She was, however, to give a major speech at the Congress in Madrid—"The School Libraries of the United States." With her on the adventure were three other state librarians, among them Clara Baldwin, veteran of the English bicycle tour forty years earlier. Both Nazi Germany and Stalin's Soviet Union were well represented at the Congress. Their spokesmen proudly proclaimed how their governments were using libraries to achieve national goals. Gratia took notice, for she had always preached that libraries should be a tool to educate for the nation's common good. Probably she had not earlier imagined that national goals might not always be "good" goals. But after Madrid she never again spoke of a nation's goals without specifying the importance of ethical and moral values.

Gratia returned home with two invitations that she expected to comply with, for retirement was not far off—one from the Vatican librarian to visit him in Rome and the other from the librarian of the Royal Swedish Library in Stockholm. Gratia would never make another trip to Europe, but over the years she would engage in a lively correspondence with both of these faraway colleagues.

On her way home, Gratia stopped off in Chicago, ostensibly to report to ALA headquarters on the conference, but in fact to visit Wellington. In the spring of 1935, he abandoned his nomadic life on construction projects and took a position in Chicago, as property manager. This was the beginning of a career that would carry him through life, bringing satisfaction to himself and to his mother. Gratia certainly had always hoped that Wellington would settle in Minneapolis, but in the 1930s one moved to where the jobs were.

In Robbinsdale, "Marie's" house continued to be overflowing with occupants. First of all, the head of the Hospital Service Department, Elva Bailey, had come on hard times. Gratia invited Mrs. Bailey to move in—now four librarians, brother Theo, and Mrs. Black, the maid.

At the library, hiring was in full swing—the hiring of WPA workers to augment the library staff. These workers were paid directly by the federal government, although their work supervisors were in the library staff command.

Thursday evening, September 26

My dear Son,

My letter last week just crossed yours, and I have been too busy to write since. I've needed a good deal of rest besides. These federal WPA projects are very wearing. I am hearing tales of woe, interviewing many poor unemployed people, none of whom are capable of doing library work, until I get heartsick and exhausted. It might as well have been me that was suffering for work. It is no fault of mine that I have always had a job, a good many better people than I have been thrown out. Well, I am thankful for my good fortune.

The $20.00 which you sent was checked right into your bank account. You now have $53.00 there, and have paid your own insurance premium in April and July, besides paying your union fee

> and living. I think that is a pretty good record. But of course you should keep it up—for you may lose a job too. . . .
>
> Aunt Marie has your letter this week. Sorry you had such a time with hay fever. I wish you would have some serum injections in time next year.
>
> . . . Affectionately, Mother.
>
> Poor Mrs. [Grace] Wiley. She has had a blow. I think there is much history behind it. She has had a collapse. Her mother has written me.

Grace Wiley had been fired from the Brookfield Zoo after a gardener found one of her most deadly snakes curled up in a pile of leaves outside the zoo building. Her reputation well tarnished, Mrs. Wiley took her snakes to Los Angeles. There she displayed them from time to time and leased them occasionally to the film studios. Grace Wiley died suddenly within a few years, after being bitten by one of the snakes. It was a sad end for this exceptional woman who had no peer when it came to understanding the curious world of a reptile.

On November 29, Gratia celebrated her sixty-ninth birthday. From Chicago, Wellington telegraphed flowers and Gratia wrote back immediately:

> November 29
>
> Thank you, my dear son, for the glorious bunch of chrysanthemums, which reached me today on my birthday. I appreciated them very much as I do every mark of your affection and thoughtfulness. I only scold you about the things which make me worry over your future and your success. But I always love your kind generous ways, which lead you nevertheless into over-much spending. . . . The Library Staff gives a dinner party for me next Saturday night. Will write more next time. Many thanks. Lovingly, Mother.

And indeed the staff did put on a magnificent party, in the art room of the library. The event was complete with a mimeographed booklet, including cover portrait of their chief and an abbreviated biography. The toastmaster was staff member Glenn Lewis, who would later be the staff's overwhelming choice as Gratia's successor. The "presentation" was by Mabel Bartleson, her final act of fidelity to the woman who through all the years had sheltered her from an undeserved past.*

In December, one of Gratia's librarians—not a close friend—was moved to put on paper her feelings not only about the library, but also about its chief.

> Minneapolis, Minnesota
> December 22
>
> Dear Miss Countryman:
>
> Because the Christmas season is a time to open our hearts and tell what lies there, I want to take advantage of it to tell you—above all others—what happiness has come to me through my work in the library and through you.
>
> Perhaps I do not need to tell you that my work is a joy, that for me it is not work, but a fulfillment. I believe you know that; but about my feeling for you, you could not know unless I told you. Naturally, it is a little difficult to put into bare words all that feeling, because it seems like an intrusion, but the dignity with which you have endowed all my efforts by your warm friendliness and cooperation and inclusion as one of your own, coming at a time that had become bewilderingly and surprisingly hard and dark for me, has brought me to what I feel is one of the happiest phases of my life. I feel, without reserve, that I owe this great blessing to you, and I want you to know how I value it and my association with you. You have quietly and consistently "held up my hands" in everything I have tried to do. I am not unmindful of that. . . .
>
> You have somehow not treated me as a stranger and a newcomer but as one who is welcomed home. I wish you every happiness for the new year. Very sincerely yours, (Mrs. J. E.) Mabel Oren.

*Harry Hayward and the Kitty Ging murder.

Gratia's last Library Board Meeting, November 1936: left to right, President E.C. Gale, Gratia Countryman, Archie Walker, Mrs. Philip Erickson
Source: Minneapolis Public Library, the Minneapolis Collection

Farewell

My best wishes to all the library staff for the coming year, not only to the staff as a whole, but to each and every individual member of it. You have always been a wonderful working group, but chiefly because you have each in your particular place promoted the best development of the library. You have made it yield the best service possible to each person who came to use it. You have made its reputation, and it will be you as a group and as individuals who will continue to make its reputation. . . .

Gratia Countryman
December 27, 1936

1936. The city of Minneapolis had specific rules covering women employees. They were required to retire at age sixty-five, but the requirement could be waived annually up to age seventy. In Gratia's case it had been waived year after year. But this was the year of her seventieth birthday, meaning retirement was indeed at hand. Gratia would have liked to stay longer. She never really felt her work was finished, and certainly the "worst of times" in the nation's economy were still very present. Gratia probably thought also of her personal economic situation, for she had already embarked on her retirement project—the Wetoco Dairy and Poultry Farm, an enterprise that would require constant capital investment.

In spring the library board appointed a search committee. It was rumored that Miss Countryman wanted an outsider to take over, even as her staff expected one of their own—namely, Glenn Lewis—to succeed her. How much credence the rumor held will never be known. After a long wrangle on the divided library board, Carl Vitz, a librarian from Ohio, was selected as fourth director. Happily for many on the staff, ten years later Glenn Lewis would become the fifth chief librarian.

Beginning in September, the Gratia Countryman fetes were

under way. It seemed as though every organization in the city wanted a farewell talk from the retiring librarian. *The Minneapolis Journal* published a major feature article by reporter Bess Wilson. The article itself became a classic for journalism. It began:

> "Behind Miles's, Darius Miles's that was, I asked an Irishman how many potatoes he could dig in a day, wishing to know how well they yielded. 'Well, I don't keep any account,' he said; 'I scratch away and let the day's work praise itself.'"
>
> So wrote Thoreau in his journal on September 24, 1851. And I remembered these words the other day when I let my mind go over the years of Gratia Countryman's work in Minneapolis, those years which are coming to such a triumphant close the first of the new year. Gratia Countryman has had no need to "keep any account." Certainly she has "scratched away." Most certainly of all, her "day's work has praised itself."
>
> Her "day's work"—all the days there are in all the years that have stretched ahead from that day in 1889 when she became part of the library system of Minneapolis, then a pretty small system in comparison to its reach in 1936. . . .
>
> When I made up my mind that I was going to give myself the pleasure of writing about this Gratia Countryman of ours, I let my mind slip back over the years I have watched her work, have stood on the fringe of her acquaintanceship, I tried to get as far back as the very first contact with her.
>
> As nearly as I can remember it came one day when I was sent by *The Journal* to get from Miss Countryman a statement on one of the important civic problems of the moment. I found her at a hotel having luncheon with one of those committees on which she has always done such yeoman service for Minneapolis. She left the luncheon table and came to talk with me.
>
> The matter in hand took about three minutes—certainly not longer. Miss Countryman knew exactly how she felt about the question, exactly what she wanted to say. She said it tersely, precisely and briefly, dictating slowly so that my clumsy longhand could get the words as she spoke them. Then she looked up with a smile and said, "You won't let your paper change that, will you?

That's exactly what I mean, and I trust you to see that I am quoted accurately. . . . "

So powerful was Bess Wilson's tribute to Gratia that speakers throughout the community began to attribute to Miss Countryman the phrase, "Let the day's work praise itself," forgetting that it was written by Henry Thoreau and later picked up by Bess Wilson.

On the first Tuesday of November, Franklin D. Roosevelt was elected for a second term as president of the United States. Wrote Gratia shortly after the election:

Wednesday evening

My dear Wellington,

. . . I was interested in your reaction to the elections, and now that they are over you realize how many people agreed with you about Roosevelt. I don't think there has ever been an election where a presidential candidate carried 46 states, the only other two being among the smallest in the U.S. Even big manufacturing states, with great industries and utilities, like Massachusetts, Michigan and Pennsylvania, were for him. It is most astonishing.

But I also voted for him, for I didn't think [Alf] Landon was big enough, and every time he made a speech he lost votes. [William] Borah would have run better, but he was a little old to bear so great a burden as the presidency. Now Roosevelt will have a chance to finish up some of the plans he has begun, and I shall be interested in watching whether he turns to the left or right. It will depend upon his wisdom in choosing advisors. I don't think he was fortunate in the personnel of the Commission who have been trying to settle the longshoremen's strike.* We are going to feel tragic results of that strike if it isn't settled.

---

*The Longshoremen's strike to which Gratia refers began October 29, 1936, on the Pacific Coast, following failed negotiations between the ship owners and the several unions representing longshoremen and other maritime workers. These negotiations had been both facilitated and monitored by President Roosevelt's newly appointed Federal Maritime Commission. On November 6, the Atlantic and Gulf Coast longshoremen also went on strike. Thus, for eighty-six days, international trade with the United States came to a complete halt. The east coast strike folded the end of January 1937, with the ship owners having "won." The west coast strike was settled February 7, virtually a total victory for the workers. The battle as to which union should represent the longshoremen and other maritime workers would continue for another decade, with Communist influence and control as the primary issue.

> I closed up the cottage last Sunday. It was too cold to go up any more, and I drove down in an icy slush. We rented a trailer and brought down a big load of wood to Aunt Marie. . . .
>
> I haven't heard from Aunt Lana since I came home, but Uncle Theo is there now [in California] and I hope he will write often. Constance and Gilbert were down last Saturday, and I think Constance will go to California and stay until I can get there. She is so worried that it will relieve her to go out. . . . Lovingly, Mother.

The rest of November and all of December became one round of celebrations. Gratia succeeded in upstaging the major ones by putting on her own seventieth birthday party, November 28 at the Walker Branch Library. She invited the entire library staff, some three hundred people, including about a hundred WPA workers. Each person received an engraved invitation, and most responded on their best note paper, as one would do for a wedding invitation.

Clearly Gratia Countryman intended to have the last word, for at the party she announced her farewell gift to the staff—a new employee cafeteria and restrooms, ordered a few days before her retirement and to be installed by the end of the year.

Two days later—one day after Gratia's forced retirement—the library board voted her "Librarian Emeritus [sic] with a desk and the privileges of the office for life."

The formal testimonial dinner was held in the Nicollet Ballroom on December 10, attended by 450 people. It was a black tie affair with front-page headline and pictures in the next evening edition of *The Minneapolis Journal.* The arrangements committee, representing some fifteen organizations, cut across all lines and interests in a city that was increasingly divided politically—the Farmer Labor Party on the left and the Republican Party on the right. The superintendent of schools and the president of the library board each made formal remarks. The major address—"A Successful Woman"—was given by the well-known Minnesota author Margaret Culkin Banning. The

Roosevelt High School string quartet provided music, while the St. Paul Book & Stationary Co. contributed banks and banks of flowers.

Among the many messages read at the dinner was a lengthy one from the Librarian of Congress, Herbert Putnam, who had hired Gratia at the Minneapolis Public Library before it ever opened. His tribute read in part:

> . . . I well recall the circumstances of [Miss Countryman's] beginnings at the Library, after her graduation from the University of Minnesota, and the confidence in her qualities expressed to me by the highest authority—President Northrop himself, who had seen them emerge from the main body of students. And I recall very vividly the impression she at once made upon me, which continued throughout my official relation with her, and has continued since . . . the impression of an unusually competent mind poised upon a singularly steady character.
>
> Such a combination—of mind and character equally lucid, equally sincere, equally reliable—was certain to prevail, and it did. . . . Not among the aggressives of the profession—her modesty has precluded—she has always met the occasion.
>
> You are, I believe, to honor her with a banquet on December 10th. I am sure that she dreads it; but equally sure that in the experience she will relish it—for the cordiality of your appreciation of what she has been, and done, and the good will toward her future as an Emerita.
>
> I wish indeed I might be there. Faithfully yours, [signed] Herbert Putnam.

On New Year's Eve, Gratia boarded the train for Ontario, California, where sister Lana lay ill—very, very ill.

Part VII. Librarian Emeritus

"Miss Farmer"

Once I was introduced to a man, new to the city, who boasted to me of his technique for remembering names. He claimed to memorize them by association. When I met the man again some time later, he confidently greeted me as "Miss Farmer."

Gratia Countryman (with a twinkle in her eye), undated

1937. Retirement began badly for Gratia Countryman. She arrived in California only to find that her sister Lana was sicker than anticipated. Yet it was comforting to find brother Theo nursing his sister as he had once nursed his father during Levi's last illness. Lana was suffering from incurable cancer, which had been misdiagnosed over a period of several months, and at this late stage there was little to be done. Still, the last weeks witnessed a family gathering that had not occurred since before the death of Levi. Constance came from Duluth, with daughter Virginia. Son Edwin was already there, for he had been a companion to his grandmother during all of his high school years.

Thus a long, leisurely family farewell preceded Lana's death. Afterward Gratia turned to her absent son.

Ontario, California
Sunday, May 9

My dear Wellington,

A box of very beautiful flowers was delivered to me today for Mother's Day from my dear boy. It touched me very much to have you remember me, especially just at this time when I am feeling very lonely without my little sister. Because the long-ago days, when she was my constant playmate, keep coming back to my memory. You did not know her very well, but I find that nearly everybody in this town knew her and loved her. The teachers tell me that she has long been the best-loved teacher at Chaffey and that her influence and inspiration have been left upon hundreds of her pupils, many of whom took Latin just to have a class under her.

Constance and I both thank you for the sympathetic letters you wrote us; I shall always keep mine.

We are now going over all the trunks and shelves and treasures left in the house. Some of Mother's things are still here, but I just have to forget sentiment and be practical. There is no use in being too much attached to things, even if they do have association.

We expect to rent the house and are getting it painted and papered. When Gilbert [Buffington] comes out, he will take the family back. But Theo and I will start back about May 22nd. I may not write again.

I am sending you a little package of walnut meats to munch on. Affectionately, Mother.

It was not until after the first of June that Gratia finally found her way home to Minnesota and up to Wetoco Lodge, with the intention of beginning her new life as a farmer. Over the previous years she had acquired several pieces of marginal land across the road from her lakeshore property. It was mostly pasture and woods, and altogether the pieces totaled fifty acres. The site that would evolve into the Wetoco Dairy and Poultry

Farm was a quarter mile from Wetoco Lodge. It was known as "Gus's place," and its only distinguishing feature was a squatter's shack. This site was the candidate for Gratia's ambitious plans. But the late summer start had taken its toll. Very little had been accomplished before Gratia arrived, and whatever had been done wasn't working out quite as planned.

Wetoco Lodge, Onamia
Sunday, June 20

My dear Son,

I was so glad to receive your letter . . . I also want to assure you that I did not forget your birthday, although I did not send you anything or even write. Aunt Marie was writing and I was up to my ears getting things going up here at the lake.

No, I am not doing all the work. I have Mrs. Boxell's youngest daughter to help. She cannot cook; but she is eager to please and can wash dishes, fix vegetables, sweep, make beds, etc., which is lots of help.

I have quite a herd of animals. My good cow, a yearling heifer, a baby bull calf, and a little pig. . . . I got [the pig] because the calf couldn't drink all the skim milk, and I shall sell him anyway in a couple of weeks while he still counts as veal. I have a very good high school boy—a cousin of the Boxells—helping me. He milks night and morning, and gives me half a day each day. So we are getting caught up.

It rains the whole time, so Uncle Theo and I have to stick in garden seeds between drops. It isn't a good thing to work in soggy grounds, but it is the only way we can. Our first plantings are up, and so are the plantings up on Gus's place.

But the mosquitoes are terrible, just rising in clouds around us whenever we step out, and we just naturally bring some in. They are an unmitigated pest. The woods are heavy in foliage and the wild flowers have been beautiful. I love it up here, but I am hesitating about developing it as I hoped to do. I don't like to be away from home for six months of the year. I go back and forth every week to see Aunt Marie, but I am rather lonesome.

Aunt Marie is to be alone for two weeks. Mrs. Bailey has gone to Prescott, Miss Macdonald to the ALA in New York, and Mrs.

Black [the maid] has a month's vacation. I tried to have Aunt Marie come up here with me, but she couldn't leave her peonies. I don't blame her, after she has labored with them. She has a little girl in evenings to stay overnight, and I shall drive down every week. I got a little 1934 Plymouth coupé to use up here, and it is very handy and saves the big car. . . .

Mr. Benson is coming over this week to connect up the gasoline engine and pump, and the boy is putting out the dock. I am going down to Milaca to see the County Engineer about fixing the road past Gus's place. I tried to get around there the other day but was stuck for 3 hours with 4 men trying to pull us out. . . .

Will be most glad to have you spend your vacation here and will furnish trees or a wood pile for you. Edwin [Buffington] wants to come and practice his muscles, too, but I don't know when.

3243 France Avenue
August 6

Dear Wellington,

I have been at home for nearly a week, for the various ailments of my family. When I came down last Saturday, I found Aunt Marie quite ill. As usual she had been overdoing and working herself to the limit. She had so much nausea and dizziness that we called her doctor and decided to take her to the hospital. She was perfectly willing. It is only what I have been expecting for several years. I knew she would have to break before we could do anything with her. Well, we had a consultation on Sunday morning and have been giving her a complete clinical examination. . . . The doctors order her to remain in bed in the hospital for several weeks and then more rest somewhere for several months. Then if she always stops when she is tired and never lets herself get fatigued, she may go back to work. I am terribly worried about her, but then I have been for a long while. . . .

Miss Macdonald has been in another hospital getting her tonsils out, but she is home again and I will take her to Mille Lacs on Saturday for her vacation, but I will come back again early in the week.

Just when are you planning to come up? I'm saving some trees purposely for you to reduce on. If I knew the day you were to arrive, I would try to meet you here at home and take you up. . . . Will be seeing you soon. Lovingly, Mother.

Wellington did come up to spend his vacation. He kept the pump motor in good repair, cut down trees and brush, chopped wood, and even built an elaborate parking circle for Gratia's car. As Gratia long observed, Wellington was made for the out of doors. Over the years, the best times between mother and son were their times together at Wetoco Lodge, and when it came to Wellington's future, Gratia was quietly spinning fantasies. Once the farm came into its own, he would leave Chicago, come up and take over the enterprise, with the idea that it would one day be his.

Onamia
Thursday, September 16

My dear Wellington,

I have just been packing up your clothes to send to you. I couldn't bear to send you dirty clothes, so I had them washed and have taken a few stitches here and there. You will be surprised to see your old Pillsbury [Academy] bag, over which we fought and bled because you just wouldn't ship your dirty clothes.

Well, the farmer has begun work. The young man decided not to take the job, but just the day before the older man from Anoka [Mr. Strong] decided to take it. He is not going to bring his family up this winter, but is going to "bach" it. He says he has lived alone many months at a time, knows how to cook and isn't particular. He takes hold like an experienced man. He can do anything, build buildings, wire them, do plumbing, etc. But most of all he is an experienced chicken man, so we will specialize on that.

We have been talking over our barn and chicken house, and he wants to combine them. The slope down hill below Gus's old shack will allow the cows to be in a high basement and the chickens over them. I've told him to draw plans, estimate the lumber and cement, etc., so that I can get prices, and then we will get foundations in right away. I expect to be up here until November 1st anyway.

I give him $50 a month. He will do all the building, except when he needs an extra man. After profits begin, then I pay him nothing, but he shares 50-50 in all profits.

The calf has acted like the dickens since you went away. She jumped the fences, got into the garden, and had to be corralled and tied with a stout rope. It is up to the new farmer to take her again to the bull. I wish him joy.

It has been lovely up here lately. Elizabeth Bray, Mrs. Bailey, and Genevieve came up last Sunday and it was lovely. . . . Tomorrow I am going down to Minneapolis to attend a party for Miss Bartleson who is retiring. . . . Mr. Moses . . . talks of putting in electricity and will give me a wire off his transformer if I will put in the poles from the cottage. I can use as much or as little as I wish at his rate. I'm considering it. The engine won't go because the new battery has gone dead. The fan on the car is fixed. It needed an extra piece. Yours, Mother.

Wellington's Marriage

My dear Miss Countryman . . . . I cannot accept your gracious invitation for next Sunday afternoon. . . . Will you please give Wellington and his bride my very cordial congratulations and good wishes. And I congratulate you most heartily on what seems like a consummation of this beautiful service on your part. What a list of good deeds, private and public, you can think back upon in these days of odium cum dignitate, *which I trust may be prolonged for many happy years! Sincerely yours, Edward F. Waite.*

May 23, 1938, from the Juvenile Court judge who awarded Wellington to Gratia back in 1918

1938. By spring the Wetoco chicken house was finished and in operation, for Gratia relied on Mr. Strong's poultry expertise and invested mightily in the chicken venture. If anything was amiss in the arrangement, it was that Gratia, the owner and investor, had too many facets to her life. April was taken up with her responsibilities as chairman of the International League for Peace and Freedom National Conference, to be held in Minneapolis during May. And annually, in April, she was involved with the spring banquet of her old Delta Gamma Fraternity. She considered herself personally responsible for the young women who were graduating, and in this spring of 1938, as toastmistress, she selected the speakers from among them and coached each one individually. Always on her mind was Marie Todd, sometimes better, sometimes worse, but overall slowly fading away.

Closest to Gratia's heart, however, were rumors from Chicago that Wellington was planning to get married. The prospective bride was one Dorothy Whitstruck, whom Wellington had brought up to Wetoco the previous summer. With all of this to engage Gratia's interest, Mr. Strong and the chicken operation were pretty much on their own.

Robbinsdale
April 15

My dear Son,

Well, the Delta Gamma banquet is over, and my toastmistress's duties for that. . . . the [National Peace] Conference will soon be over; then I will have to think of the summer's work on the farm. . . . I haven't seen the chickens since I took them up, but Mr. Strong reports that they are growing splendidly and I am anxious to see them. I have a good deal of capital tied up in the venture. . . .

The money you sent me was a windfall. I didn't expect it, and I was a little worried over expenses here. Aunt Marie of course hasn't had any salary to speak of for a good many months. I have sufficient for ordinary purposes, but of course Mr. Strong's salary and the initial expense of chickens, feed, etc., has eaten into my resources very fast. I was mighty glad to get that lift. I am looking into this federal housing arrangement to see if I can get some long-time loan for a little house on the farm. . . .

Mrs. Bailey . . . told me that you were considering marrying Dorothy. I just want to say that I liked Dorothy very much. And if you feel that she is the one for you and that you two can make a successful life together, I shall welcome her as a daughter. I care only for your happiness in such an event and the consequent happiness of your wife.

I shall feel much relieved if you have a wife whom you love and who will make a home for you. Dorothy seemed to me a very sensible fine woman, though of course I saw her such a short time. And Wellington, if you and she feel sure of each other, don't wait for marriage. You are both getting older, why lose time. . . . You could get along on what you earn, especially if Dorothy kept working until these hard times are over. Now perhaps I am too curious, but won't you tell me how matters stand so that I can write to Dorothy.

Aunt Marie remains about the same. She went down to the library this morning, but she stayed but an hour and was very tired when she came back. She is in bed now. The doctor thinks she is improving, but her blood pressure goes right up when she does anything. . . . This is Mrs. Black's day off. I'm perfectly well and strong as ever, can outwork the others. . . . Lovingly, Mother.

Tuesday, April 19

My dear boy,

Your letter just arrived has made me very happy. I have long hoped that a woman whom you could love and respect would appear. And I am sure that Dorothy will answer these qualifications. You have been brought up among people who valued the really valuable things of life, and had high standards, morally and spiritually. You have long shown that you also have high standards, and I have been proud of the little boy I have raised.

Now about the time of your marriage. You just couldn't be married without me, and I am a little puzzled as to how I can manage on May 1st, for the [Peace] Conference lasts all day on Sunday, May 1st, and as local chairman I am responsible for any arrangements that might go wrong. I have another thing to suggest. Please think it over with Dorothy and let me know.

I would like to have you married at home, here in Minneapolis. . . . We would like to take Dorothy in, and have her become our daughter right here where your best attachments are.

If you cannot get a day off, could you come up Saturday night, have Sunday with us, be married here and return Sunday evening. I will take care of wedding expenses as far as ministers and eats are concerned. Gilbert and Constance could probably drive down [from Duluth], and you could have Don or any other old friends. Chiefly I urge it because Aunt Marie could not go down [to Chicago], and it would be more expensive for the rest of us, several of us, than for you two.

But if you think this is not wise, I am afraid you would have to postpone it for a week, for I have to be at a big convention banquet on Saturday night and to be on hand Sunday morning at a conference. Talk it over right away with Dorothy and let me know your decision. I would so love to have you married at home. . . .

And, by the way, I think you sent me $5 while I was in California that wasn't reckoned in, so that you owe me nothing. . . .

I am so excited, I can scarcely write coherently. I presume I shall think of a lot of things I want to say. But please do tell me Dorothy's other name and her address. I want to write to her. Lovingly, your Mother.

April 21

My dear Dorothy,

I am so happy over Wellington's glad news that he is going to marry you. When you were up last summer, he did not encourage me to think that you and he had any serious intentions, although I asked him. As I had had no further intimations on the subject, I had almost decided that you were only a good companion with whom he enjoyed himself. . . .

I am sure that he has shown you my letter to him and you already know that I am more than pleased. I have not seen much of you, but I am perfectly satisfied with what I did see and know that I shall take you into my heart as Wellington's wife.

Wellington is as dear to me as a son could be, even if [he] is an adopted son. And I am very proud of his manliness and his standards. He has not always been ambitious and was rather slow in developing any interests. I never could push him. He had to learn things for himself. But he is one of the most loyal boys I ever knew—to his friends, to his family and to his own ideals. He is to be trusted and I am sure he will be tender and loyal to you. You in your turn can awaken ambitions and give him the kind of incentives which he needs. He has always loved children, he has always

WETOCO POULTRY FARM

RUFUS F. STRONG, Manager
TELEPHONE: 8F2

Tuesday.
ONAMIA, MINN.

My dear Boy

I'm just writing on this paper to show how business like we look. I decided not to have my name on it at present.

We now have 700 fine big chicks with 1100 Eggs now in the incubator.

But I am writing to thank you for the gorgeous big bouquet that reached me Mothers Day with a message from you. It consisted of pink snapdragons of various shades and big pink peonies. It was and still is very beautiful. Thank you very much and thank Dorothy for her thoughtfulness in sending a card.

We have not been up to the farm since Good Friday. It has rained constantly, and the wood road

has been almost impassable. Mr Strong
Called me on the phone this morning
and begged me to come up. he said
the roads had been fixed. So Theo
and I are going up tomorrow. Theo
will stay.

I am not planning ~~of~~ to stay
up there this summer. I just
Cannot be away from Aunt Marie.
She scarcely gets up at all these
days, except for dinner at night.
She just likes to lie still and rest
which seems to be what the doctor
wants. I'm very much puzzled about
her. She seems to need an incredible
amount of sleep. Anyway I cannot
leave except for a few days at a time.

Here is a clipping that appeared
in the Christian Science Monitor. It
seems queer that they should give
me such a tribute after I have stopped
work. Another fine Editorial about me
Came out in the San Antonio Texas
Paper, followed by one in our Journal.
Why this sudden bunch of publicity I don't know.
Much Love to you both. I'm waiting
to hear your plans — Lovingly — Mother.

Handwritten letter from Gratia to son Wellington, May 1938

Source: Wellington Countryman

been gentle with animals, especially little young things, and he is affectionate and kind.

I am rejoicing that he has found someone to whom he can give the best that is in him. And who will give him a home and home interests and the love that any human being needs. . . .

My home will always be home to you both, as it always has been to him, and I hope this summer vacation will be spent at the cottage on Mille Lacs. Bless you both, Affectionately, Gratia Countryman.

April 24

My dear Dorothy,

. . . I am rather glad you have postponed the wedding. . . . The Decoration Day plan seems much wiser to me and will give us all time to plan. Of course I had thought about the license and intended going down to the Court House to make inquiries. . . . I believe Wellington should get his doctor's certificate and buy his license there in Chicago. It is a good law, meant to protect women. Then I will find out as soon as I get this conference off my hands what the Minnesota license law is.

I believe it would be better to have the marriage ceremony here at Wellington's home, say on Sunday afternoon, then take my car up to Mille Lacs and stay there by yourselves over Decoration Day. I will have had time to clean up the cottage and get provisions in. It doesn't seem to me productive to have the wedding or the wedding party up there. I could take care of young people up there, but could not make older people comfortable. . . .

After I have found out about the license, I will write again, and we will then make definite plans. The family is quite excited about it all and very pleased. Yours affectionately, Gratia Countryman.

Tuesday, May 10

My dear Boy,

I'm just writing on this paper to show how business-like we look. I decided not to have my name on it at present. We now have 700 fine big chicks with 1100 eggs now in the incubator.

But I am writing to thank you for the gorgeous big bouquet

that reached me Mother's Day, with a message from you. It consisted of pink snap dragons of various shades and big pink peonies. It was and still is very beautiful. Thank you very much, and thank Dorothy for her thoughtfulness in sending a card.

We have not been up to the farm since Good Friday. It has rained constantly and the wood road has been almost impassable. Mr. Strong called me on the phone this morning and begged me to come up. He said the road had been fixed. So Theo and I are going up tomorrow. Theo will stay.

I am not planning to stay up there this summer. I just cannot be away from Aunt Marie. She scarcely gets up at all these days, except for dinner at night. She just likes to lie still and rest, which seems to be what the doctor wants. I'm very puzzled about her. She seems to need an incredible amount of sleep. Anyway I cannot leave except for a few days at a time.

Here is the clipping that appeared in the *Christian Science Monitor.* It seems queer that they should give me such a tribute after I have stopped work. Another fine editorial about me came out in the San Antonio Texas paper, followed by one in our *[Minneapolis] Journal.* Why this sudden bunch of publicity, I don't know.

Much love to you both. I'm waiting to hear your plans. Lovingly, Mother.

Friday a.m.

Dear Dorothy

. . . I got all the information about the licenses. You can be married here on a Minnesota license, even if you are both nonresidents. There is a condition that the license must be secured 5 days in advance, but they will waive that 5 days for us. If you get in on Saturday before 12 noon, you can get the license at the regular place. But if you get in at any time up to 8 or 9 P.M., they will give the license certificate to a deputy clerk and you can go to his home to sign for it. They will choose the clerk who lives nearest us. So much for the license. . . .

Aunt Marie is pretty tired, and I shouldn't wonder if we should keep our list of people down, but even then there can be all the closest relatives and friends as follows: . . . [totaling 26] There could be 8 or 10 more if you both wish more, or these names could be cancelled if Well wants to cut out any of them. . . .

If Well has no minister friend here, and I cannot think of any, then I am sure you will be satisfied with Mr. Aanestad, our old neighbor, but you must let me know. I am afraid a morning wedding would be difficult. Every minister will be at his pulpit. . . .

I've been up to the Lake this week and am going up again next week to have the cottage cleaned. But I have no maid this year and am not staying up there all the time. But I think we can make you comfortable: Can you help me cook? Affectionately—Mother-to-be.

Wednesday p.m., May 18

Dear Son,

. . . I have again called up the license bureau. I am to get the waiver of the 5-day advance license, this week. So you will get your license anytime on Saturday. . . .

The plan as we think it out would be: Arrival Saturday morning; attend to business Saturday morning; lunch downtown perhaps; dinner at home; Mr. Aanestad Saturday evening; Sunday breakfast at home; get house ready; dinner at some nice place to leave house free for maid preparing refreshments; marriage ceremony at 4 P.M.; Miss Macdonald play the wedding march. (Does Dorothy want Virginia [Buffington] as flower girl, to hold her bouquet when the ring is put on? Virginia would love it.); reception, simple refreshments; drive to Wetoco.

Probably Miss Macdonald, Theo and I would drive up too. You will need someone to get meals and help out, but we won't molest you. Perhaps we will take dinner at the resort to save work . . . I was going up to Wetoco today to clean up this week, but the hard rains have drowned the wood road. . . . Have I said all I want? Well, I guess so. I'm so glad you are being married, and to such a fine girl, and are to have a real home—bless you. Lovingly, Mother.

The wedding went off on May 29, just as arranged, and in the evening four Countrymans—two of them newly wed—plus Genevieve Macdonald, drove up together to Lake Mille Lacs and Wetoco Lodge.

Back in 1917, Gratia's niece Constance married Gilbert

Buffington in Minneapolis, with the reception in Gratia's grand Lynnhurst home. Afterward Constance and Gilbert took off in their automobile for a honeymoon in the Wisconsin countryside. Following their vehicle was a second automobile, driven by Aunt Gratia, with passengers Wellington, Marie Todd, and Marie's aged mother. Wellington was to stay with the newlyweds. Gratia thought the rest of them ought to make the drive also, just to enjoy a country adventure. Now in 1938, after the wedding reception in Gratia's home, the honeymoon crowd was somewhat smaller. They all fit into a single auto. That honeymoons were usually meant for just two disturbed Gratia not one whit. In her eighth decade of life, she continued to be uplifted whenever love conquered. Why not rejoice and partake!

The WPA Project

> *May 16: This afternoon went to St. Paul to consider taking a WPA position as supervisor of a project to index the newspaper. Can't decide whether to take it. . . . June 17: Spent the morning on a WPA project getting it in shape. August 19: . . . Went again to town to get a social security card. Necessary for the WPA project. . . . August 26: Am on duty for my new job, which promises to be hard but interesting.*
>
> Gratia Countryman's day book, 1938

1938. Wellington's wedding was the last great event in Marie Todd's life. Gratia knew what awaited her once she was back in Robbinsdale and at her desk—a letter of resignation to the new chief librarian, on behalf of Marie, who could no longer handle her own correspondence. Marie was just sixty years old.

June 13

> Dear Mr. Vitz,
>
> I am writing for Miss Todd. She feels that she should retire on July 1st. She feels that she will not be able to work any more; her only regret in leaving so soon, being that she has a lot of loose ends which she had hoped to clear up before leaving. . . . Sincerely, Gratia Countryman.

From July on, Marie required round-the-clock care. There were day nurses and night nurses, with a nurse's cot set up in the living room. This illness was already several years old, and so much working time had been missed that Marie not only could not pay her mounting medical bills, but also could not make payments on the mortgage that Gratia held. Gratia on her part picked up all Marie's bills, medical and otherwise, and reluctantly secured second and third mortgages on the property as expenses mounted.

Under such domestic circumstances began Gratia's new career—organizer and supervisor of project No. 6681, Work Projects Administration, under the Minneapolis Public Library. Gratia couldn't do it alone, of course, so she recruited two assistants, one currently employed at the Minneapolis Public Library, the other a younger woman, formerly a librarian at the Minneapolis Public Library, now the wife of a struggling attorney and mother of two small daughters. These two assistants were Genevieve Macdonald and Irene Melgaard Hauser. Gratia and "Vieve" of course were already a team, each understanding the other without words ever being spoken. In the case of Irene Hauser, this WPA project transformed a relationship of mutual respect into an intimate friendship that eventually comprised the entire Hauser family, a friendship of which there is yet more to say.

To celebrate her new career, and to ensure adequate transportation in all seasons, Gratia bought a new blue 1939 Buick. It would be the last of the several automobiles that had carried her through her busy life, and by all accounts her favorite.

At the indexing project, there was very little to suggest the comfortable intimacy of the Minneapolis library. First of all, the project spaces were the empty classrooms of Trudeau School in southeast Minneapolis. Originally, Trudeau had been a school for truant children, then a "fresh-air" school for tubercular children. It was finally closed and abandoned by the school board. In 1938 the Federal Government leased the building as the site for this WPA project, planned to employ two hundred white-collar workers.

The project was designed to use the talents and skills of unemployed "professional" workers. A curious aspect of the Great Depression was that at the beginning, the blue-collar workers were hardest hit, later followed by the clerks and administrators, and finally increasingly by "professionals," as defined in those days. The men and women assigned by the WPA employment office to Trudeau School included unemployed teachers, small business owners, managers, stockbrokers, bankers, lawyers, writers, musicians, and an assortment of clerks. They came in all races. The supervisors met familiar faces—men and women who previously had strolled on Minneapolis's Nicollet Avenue. These former captains in the world of finance and one-time department heads in retail stores more often than not were dressed in threadbare coats and mismatched suits, but never mind that.

Little by little an esprit de corps evolved among the motley crowd. It began with Gratia Countryman's leadership, and it was nurtured by their common involvement in the immensely interesting tasks at hand. Gratia first outlined the project in a brochure that was presented to each new employee and made available to the many visitors who streamed through the project doors.

> *The Purpose of an Index* is to point the seeker to the very place where the desired information is found. A newspaper index similarly points to the date, page and column in the paper where the news item or advertisement about a place, person or topic sought may be found. . . .
>
> *The Scope of our Index:* . . . This newspaper index therefore will be an alphabetical list by subject of all items connected with Minnesota which have appeared in the columns of *The Minneapolis Journal.* It will index activities of Minnesota people whether performed in the state or outside; the progress of industry, such as lumbering, milling or the grain industry . . . It will index political news, editorials, sports, crimes, accidents, obituaries, labor activities, churches, farmers' institutes, personals, etc., of any town in the state . . . It will also index advertisements . . . commodities offered for sale, household utensils, clothing styles, methods of travel and railroad schedules, new inventions, amusements and legal notices . . .[26]

The indexing began where *The Minneapolis Journal* began, with the first issue of November 26, 1878. Simultaneously, and also on the Trudeau School premises, the task of microfilming the actual newspaper pages commenced. The two aspects of the project went hand in hand, for without permanently readable newspapers, a newspaper index was of no value.

The project was not full time, but rather 110 hours a month, as decreed by WPA administrators. Gratia developed a complicated monthly scheduling system so that employees could work full days and have "cushion" days added to their weekends. For every new employee there was a two-week classroom training period, with a manual of rules, a blackboard, and indexing exercises. Irene Hauser's great contribution to the project was the fifty-page mimeographed and bound *Manual of Instruction*, a complete tutorial of indexing, with specific application to the project, as defined by Miss Countryman. Gratia was enjoying her new career, though it was a far cry from the career in agriculture that she had carved out for herself a year earlier.

In this fall of 1938, one might say that across America a great tide was turning. The evolution of Gratia's own mindset was not atypical of the nation at large. For nine years she had witnessed the deterioration of the domestic economy, made especially visible through the increase and change in library demands. The public library WPA program that augmented the staff by more than a hundred workers had brought Gratia in touch with the individual disappointments, and tragedies, that defined the Great Depression of the 1930s. In 1936 she had shared the hopes and fears of other Americans, abandoning her historical Republican roots to vote for the Democratic president, Franklin D. Roosevelt, now in his second term.

This October, two years later, Gratia was being forced to reconsider another long-held tradition—her devotion to the worldwide peace movement. This movement grew out of the seemingly senseless loss of young men's lives in the trenches that characterized the First World War. The campaign for women's suffrage, which finally achieved success soon after the war, evolved easily into a quest for the end of war in general. Gratia was an early and active member of the Women's International League for Peace and Freedom. The year 1938 capped her participation in this peace movement, by bringing the National Conference to Minneapolis and providing a forum for her definitive speech on world peace. It would be her last speech on the subject, for the Second World War was already looming on the horizon.

As early as 1935, Gratia was made keenly aware of developments in Germany, under Adolf Hitler. Quite suddenly, at the library there had been increased demand for German-language books, especially the kinds of books that intellectuals and other highly educated people would care to read. It turned out that these new readers were Jewish refugees from Germany, the earliest victims of the German policy that would take on a name in history—the Holocaust. If that wasn't enough to raise questions, Gratia was made keenly aware in other forums, especially through her work with the National Council of Christians and

Jews. As with many of her compatriots, world developments were causing Gratia Countryman to rephrase long cherished ideals. From her daybook:

> October 26: Went to foreign policy meeting tonight, all the family including Marie. Talks on Germany and Czechoslovakia over which there is much concern. Germany is a beast, greedy, tyrannical. Talks were good.*

> December 20
>
> Dear Dorothy and Wellington,
>
> I sent a little package to you, but I'll also write a little Christmas letter, especially as I am feeling very blue about Aunt Marie. If I had had the slightest idea of going to Chicago [for Christmas], it would have been dispelled this morning. She has been growing much stronger this past week or so, sitting up in a chair for a few moments at a time, and walking with assistance to the bathroom. This morning the night nurse took her to the bathroom, and while sitting on the toilet, she had another slight stroke, like a deep faint, and I thought she was gone. But she has come out of it now and seems perfectly rational—well, no, she is confused when she talks, but she knows us all and knows that I haven't gone to work as usual.
>
> I am waiting for the doctor, although he has warned me repeatedly that she might slip away any minute with a brain hemorrhage. There is really nothing that he can do. I feel just heart broken, and yet, as I look back over the past ten years, I can see that it has been coming on and that she has been unaccountably irritable and unreasoning—just pushed by this blood pressure stimulus. . . .

---

*On October 1, 1938, the leaders of Great Britain, France, Germany, and Italy met in Munich, Germany, on invitation of Italian dictator Benito Mussolini. There, the leaders of Great Britain and France signed an agreement with Adolf Hitler, allowing Germany to seize the western portion of Czechoslovakia, with German troops occupying the territory immediately. No representative of Czechoslovakia was permitted to speak at the conference. In return for this "gift" of western Czechoslovakia, Hitler agreed to make no additional land claims in Europe. Within six months, Hitler broke the agreement, and German troops seized all of Czechoslovakia

I am busy all day long with this very interesting project which I have organized for the library. I have 115 people now, and will take on about 50 more, I think, after New Year's. As usual I am on public committees and trying to do welfare work—just now it is helping to plan a big benefit to raise money for the refugees, which that fiend Hitler keeps increasing. I read letters which the Czechoslovakians are getting from their starving, freezing relatives and my blood boils. Literally millions will starve or die with exposure this winter. A big boycott movement is spreading from coast to coast against German, Italian and Japanese goods. I hear that big concerns like Kresges have not ordered from Japan in two years. Just now there are six big loaded freighters tied up in San Francisco because Japan cannot pay for the goods. So the boycott is beginning to tell.*

Well, this is no Christmas letter, but we certainly have something to be merry about, that we live in America. I'm having a big Christmas party for my big W.P.A. family next Thursday. They are all such good sports, even if their fortunes and jobs have gone. So I'll be merry with them if Aunt Marie stays with us. Bless your hearts says Mother.

Wednesday evening, December 28

My dear Dorothy,

It made us so happy to have Wellington here over Christmas. Aunt Marie enjoyed every minute that she was with him. And I want to thank you for letting him come. Not every woman would have let her husband go on their first Christmas. It was very fine of you and I appreciated it. It was the finest present you could have given us. But I thought my bag was beautiful. I shall use it with much pleasure. It was just about time for another. I will now demote my previous bag to more common uses.

I shall soon be preparing to busy myself in another way. I always did like to make baby clothes, but it will be quite an exciting thing to make some for my grandchild. And am I happy about it! You were so wise not to wait longer. The years pass quickly, all too

---

*In 1937 Japanese forces invaded China, and by the fall of 1938, a large portion of that nation had been conquered and occupied by Japanese forces, with massive loss of life to the Chinese civilian population

> quickly, and it is a joy not to lose, but to have as many years as possible.
>
> Wellington will tell you about Marie. She suffers no pain, but she seems to be gradually slipping away. My heart is torn. I don't see how I can get along without her. We have been together for a lifetime. I keep hoping for a miracle to restore her. Miracles sometimes happen. . . . Lovingly, Mother.

Granddaughter Alta Marie

> *Alta Marie is the name chosen for the new daughter of Mr. and Mrs. Wellington Countryman, now of Chicago. The baby was born June 28. Mr. Countryman is the adopted son of Miss Gratia Countryman who has just returned from visiting him and his family in Chicago.*
>
> *The Minneapolis Journal,* July 9, 1939

1939. The newspaper indexing project was growing and succeeding. By March there were two hundred workers, and still Gratia had it all under control. To undergird morale and increase communication, she created the *Indexer,* a semimonthly house organ written by and for the workers. Issues varied, but always they included pieces out of the newspapers being indexed—items that one or another worker found especially amusing. There were also feature stories on this or that worker —for instance, a renowned Ojibway chief who was on the project. And always there was an editorial by the director herself:

> Our project is the best project in the city, best for any reason you might name. Its permanency and use for posterity alone makes it not only one of the best projects financed by the WPA here, but *the* best. Working conditions are best, qualifications and eligibility highest, and the honor system is applied and used almost entirely. So why not keep the trust placed in us and show our appreciation by keeping the cost of production down. Let us keep our project

the best in the city, by earnest, serious, studious application to work which is by no means monotonous nor boresome. . . .[27]

Trudeau School and the indexing project became showpieces of the local WPA administration. A continuous stream of visitors came through to watch the workers at their chairs making notes from newspaper sheets that hung on large vertical boards. The three supervisors moved from board to board, answering questions and making suggestions, for indexing always requires an element of judgment, the kind that comes only from experience. Trudeau School was a busy, humming place in the spring of 1939.

Down in Chicago Wellington and Dorothy were awaiting the arrival of their first child and fretting that Gratia had not yet visited them in their modest apartment. Indeed Gratia was glued to Minneapolis and the WPA project, but in this spring of 1939, her heart was filled with the expectation of a grandchild. For Wellington's birthday she shipped to Chicago a deluxe baby buggy. Wellington's own heart swelled in appreciation.

4324 Drexel Boulevard, Chicago
June 1

Dear Mother:

Your gift has certainly solved the baby buggy situation, which had been given some serious consideration. As for combining my birthday gift with it, I find that anything for the new arrival is the same as a gift to me. A year ago I never would have believed that I would be a prospective [father] by this time. The nice thing about it is that after a year's marriage I wonder what I was doing up to that time, just existing? I can frankly say that life is starting to have some real meaning. . . .

Well, to add my wistful wishing to Dorothy's, when are you coming down to Chicago? We can put you up. Anyway I want to plant a nice big kiss on that curly topknot of yours, seasoned with

> a gentle bear hug, and of course you can sit on my lap providing your feet don't drag. . . .
>
> Again I thank you for the magnanimous gift, which came like manna from Heaven. Although I must tell you that your hitherto improvident son is solvent to a surprising degree, with both doctor's fee and hospital charges waiting in the bank for the eventful day.
>
> Love to Aunt Marie and the family, Your son, Wellington.

There was no vacation time at the WPA, but fortunately Alta Marie Countryman arrived on June 28, shortly before the Fourth of July holiday. On July 1, Gratia drove her Buick down to Chicago, never dreaming that she would return a few days later to find the WPA on strike.

As a matter of fact, in the weeks preceding the event, there had been a restlessness among WPA workers throughout the nation. Congress was becoming impatient with an increasing rate of unemployment that just wouldn't quit, in spite of the thousands of WPA projects across the nation. A perception was growing that productivity on these projects was low and falling. The program simply wasn't stimulating the economy as had been expected. In some places, WPA projects, especially those involving the building trades, had been organized into labor unions. This was certainly so in Minneapolis and St. Paul. In fact, Gratia had earlier noted in her day book, "My WPA people are forming a labor union, much excited about it. I don't quite like it."[28]

On Wednesday, July 5, workers arrived to see a posted notice explaining the newly passed Emergency Relief Appropriation Act of 1939. The notice announced an increase in the number of hours of work required each month with no increase in pay, hence a decrease in hourly wages.[29] This was the spark that ignited the strike. Striking workers and their supporters formed picket lines at each project site and urged workers not to return to work the following day. Within the next three days, many WPA project sites closed down for lack of workers, but not the

Trudeau School site. Gratia, Genevieve, and Irene Hauser reported daily for work, along with most of the other workers. They walked through unfriendly picket lines but noted that not one of their "indexers" was on the line. Still, it was an unenviable plight. The situation deteriorated over the weekend, and by the following Monday, violence broke out at several sites. On July 14 the mayor of Minneapolis warned the WPA administration that he could not guarantee police protection at the WPA project sites.

Reluctantly, the WPA administrator ordered all projects in Minneapolis and St. Paul closed down. Wrote Gratia to her son and daughter-in-law:

> Saturday, July 15
>
> My dear children,
>
> I am so anxious to hear from you. I want to know that Dorothy and Alta Marie got home safely. I want to know if Dorothy can nurse the baby, and whether the one breast developed any troubles. . . .
>
> We have been so busy going through strikes up here . . . None or few of the WPA people are striking, but the gangster group are doing the striking and picketing in the name of the WPA. My project has been open, and everybody has been on the job, with mobs of picketers outside our doors.
>
> But last night one project was so badly treated, one man killed and 20 or more wounded, that all projects are closed on Monday. The "G" men are here in numbers, trying to get evidence on the leaders. It is quite exciting. With love, Mother.

Not until July 21 did workers return to their projects. The strike was settled in the office of Minnesota's new Republican governor, Harold E. Stassen, a man whom Gratia had enthusiastically supported in the fall elections of 1938. The settlement was hardly a victory for either side. It was simply an agreement that striking workers could return to their jobs without penalty.

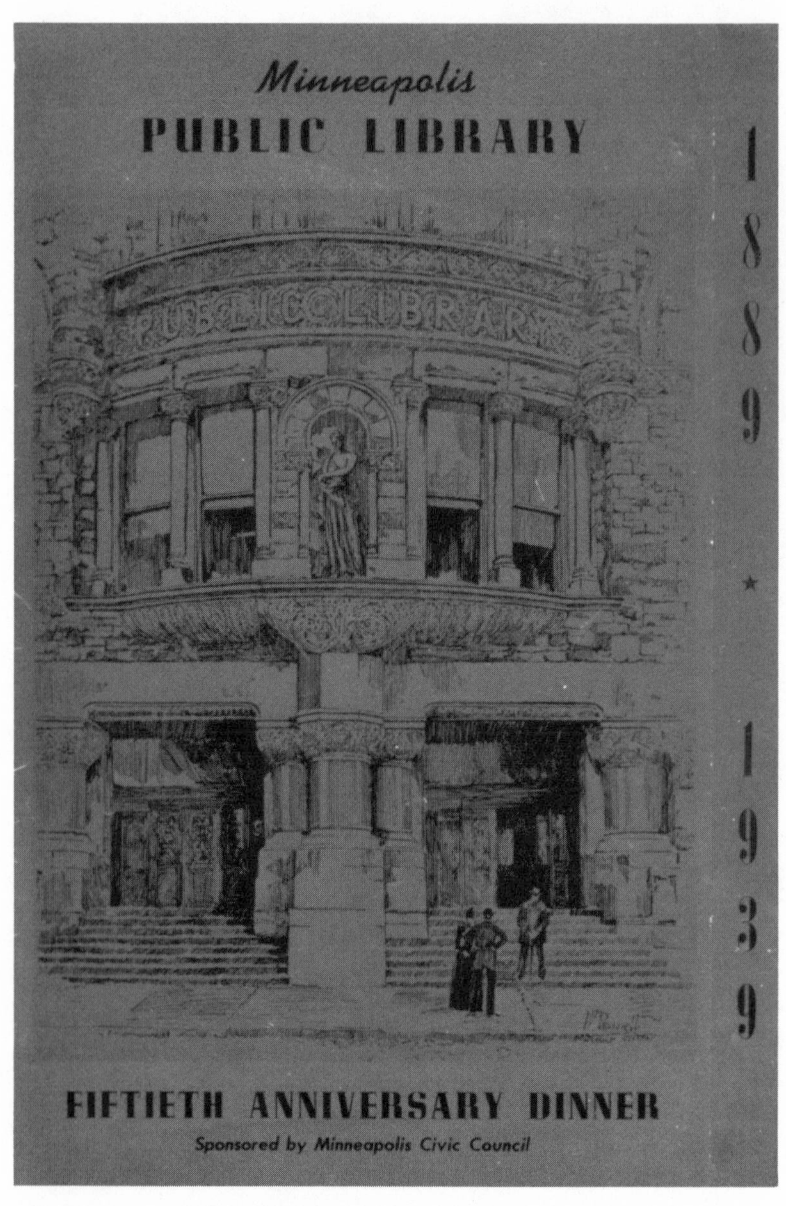

Minneapolis Public Library Fiftieth Anniversary Program, 1939
Source: Virginia Buffington Shaw

September 13

My dear children,

I'm neglecting you, but I don't mean to. The days and nights just slip away. My work goes on day after day, and at night I am tired. But two weeks ago I had five consecutive days, so with the doctor's permission I bundled Marie and her nurse and Mrs. Black and went up to Wetoco for that period. Mrs. Bailey was at Prescott . . . and Genevieve wasn't yet back from her vacation, so we could all go. It was lovely weather except the last day. Our Marie could be out on the porch in her favorite chair. The cool days and nights Theo kept grate fires going. Marie stood the trip very well and we thought it gave her a nice change. This week, however, she has taken a bad turn. She didn't know me, when I came home from the lake this Monday and has seemed dazed and unable to talk. She is a little better this morning and reaches out her hand to me, though she doesn't talk. It is very sad to watch the little girl gradually slipping, but there is nothing to be done but to take care of her. . . .

But oh, this war, it oppresses everybody. Hitler does need a good thrashing, but I do hope we won't have to help. War is terrible. I've about decided not to listen to the radio and get myself all stirred up. America must keep out at any cost.* . . .

And the dear baby—she is three months, nearly four, and she must have changed a lot. How I do wish you could get back to Minneapolis where we could watch the baby grow, and see you often. Lots of love to all three of you. Lovingly, Mother.

In November Gratia turned seventy-three, and in December she was feted at least as grandly as she had been three years earlier at her retirement. The event was the celebration of the fiftieth anniversary of the Minneapolis Public Library. It took place on December 16 in the Grand Ballroom of Minneapolis's premier Nicollet Hotel. In truth, the banquet was organized as a tribute to the former chief librarian. The toastmaster was Guy

*On September 1 German military forces invaded Poland. Two days later Great Britain and France declared war on Germany. This was the beginning of the Second World War.

Stanton Ford, president of the University of Minnesota, on whose right at the head table sat Gratia. Ford began the program by voicing a tribute to the Librarian Emeritus in lengthy and appreciative words. Gratia responded in kind and then presented her prepared speech, a personal assessment of the library's "Fifty Fruitful Years." To Gratia's right sat the nationally known journalist and scholar, Christopher Morley. His announced presentation carried the rather obscure title of "Streamlines in Literature." Mr. Morley's remarks followed Gratia's talk. He stepped to the lectern and began extemporaneously with the words, "Friends, Romans, . . ." and a mischievous glance to the guest of honor. Oddly enough, it was these words that would become the title when Christopher Morley's remarks were later published in a bound volume.[30]

For Gratia, the burst of unexpected appreciation was a soothing tonic in this autumn of war and Marie Todd's lingering illness.

Men and Women in Need

Dear Son,

I don't know how you feel toward me, but if you would like to write, send me a letter. Tell me all about yourself and what you are doing. It is after Xmas now. Things are bad here, not a great deal of work. Best Love, Mother. XXXX

Undated note to Wellington from Mrs. Edd V. Moore of Canada; forwarded to Gratia Countryman by the State Board of Control, and by Gratia to Wellington

1940. Wellington did not answer this gentle inquiry from his birth mother, the former Annie Magee. The reasons were complex and difficult to put into words. He considered Gratia his mother in all respects, and later would fret that he and his progeny were not part of the famed Countryman genealogy book. This volume was one of the few endeavors involving Gratia Countryman over which she had no control. One suspects that Gratia did make some sort of reply to Mrs. Moore, for months later a second letter arrived—addressed to Wellington at Gratia's address.

> Dear Son,
>
> Well it has been a long time since I wrote you last from Saskatchewan. Dad has been ill for some time. He gets a small pension from the last war. My other son is home, lost his job. He was working for Hudson Bay Company. He is 17 years old. Work is scarce here. Men are being laid off every day.
>
> Your oldest brother is in Saskatchewan, runs a small store. One sister married in Winnipeg and one at Hamilton, Ontario. We are very hard up just now. Dad thought if we came to the city, he would get a light job that he could do, but you couldn't buy one. Not like our old home town, where we were known and could get credit. I am afraid we are in for miserable times.
>
> Well, son, tell me all about yourself when you write—what you do and if you are married. Don't forget [that] I never forgot. In the still of the night I often wonder where you are and if [what] they know will affect you in any way.
>
> We can't get across the line now without a permit.* Dad says we will go back to Saskatchewan in the spring. Write me a long letter, dear, won't you. I love you just as much as the rest. You will say, I don't believe it. Come and see us if you get this letter. Lots of love, Your Mother.

This time Gratia did not immediately forward Mrs. Moore's letter to Wellington. She first wrote to him and asked if he wished to receive it. Wellington's affirmative response and declaration of filial fidelity to his adopted mother touched her deeply.

*Canada was at war along with Great Britain.

February 9

Dear Mother,

. . . In regard to the letter which you have, please send it on and I will render it the attention it merits. To me you may be assured my mother means you and nobody else. I have come to recognize the fact that the bad impulses which I have had to fight in the past are due to heredity, and it is due to the environment and influences of you and Aunt Marie that I have been able to overcome these faults. I might say that it is more curiosity than sentiment that prompts me to have any particular interest in seeing the letter. When I decided to call you "mother" I did it without reservations, as I do today. . . . Love, Wellington

Sunday evening

My dear Son,

I appreciated so much your very dear letter received this week and shall keep it always.

Aunt Marie and I didn't know much about bringing up a little boy and we made many serious blunders, but we always loved you and did our best. We felt that you had very good stuff in you and you had some most lovable and admirable traits, which cropped out early in your boyhood. If you have had inherent faults to overcome, you are no different from everyone else. We all have inherited and acquired faults which we fight more or less successfully and never wholly overcome.

I am proud of my son and what he has made of himself, with the help in late years of a good wife and the responsibility of a little child. I am sending the letter. My curiosity got the better of me and I took the liberty of opening it. I hope you won't mind. I wouldn't have thought of doing it under any other circumstances.

We have a new heifer on the farm and are expecting another in March. I'm hoping for several heifers. The man helping Richard to clear land has finished all that I can afford to pay for, and I believe it will be enough pasture for awhile. The place is far from profitable yet. I'll send you my balance sheet, which I made out for the income tax statement. But it will look better at the end of next year. I'm tired and must go to bed. Lovingly, Mother.

Enclosed in the envelope with Gratia's letter was the final communication from Wellington's birth mother. Wellington saved all the letters, but he never did write to Annie Magee, now Mrs. Moore. Dorothy would chide him from time to time for this perceived lack of compassion. His reluctance became a permanent point of contention in a long and otherwise very happy marriage.

At the WPA project there were almost as many tales of loss and distress as there were workers. With three compassionate women running the project, counseling became a natural part of supervision. From time to time in the evening a worker would show up at the home of Irene Hauser, at her invitation, to talk over some legal problem with her lawyer husband, Walter.* More than a half century later, their names and their problems are lost to memory. Just one vignette remains—the visit to the Hauser home by a gentle black man, a poet by the name of DuBois. He needed to make out his last will, for he was ailing badly and expected to live only a few months longer. And why did Irene Hauser still remember his name after so many decades? Because she had asked him if he was related to the famed African-American educator and leader William DuBois, and indeed he was.

As involved as Gratia and her assistants were with the lives of the other WPA workers, these relationships would fade once the project closed down—all but one, that is—and that was with Blanche Molineux Scott. No one who ever worked at the newspaper indexing project would forget Mrs. Scott. She was a thin little woman, close to sixty-five years old, with hennaed red hair and heavy makeup, especially around her eyes. Winter and summer she came to work in the same broad-brimmed hat, black wool cloak, and wool skirt, cut short above the knee and quite contrary to the prevailing styles. Blanche Scott's

*Irene and Walter Hauser were the parents of author Jane Pejsa.

coworkers at Trudeau School might have been more sympathetic were it not that she was simultaneously haughty and fearful when it came to other people. As it was, she appeared to hold her fellow workers in such contempt that Gratia assigned her a space quite apart from the others. Yet Blanche Scott worked well and intelligently, preparing the indexing slips with an elegant, yet readable, handwriting. She became one of the most dedicated and productive workers at the indexing project.

From her looks, one could guess that Mrs. Scott had at one time been very beautiful and perhaps quite elegant, for she spoke in a voice and accent that reminded the listener of the East Coast elite. And so she had been—so beautiful that in 1899, when her husband was on trial for a society murder in New York City, the *New York Times* was moved to describe her daily—what she wore in the courtroom and how she comported herself.

Mrs. Scott, the former Blanche Chesebrough, had been an aspiring New York singer before marrying one Roland Molineux, the son of a well-decorated Civil War general. As Gratia became better acquainted with this enigmatic woman, she came to understand that the haughtiness and apparent disdain for her fellow human beings grew out of a desperate fear—fear that they would learn of her first marriage and of her indiscretions that had led her husband to murder his best friend. There had been two murders—by cyanide—and two trials. In the end, Roland Molineux was acquitted, but there was no doubt in Blanche's mind and in the public perception that he was guilty.* Immediately after Roland's acquittal, Blanche fled New York, divorced him, married a lawyer in Sioux Falls, and subsequently moved to Minneapolis. Her second marriage was equally disastrous, ending in divorce after her only child died.

*Blanche Molineux's courtship and marriage, along with the murders and trials, are well documented in *The Molineux Affair* by Jane Pejsa. Minneapolis: Kenwood Publishing, 1984.

Before the 1929 stock market crash, Blanche Scott lived in a fine home on Minneapolis's posh Park Avenue. Yet she shied away completely from society. By 1930, she had lost her home and was penniless. For a few years she became companion to a former Minnesota governor. He supported her in one of Minneapolis's older residential hotels until he died. After that Blanche Scott fell into absolute destitution and was convinced that she had also lost all respectability. Little by little she confided her tragic life to the three women—Gratia, Genevieve, and Irene—a life deriving not only from her own bad decisions but also from betrayal by others. For these same three women, individually and as a team, the spiritual recovery of Blanche Scott became a high priority.

It began with invitations to the Hauser home at Thanksgiving and at Christmas, followed by summer weekends at Wetoco with Gratia, Genevieve, and Theo. The WPA association was but the beginning. The friendship and emotional support for this tormented woman would carry through for well over a decade, as long as Blanche Scott lived. Such was the human legacy of the WPA project.

In October Gratia and Genevieve left Marie in the care of her nurses and drove up to Wetoco to join Theo for an autumn farewell to Lake Mille Lacs. With her deep feelings left unsaid, Gratia wrote in the Wetoco diary, dated October 12–13: "This October 12 is Marie's Birthday. She was here two years ago on her birthday."

On Gratia's return to Minneapolis, the final realization came that she could no longer care for her "little Marie." On October 22 she brought Marie to the hospital, where Marie died on November 25. Months before Marie's death, Gratia had already written a fitting tribute.

> Marie Annette Todd, for 33 years head of the Art Department of the Minneapolis Public Library . . . Miss Todd was deeply interested in social and humanitarian work, belonging to many local

> and national organizations that promoted better human relationships and social conditions. Kindness, sincerity, self-sacrifice, patience and integrity were her characteristics. Gardening, bird lore, and amateur photography were her hobbies in an otherwise studious and busy life.
>
> Because of Miss Todd's far-sighted vision and ideal of superservice, the Art Department grew to be one of the largest and most useful in this country. The collection of art books, many of them rare and expensive, numbered about 21,000 volumes at the time of her retirement. . . .
>
> Always original in her ideas, Miss Todd was not content with traditional library services, but soon started circulating picture and lantern slide collections, thus becoming a pioneer in the field of visual education. These collections grew steadily until at her retirement they numbered about 250,000 pictures and 32,000 slides, with a combined annual circulation of over 200,000 items. . . . In all these acquisitions she sought unexcelled quality rather than quantity. Now seldom a day goes by without expressions of appreciation by patrons for these unusual and helpful services.

So ended Gratia's lifelong relationship with Marie Todd. From the beginning it had been a blending of opposites, but in the end it was an extended odyssey of caregiving. Something was bound to change after Marie's death, and so it did—a metamorphosis in the relationship between Gratia and Genevieve. In the past Gratia had always been in charge, with Genevieve her elegant, competent, and witty subordinate. There was no denying that Gratia was totally exhausted from Marie's long illness, as she admitted more and more to being tired. Worst of all, her eyes were failing. She was little by little leaning on Genevieve. To Genevieve's consternation, Gratia could not bear to give up driving, for her love affair with the automobile had not waned one bit. And finally, without the demands of Marie and her nurses, Gratia could no longer justify keeping a maid. If Gratia was in charge at the WPA, Genevieve was increasingly managing at home.

Birthday Celebrations

How swiftly the years do pass. It seems no time since Aunt Marie and I talked it all over and decided we would love to add a little red-cheeked boy to our family. It is just yesterday that a gay irresponsible little boy lost his shoes out of the car and left them down by the creek. And gave short careers to puppies and rabbits, but played with squirrels on his shoulders and toads in his pockets. There are more happy memories than anything else, and you are a dear and I love you.

From Gratia to Wellington on his thirty-third birthday,
June 10, 1942

1941. Gratia left the newspaper indexing project, having resigned when she underwent cataract surgery. Genevieve carried on at the project, under a new director sent over by the public library.

On December 8, the United States declared war, against Japan in Asia and the Pacific and against Germany in Europe and Africa. For the next four years, this Second World War would be the driving dynamic for the entire nation.

1942. In the middle of the year, the WPA indexing project was closed down. Many workers had already left the project to take jobs in the private sector. Unemployment virtually disappeared in a few months, as the United States built up its military force of men, machines, and supplies. Genevieve took the opportunity to retire from the Minneapolis Public Library, from which she had been on loan during the entire WPA project. It all happened so quickly that Gratia's grand indexing project fell short of its goal. The final report laid out both its success and its stunted finale.

> The project indexed all state and local news, editorials, and advertisements contained in *The Minneapolis Journal,* a complete bound file, which is owned by the Minneapolis Public Library. The index began with the first issue of November 26, 1878, and continued through 1900. (Indexing actually was completed through 1939, but the project closed before the editing of the additional cards was done.) The final form of the index was a card index on 3×5 standard catalog cards. They were arranged alphabetically like a dictionary catalog of a public library. . . . This permanent card catalog now belongs to the Minneapolis Public Library.*
>
> The entire file of newspapers from 1878 through 1939 was microfilmed on the project. The filming produced a negative master film from which any number of positives may be taken. . . . It will be difficult to name all of the groups that will use this index, as difficult as it is to foresee the unusual requests that come every day to a library.[31]

Gratia hated to leave tasks unfinished—especially professional tasks—but this last one, which had so stimulated her, was now far beyond her control. Instead she turned her attention to the Wetoco Poultry and Dairy Farm, in which she had already invested far too much money. Besides the innovative chicken house cum cattle barn, she had built a home for her tenant farmer—a house designed by architect and old friend Hiram Livingston, who would never compromise when it came to quality and detail. Her library pension simply couldn't handle it all.

> April 24
>
> Dear Children,
>
> I have neglected you very badly. I'm sorry, but I am lazy. . . . I have been trying to keep house, but I don't do much but get the meals for Theo and Genevieve. A woman comes to clean, and I get

*In 1994, the WPA card catalog index is located in the Humanities Division of the central library and is used extensively.

on by lying down every afternoon. I've been out raking in the yard in preparation for helping Theo make the garden. I'm afraid I won't be as much help as usual.

We went up to the farm two weeks ago. The ice was piled around the shore, some places in front of the resort were 20 feet high.

Buttercup has a heifer and Daisy has a heifer, but Pansy, the new cow, lost hers. I don't see why, but I now have eight head and Gloria will have hers in July. Four hundred chicks are going up next Monday—the large variety. The other hens still lay three or four dozen a day. . . .

I hope to go up to Wetoco to stay about May 15. Mrs. Brandt is painting the kitchen linoleum and cleaning the cottage, and Paul is plowing a new hay field. This week Richard has a man to help him put in fence posts.

If Wellington has any idea of making Wetoco pay, he might look over the enclosed statement for last year. If he was with me so I wouldn't have to pay so much labor, we might break even. By the way, if he wants to take out stumps, we can get some dynamite sticks and blow up a few in the new pasture.

When are you planning to come up? I would be glad to have Dorothy and Alta here as long as Wellington can spare them. Dorothy would have to help me, as I am not very strong, but we have to live simply nowadays. And our bills are being cut to the bone. What do you feed that hearty man, Dorothy, and keep bills down?

We are hoping to rent out the Robbinsdale house for four or five months and stay at Wetoco. Other people seem to rent theirs without harm to furnishings . . . Theo is having a bonfire just now. Our tulips are in bloom, and the plum trees are pure white. But we need rain very badly. Love to all of you, Mother.

Unfortunately, this became the summer of the great disaster and the beginning of a general demise at Wetoco. Gratia's pride and joy was turning out to be the herd of well-bred Guernsey cows. These animals were raised so carefully and in such cleanliness that the whole south shore of Lake Mille Lacs, including guests of neighboring Izaty's Lodge, drank Wetoco farm milk, unpasteurized. Gratia's only regret was that her father, Levi—the farmer idealist—was not there to share in her accomplishment.

Late in summer, one of the herd became ill and the local veterinarian was called. What he found was that not only the sick cow, but the others as well, tested positively for brucellosis, or Bang's disease. By law, Gratia's entire herd had to be slaughtered, within days. The financial blow was the death knell for the farm, and Gratia would never fully recover from the setback. Still, the Wetoco poultry venture limped along by leasing grazing land and selling the hay crop.

1943. Gratia contracted pneumonia and was hospitalized. Fearing that her recovery might be prolonged and possibly incomplete, she gave a general power of attorney to Genevieve Macdonald. Gratia's hospitalization made the newspapers in Minneapolis. The owner of Izaty's Lodge no doubt read the news, for he contacted Genevieve and made an offer to buy the pasture land and hay field. Unaccustomed to business and perhaps overwhelmed by the responsibilities conferred on her, Genevieve promptly accepted the initial offer—a minimum offer at best. Gratia recovered fully from her illness and was devastated to learn that most of her farm had been sold off "for nothing." It was bitter medicine and it had a permanent, though unspoken, impact on the relationship between the two women.

1945. The Wetoco farm was gone—both the worries and the joys—but retirement turned out to be not at all unpleasant. There continued to be a never-ending round of educational and social events. Gratia's mind was amply challenged, with the College Women's Club, the Peripatetics study club, League of Women Voters, foreign policy meetings, and the always stimulating conversation among her oldest friends, the retired librarians. They called themselves the "Ex Libs," and they met monthly for luncheon in each other's homes.

If Gratia's eyes were failing and her driving erratic, her mind certainly was not. Genevieve managed the reduced household, and together the two women managed Theo. Major holidays were now routinely celebrated with Irene and Walter Hauser, their daughters, Susan and Jane, and always Blanche Scott. Theo was close to ninety, but he still went to Wetoco Lodge for the summer, gardened, brought in the ice, carried the wood, and did his best to keep the cottage open. Genevieve and Gratia still drove up for long weekends as their busy Minneapolis schedules allowed, often with Mrs. Scott in tow.

And every summer the Buffingtons from Duluth came down to Wetoco for a week—Constance, Gilbert, and Virginia—without Edwin, for he was married and serving his nation in uniform during these years of the Second World War. Likewise, the Hausers from Minneapolis drove up for their week at Wetoco. In 1945, it was at Wetoco Lodge that the Hauser daughters first heard the news of the Hiroshima atomic bombing. With no radio in the cottage, they sat in their father's automobile under the trees and listened on the car radio. And it was at Wetoco that the Hausers and the Buffingtons first become acquainted—an acquaintanceship that forty-seven years later would be the principal catalyst in this life story of Gratia Countryman.

Late in 1945, Carl Vitz announced his resignation as Minneapolis's chief librarian to become director of the Cincinnati Public Library. In Minneapolis, he had both supporters and detractors. Thus his pending departure opened up old wounds and kindled new hopes among the library staff. Almost a decade earlier, when Gratia retired, Glenn Lewis had been the "staff" candidate for the position. He was still on the staff, and his name was being bandied about again. Gratia continued to have a mind brimming with library ideas, along with a chronic disappointment that Mr. Vitz had never asked her for them. This time she took the initiative, offering Glenn Lewis her support and taking the opportunity to share her library concerns. He responded:

November 21

> Dear Miss Countryman,
>
> Thank you for your frank and generous letter.
>
> As the time approaches when the Library Board must make a decision, I am more and more aware that I shall have a great deal to measure up to if I am appointed to what I consider the finest position the City of Minneapolis has to offer. I always admired your understanding of your staff and your grasp of the people, organizations and neighborhoods in Minneapolis—in short, the city's needs in a library way, and I can assure you that if the Board decides in my favor, I am going to seek your counsel at the first opportunity. Yours sincerely, Glenn M. Lewis.

1946. Gratia's eightieth birthday celebration was a week-long affair, beginning with the arrival of niece Constance from Duluth. With Constance, Gratia began sorting family keepsakes and pictures—going back to Levi and Alta Countryman, and even further. It was time to begin letting go.

The first of the birthday events was on Tuesday, November 26. As Gratia had done so successfully in 1936 on her seventieth birthday, she did her best once again to upstage the others. She invited her old friends of the Library Luncheon Club to the Young-Quinlan tea room for lunch. Young-Quinlan was Minneapolis's exclusive store for women, founded by Gratia's old friend Elizabeth Quinlan and without doubt the most elegant building on Nicollet Avenue: Having lunch at the Young-Quinlan tea room was next to having lunch at the most exclusive club in town. The joy was that this tea room, with its indoor flowers and bubbling fountain, catered to a public that was both discriminating and thrifty. Gratia may have been hostess that day, but the guests turned the tables on her with their own cards and gifts.

Wednesday evening Gilbert Buffington drove down from Duluth, and on Thanksgiving morning, Wellington arrived from Chicago via the night train. The family had Thanksgiving/birthday dinner out, and Wellington took the night train back to Chicago. Afterward Gratia wrote, "Wellington came just for the day (bless him)."[32]

Friday morning, Gratia spoke at the library's North Branch, and in the afternoon the library staff entertained her with coffee and a birthday cake. Then two evenings later, Irene and Walter Hauser put on a private birthday dinner at their home. Guests were the new chief librarian, Glenn Lewis, and his wife; architect Hiram Livingston and his wife, Florence, one of Gratia's librarians; Professor Harold and Marie Deutsch, good friends and summer neighbors at Lake Mille Lacs; and of course, Genevieve Macdonald.

Gratia's eightieth birthday was noted in *The Minneapolis Journal,* which led to an avalanche of cards, telegrams, airmail letters, and telephone messages, more than a hundred and fifty altogether. Wrote Gratia in her day book:

> Have stood the excitement very well and seem much stronger than last year. Genevieve too seems well, but gets tired easily and has to rest. We wish we could go South for the winter, but we are thankful for home and for fairly good health and hosts of friends.[33]

Part VIII. Compleat Woman

Leave-taking

Genevieve drove up to town and lost her voice. . . .
Genevieve has [had] a stroke. We are stunned.

Gratia's daybook, August 26, 1947

1947. This year would be one of farewell to "Marie's house" in Robbinsdale, farewell to Minneapolis, and farewell to Wetoco. It started out in an ordinary way— a cold January, trouble with the automobile, and consequently missed luncheons and meetings. Genevieve had taken over the driving, and now the blue Buick was eight years old. When it was in the garage, as it often was, Genevieve could take the streetcar, but Gratia simply wasn't up to riding public transportation any more. When the automobile was in order, there were trips downtown to fit and refit Theo with a hearing aid. Gratia was preparing him for Walker Home, a Methodist senior's residence founded years earlier by the wife of T. B. Walker. With Gratia leading and Genevieve driving, Theo was taken over to Walker for an interview. He was accepted, and now began Gratia's at-home tasks—to take an inventory of Theo's clothes, select those that should go with him, sew name tapes on everything, including linens and towels, select furniture from the Robbinsdale house to go along with him, all in all to prepare for this major change in Theo's life. Gratia made all the decisions in her efficient business-like way and together with Genevieve carried them through. The adaptable Theo went along with it all and moved placidly to the Walker Home. For the first weeks, there were daily trips to Theo's new home, with Genevieve at the wheel, then every other day, and finally weekly visits to Walker Home, for brother Theo—Offie of Gratia's childhood— adjusted well. In fact, he seemed happier at Walker than he had been of late at home.

All through the spring, life was as busy as it had ever been. Though Gratia complained about her lack of energy, she still participated mightily. There were luncheons, dinner parties, the regular study clubs, Maurice Evans in "Hamlet," Lawrence Olivier in "Henry V," Barbara Ward speaking at the university, concerts, church, and Theo's ninetieth birthday. For Theo's celebration, Constance, Gilbert, and Virginia drove down from Duluth and it became a genuine family gathering.

In July Wellington, Dorothy, and little Alta Marie joined Gratia and Genevieve for a vacation at Wetoco. But it was only a week, for the two older women returned to Minneapolis as soon as the young family left for Chicago. Genevieve could not manage the cottage without either Wellington or Theo around, for Gratia's physical strength had waned badly. Yet Gratia put up apricot, orange, and pineapple preserves, and on the hottest day of the month celebrated Genevieve Macdonald's birthday by inviting old friends for dinner and bridge.

All of that came to an abrupt halt in a severe late summer heat wave, as recorded by Gratia in her day book.

> **August:** Terribly hot, nearly 100. . . . Very hot indeed. Just try to keep quiet. . . . Genevieve gave a luncheon at Young-Quinlan. . . . Called on Theo. . . . Got Theo and took him to the doctor. He seems to be getting blind. . . . At Dr. Ward's for further examina-

tion. Don't seem to be strong. Dr. Ward here, says for us to go up to the lake tomorrow. . . . Very hot. So we started and took Mrs. Scott with us. A very hot ride. . . . Slept under a blanket last night but won't tonight. . . . Turned cooler. Had a little fire. . . . Genevieve drove up to town and lost her voice. . . . Genevieve has [had] a stroke. Roy Horton drove us to town [Onamia] to Dr. Vik. We are stunned by it. . . . Drove back [to Minneapolis]. Genevieve in an ambulance and Roy drove my car. Constance and Virginia came down. . . . Took Genevieve to Fairview Hospital. Much better care. Constance and Virginia begin packing away our things. . . . Have rented the house, as of October 1st. Went over to see Theo. . . . Packed all day, got linen and bedding packed, closets emptied.

September: Finished packing dishes and cleaning cupboards. Went to see Genevieve. Still improving. . . . Constance and Virginia go home after cleaning basement and cellar. . . . Salvation Army takes a truckload. . . . Genevieve getting along fine [at hospital]. . . . Mrs. Scott goes to see Theo. . . . Been cleaning out my desk, am packing and writing letters. . . . Genevieve is brought home, needs only rest and quiet. I am very happy. . . . Mrs. Scott goes home. Will miss her, but can get on better alone. . . . The Hausers here this evening. Clara Baldwin and Mrs. Black out to see us. . . . Mrs. Scott over to lunch. . . . Last packing. Gilbert comes. Go out to say goodbye to Theo. . . . Finish packing. George Smith helps Gilbert, using my car. . . . Start at 8:00 AM for Duluth. George Smith drives up to bring our things. He drives my car back to keep for winter. . . . Settled in Duluth.

So brief and direct was Gratia when it came to reporting her final leave-taking from home, from Robbinsdale, from Minneapolis, and from all that the community had meant in her lifetime.

The Buffingtons of Duluth

. . . We do not know what a day may bring forth, but we are sure that we are facing great changes. It may be that we are on the threshold of the greatest forward step that man has ever taken. It is not behind us, it is ahead of us. God grant our statesmen great wisdom.

Gratia Countryman on World Government, January 31, 1949

1948. Gilbert and Constance Buffington owned a substantial home on Duluth's Superior Street, out from the business district. The back of the property looked out onto Lake Superior, with its singular beauty expressed in wind, fog, incredible waves, and miles of ice, all in season. It was to this home that Gratia and Genevieve were welcomed in the fall of 1947.

There were two Buffington children. The older was Edwin, now twenty-seven years old, who as a youth had been sent to California to live with his grandmother that she might not be lonely. A geologist by education, Edwin had served in the Second World War, and was now married and settled in San Diego. The younger was Virginia, nineteen years old and a sophomore at the University of Minnesota, living at home only during vacation times. For the most part, the parents were alone in the house, both leading such busy lives as would rival Aunt Gratia, even at her prime. Gilbert owned his own insurance agency, with all the busy connections this entailed in a city of 100,000 that behaved as if it were a Minnesota small town. Gilbert was especially active in the Episcopal church, which one way or another demanded his services at least one night a week. At home he changed some sixty storm windows to screens in spring and back to storm windows in fall. In spring he also cleaned the basement and prepared the garden, then mowed the lawn all summer, and shoveled the walks in winter. In spite of all that, Gilbert Buffington was one of the most generous men in the community—generous of his time, his money, and his counsel. The beneficiaries of Gilbert's generosity were legion, and they had always included members of his wife's own family, not the least of whom were Gratia and Wellington Countryman.

Constance Buffington was a civic leader in Duluth with major responsibilities in the League of Women Voters, the College Women's Club, and the church. Still she found time for the Duluth Women's Club, Daughters of the American Revolution, Delta Gamma alumni, and local charity work. These activities were outside the home. On Superior Street, Constance managed a garden—both flowers and vegetables—cooked, made preserves, baked, sewed, and generally did her own house cleaning. Within such an environment did the two elderly ladies from Robbinsdale make themselves at home. Constance and Gilbert turned over to Aunt Gratia and the partially paralyzed, almost speechless Genevieve two bedrooms, connected by a bath and overlooking Lake Superior. Gratia settled in quite well with her companion/patient. Daily she dressed Genevieve, read to her as her eyes would allow, mended her clothes, wrote letters for her, and brought her down to meals. Gratia still had faith that Genevieve would "come back," so to speak, and keeping the frail patient integrated into the family was her major objective. But Gratia still had energy for more. Her daybook was filled with garden work, baking, preserving peaches, and attending all manner of meetings with Constance. Sundays were Gratia's moment alone with Gilbert, for he always took her to church with him. Gratia might fret that after years of good Presbyterian preaching in Minneapolis she found Episcopal preaching in Duluth rather wanting. She might write this in her day book, but she would never share these feelings with Gilbert. Occasions alone with this lovable and competent man were just too precious.

The sunshine of the Buffington household was daughter

Virginia. Gratia's daybook entries indicate anticipation of Virginia's every arrival from the university down in Minneapolis, joy in her presence, and invariably, "Virginia left this evening. I am lonesome."

If there were any problems in the household, they stemmed from Constance's frustration over Gratia's love of cooking and her inability to stay out of the kitchen!

Besides the general decline of Genevieve, the swift departure from Wetoco and Robbinsdale continued to frustrate Gratia. One could deal later with the house in Robbinsdale, for it was well rented to an acquaintance. But Wetoco stood alone, having been abandoned in haste, and Gratia was anxious, as if for an absent child.

Very early in the year, buyers for Wetoco came forward with an acceptable offer—one Mr. and Mrs. Pearson* of Minneapolis—and in April the sale was completed. Gilbert and Constance and Gratia drove down to Lake Mille Lacs to empty the cottage of that which was precious to them. In her daybook Gratia recorded, "Snow, cold, ground covered. Dread going to Wetoco tomorrow. . . . Here we are starting to Wetoco at 8 A.M. Cold . . . Arrived yesterday at noon. Packed all afternoon. Then truck came this morning . . . and we drove back tired but satisfied. Good-bye Wetoco."

Back in Minneapolis were Irene Hauser and Blanche Scott, their association from the WPA years having turned into deep friendship and watchful caring. Blanche Scott was eking out an existence in her one room of an old Minneapolis house. She suffered a major heart attack in March. From Gratia's daybook: "Telephone from Irene Hauser that Mrs. Scott critically ill. . . . Letter from Irene that Mrs. Scott holding her own. . . . Letter from Theo and Irene. Mrs. Scott better. . . . Letter from Mrs.

*In 1994, the Pearsons' son and daughter-in-law—William and Jean—make their home at Wetoco, where the Countryman legend still survives.

Scott herself today. . . . Letter from Irene that Mrs. Scott worse. . . . A letter from Mrs. Scott herself."

Blanche Scott recovered from the heart attack. As a pauper in Minneapolis, she was entitled to the best medical care available and her own choice of doctor.

In May Gratia made her first trip back to Minneapolis, alone on the train, then by taxi to the public library. There she met Oscar Berg from the old library bindery, one of her longest standing library friends. They had lunch together in the library cafeteria—Gratia's farewell gift to her staff more than a decade earlier. Once again, Gratia held court while her library "girls" swarmed around her. She spent the night with Irene and Walter Hauser. The following morning, Walter drove Gratia out to Walker Home, picked up Theo, and brought him back for lunch. They all called on Blanche Scott in the afternoon, and the Hausers entertained the Livingstons for dinner. Sunday morning it was church with the Hausers, dinner at the Athletic Club downtown, and home to Duluth on the 5 P.M. train. It had been a lovely adventure, friends all around, almost like the old days.

All through summer and fall, life in Duluth held the kind of busyness on which Gratia thrived. Instead of old friends there were new friends, and Gratia adapted well, for she had an innate interest in her fellow human beings. Additionally, there was a steady stream of summer visitors. It seemed that everyone Gratia ever knew in Minneapolis made a summer pilgrimage to the North Shore of Lake Superior, especially in hay fever time and during the fall coloring of leaves. Before the age of freeways, Superior Street and the Buffington home were just a block off the main highway to the North Shore. Old friends and *their* friends would simply stop to call enroute in either direction. So frequent were the visitors that Gratia's favorite midday seating was on a comfortable chair looking out the front window.

Always Genevieve was at her side, except when Genevieve was napping, a tendency that increased as the months went by.

In fall Gratia retreated with Genevieve to their bedroom suite. There she had set up her typewriter, for she intended to write a significant paper for the Peripatetics, the somewhat exclusive study club to which she belonged in Minneapolis. Gratia's paper was scheduled for the end of January 1949, but she had completed the research months earlier and began writing in early December. From her daybook: "Lovely bright morning. Working on my paper, which I do a little every day, on 'World Government.'"

1949. Beginning in January, Gratia began to keep a true diary, writing entire paragraphs for each day and, once in awhile, sharing what was deep in her heart.

> **January:** 1949 finds Genevieve and Gratia still in Duluth, with Constance. Gratia is quite well, and Genevieve about the same as last year. She cannot talk very much, but uses her hand more. . . . I have been working on the paper I am writing for the Peripatetics on World Government. Must finish it and get it off my mind. . . . Got up early, had breakfast with Gilbert. We eat in kitchen. Then began typewriting paper and kept at it all day. . . . I typed on my paper all day, but I am very slow. . . . Constance went shopping while I typed . . . Finished typing my paper. Now must correct it, add some things and retype it. . . . This afternoon and evening I have been typing. . . . Well, have finished typing my paper, will now give last corrections and send it down in case I can't go.

Gratia did go down to Minneapolis to give her paper in person. On Saturday she and Constance took the train, and Virginia met them at the station. Irene and Walter Hauser entertained them for dinner, with the Livingstons. Afterwards they visited brother Theo at Walker Home, then stayed overnight at the Hausers', with Blanche Scott invited to tea on Sunday.

The Peripatetics meeting was on Monday, highlighted by "World Government," as read by Gratia Countryman. Afterward the members of the study club gave a luncheon at the

Woman's Club in honor of Gratia. In her diary she recorded, "I was so glad to see them all." This was indeed the last Peripatetics meeting that Gratia would attend, and the last paper that she would write.

As isolated as Gratia may appear to have been from the old centers of her life, her name was still abroad throughout Minnesota, and a month later she was once more honored for her life's work. She shared her joy in a letter to Wellington and Dorothy.

March 10

Dear Children,

I am writing to tell you of an honor I had last week. You know Minnesota is celebrating the Territorial Centennial. One hundred years ago, in 1849, Minnesota was separated from Wisconsin and together with parts of North and South Dakota, made into the Minnesota Territory. This occurred on March 3rd.

So birthday parties have been held all around the state. The enclosed clippings tell you that a vote was taken all over the state, choosing what they call the "100 Living Great" of the state. I was honored by being chosen one of the 100.

Gilbert was most pleased and insisted that Constance and I should go down to the dinner. So we did, and I invited Virginia also to be my guest. We had a very nice occasion and felt quite puffed up. The names were announced at the dinner, and the pictures appeared in the next morning's paper. They are awful pictures, mine no worse than the rest. Mine was taken in our Robbinsdale house standing by a bookcase on my 80th birthday, by a newspaper camera. They are going to issue a booklet, with pictures and a little biography of each one. I hope they will choose better pictures.

I saw Uncle Theo. He seems well although Constance thought he had failed. A very fine little woman, one of the inmates, reads to him every day, mends his clothes, goes walking with him, and is a most pleasant companion to him. I am grateful to her. . . .

We are expecting Virginia home next week for spring vacation. Lots of snow on the ground yet, but a promise of zero weather last night turned out to be 20° above.

> I find that the World Book publishes an annual to bring it up to date each year. Wouldn't you like to keep it up? If so, I will order it. Much love, Mother.

Spring in Duluth: Neither weather nor activities ever seemed to let up, as Gratia recorded details day after day in her diary. Always positive, more often than not awaiting Virginia's arrival from Minneapolis or Gilbert's return from his office, with Gilbert chauffeuring Gratia here and there, taking Genevieve for Sunday afternoon rides, Gratia reading, knitting, writing letters, helping in the garden, complaining about rabbits, and attending luncheons and meetings with Constance. If Gratia missed Minneapolis life, she hardly had time to dwell on it.

It had been a year and a half since Genevieve had her stroke and the two women were hurriedly transported to Duluth to be cared for by the Buffingtons. In Gratia's case, "cared for" wasn't quite the word she would have used. She made a modest monthly financial contribution to the household, to cover herself and Genevieve, and did her best to participate fully in the household responsibilities, from cooking to cleaning to gardening. But of course Constance had her own ways of running the busy household. Sometimes she would have preferred that Gratia simply stay out of the way, but Constance never let on. Thus Gratia never felt that she was imposing unduly on the Buffingtons, this niece and nephew whom she dearly loved.

Marie's Legacy

> *As an intimate friend of Miss Todd and the administrator of her small estate, I am sending you $2,000 as a trust fund and am stipulating that the proceeds be spent for books on art, in its broadest sense, to be added to your library.*
>
> Letter from Gratia to Piney Woods
> Country Life School, Fall 1949

1949. Since November of 1947, "Marie's house" in Robbinsdale had been rented furnished to one of Gratia's many acquaintances. All of Gratia's books, her papers, and her letters had also been left there, in the hurried departure after Genevieve's stroke. Gratia's assumption, of course, was that they would return one day, as soon as Genevieve was well enough to manage the household, and of course to drive the car.

At first, in Duluth, Genevieve seemed to have improved. She walked without difficulty and she could complete certain simple tasks. But Genevieve would never speak clearly again or recover the ability to write. By the spring of 1949, it was clear to all that Gratia and Genevieve could not go back to their Robbinsdale home. Thus, in April Gratia notified her tenants that they must vacate so that she could sell the home.

And in early May, she drove down to Minneapolis with Constance and Gilbert, to undertake the immense task of emptying the house and disposing of a lifetime of furnishings, papers, and personal treasures.

> **Sunday:** Got up 6:00 A.M. to early church and then on to Minneapolis. . . . Got to Robbinsdale home at 2:00 P.M. People called to see house all the P.M., 10 families. Irene and Walter [Hauser] called. . . . Terribly hot. . . . No one came to see the house all day. . . . Virginia here to lunch and wants a lot of things, which she can have. We packed all the rest of the day. . . . Worked all evening. All books separated. Oscar Berg came and got the books and records given to the library. . . . Man came to examine tarred roof. All is right. Our whole place looks nice. . . . Constance is a trooper. She works so hard. Virginia came over and helped. . . . Two people came to look at house, one seems much in earnest. . . . D. C. Bell [Real Estate] Agency came to appraise house, think I should get $17,000. . . . Have burned things all evening. . . . Sent table out to Theo and a lot of things over to Virginia. . . . Almost finished packing, burning letters etc. Gilbert came down tonight. . . . Gilbert here to help us. . . . Wellington and Dorothy arrived this P.M. Good to see them, am giving them many things. . . . A man quite in earnest about buying came

> tonight, believe he may be the final purchaser. . . . Mother's Day: I took the family to Curtis Hotel to dinner—a very good one. Then we all went out to call on Theo. . . . Several people called to see the house. . . . The van called for our things to send ours to Duluth and Wellington's to Chicago. We are all packed, said good-bye to our neighbors and packed up our car and came back to Duluth . . . We are all terribly tired . . . Letters from two buyers offering $14,000 for house. Refused. Have listed with Bell [Realty].

It took another two months to sell the property, for less than Gratia had earlier refused. She lamented in her diary, "Had offer for Robbinsdale house for $13,500. Don't like to sell so low, but Gilbert thinks it best."

Marie Todd had made an unusual Last Will. It included legacies to two nieces and to Wellington, and a life estate in her home for her three library companions—Gratia, Genevieve, and Elva Bailey. It provided further that when they no longer were living in the home, it should be sold and the proceeds used

> For the publicizing and promulgating of the plan known as the National Livelihood Plan for the adjustment of the social economy as set forth in the purposes and objectives of the National Livelihood Association, Winter Park, Florida; but if, after my death, it is the deliberate judgment of my Trustee that the said funds might be employed to greater advantage, and for better purposes, then I hereby authorize my said Trustee . . . to expend this Trust fund . . . for the benefit of such religious, charitable, scientific or educational corporations as said Trustee may select . . . and therein nominate Gratia A. Countryman as such Trustee . . .

After Marie's lengthy illness, there was no money to pay the legacies, nor was there any real estate, for Gratia had been forced to foreclose on the heavily mortgaged home.

When the Robbinsdale property was finally sold, Gratia chose to fulfill Marie's last wishes out of her own funds. Whether the National Livelihood Association still existed in 1949 is not clear, but Gratia chose to direct a substantial gift to

Piney Woods Country Life School in Mississippi, an educational institution for rural black youth. Wrote she:

> As an intimate friend of Miss Todd and the administrator of her small estate, I am sending you $2,000 as a trust fund and am stipulating that the proceeds be spent for books on art, in its broadest sense, to be added to your library.
>
> Miss Todd was a librarian and believed that libraries were effective educational agencies, and she believed most earnestly that education must be as universal as possible. She was Chief of the Art Department of the Minneapolis Public Library for 35 years and so was particularly interested in developing a love of art and cultivating a sense of appreciation and good taste. It was her opportunity to educate people in the things that minister to richer living.
>
> But her deep interest was in people, especially in the underprivileged. She resented racial prejudice, and I am sure she would have loved the work going on at Piney Woods Country Life School.
>
> She was a beautiful character, gentle and gracious, but courageous in spirit and firm in her convictions. She lived her religion daily in useful but unostentatious ways.
>
> There is no space here to relate the many things she did, but I am satisfied to perpetuate her work and her beliefs, in this simple gift of her money to the library of Piney Woods School.[34]

One by one, the last of Gratia's family and inner circle were leaving this world. Word came of Adda Countryman's death in Cincinnati. Adda was the widow of older brother Amplius, distanced by geography but always close in Gratia's heart, for she believed so in "family." Then soon after Gratia's visit to Minneapolis came news that brother Theo was failing. Good reason to go down to the city again. From Gratia's diary:

> **June:** . . . Dr. Ward called that Theo had fever and a little congestion in chest. June: . . . Hear Theo was better. Clara Baldwin had a stroke and is in hospital, but I had a card from her today. She is coming on well. . . . Constance and Gilbert got off early for Min-

> neapolis. They will see Theo and stay overnight at Robbinsdale, where we left a bed. . . . Genevieve and I have been alone, we garden some. . . . Genevieve does pretty well. . . . Started to Minneapolis alone by train. . . . Stayed at the Hausers. Susan Stuhr came over and also Mrs. Scott. This morning I went out to see Theo, who is quite ill. . . . Jane Hauser driving her mother and me about. . . . Irene went over to the University, where I had luncheon with my '89 class reunion. Irene took me to the train, where Virginia met me and brought me home. . . . Virginia has been doing last things before starting to England.* . . . We all went to early church, then Constance and Gilbert took Virginia to Minneapolis to start by plane in the morning. Have just had telephone call that Theo is very low. . . . Word this noon that Theo had passed away, very easily. Constance and Gilbert . . . had seen Virginia off on the airplane and had seen Theo still alive.

The Buffingtons returned to Duluth. Constance picked up Gratia, and the two women went back immediately to Minneapolis by train, to arrange for Theo's funeral. Gratia recorded:

> Jane and Walter Hauser met us at the train, took us to Davies Mortuary . . . then to Curtis Hotel for the night. Very tired. . . . Got up early, had breakfast, ordered flowers for casket. Went out to the Walker Home and packed up a few things of Theo's. Left most everything there. . . . At 1:30 funeral service, a wonderful old minister in charge, beautiful talk. . . . Many friends at service.

The ashes of Theophilus Countryman were buried at Oakwood Cemetery, situated along a pleasant rural road in the township of Nininger. Theo would be the third child of Levi and Alta Countryman to be buried there alongside his pioneer parents. Oakwood Cemetery had become a passion of Gratia's. The remnants of the cemetery association still existed, but for lack of funds the burial grounds were ill kept and subject to vandalism. Gratia gave new life to the cemetery by contributing

*Virginia Buffington was to participate in a summer program abroad, called SPAN.

funds toward a modest campaign for restoration. As Gratia contemplated her own mortality, she made plans that her own remains be buried there and that an appropriate family monument be erected.

Life went on, and in fall Gratia was busy knitting a sweater for granddaughter Alta Marie, now ten years old. If reading was increasingly difficult, somehow knitting still went along at its own pace. Gratia busied herself daily in the Buffington garden, harvesting tomatoes and root vegetables. She continued to receive unexpected visitors, for September was a favorite time for a North Shore drive by Minneapolis residents. Then it happened:

> **September 30:** This day, which has passed so happily, has ended tragically. Gilbert has been at Insurance Conference all day and to dinner tonight, but the rest of us went to the Women's Institute to hear in person [José] Iturbi—a wonderful pianist. But Genevieve fell on our front steps coming home. We called Dr. Boyer. He is afraid of a broken hip and sent her in an ambulance to the hospital for an X-ray in the morning.
>
> **October:** We have thought of nothing but Genevieve all day. Gilbert and I went to see her early this afternoon. The X-ray showed a fractured hip and a crack in the pelvis. She will not be operated on, but will have to lie quiet for a month. . . . Gilbert and I went to church this A.M. After dinner, he took me down to the hospital and I was with Genevieve for 2 or 3 hours. She is keeping very calm and cheerful. The doctor is keeping her enough under opiates to relieve pain. So she isn't suffering. . . . Rainy and very foggy. Spent the afternoon with Genevieve. . . . Constance washed and took me down in afternoon to hospital. Genevieve doing very well and so cheerful. . . . Constance took me down to the hospital this P.M. . . . Gilbert took me to hospital. Genevieve is getting on, and keeps so cheerful. But I am very lonesome without her. I don't know what to do evenings. . . . Gilbert took me to the hospital this morning and I stayed all day with Genevieve. . . . Genevieve about the same. . . . Took a taxi to the hospital. Gilbert called for me and we ate our dinner in the hospital cafeteria, which is very good. . . . October 12: My dear Marie's birthday. . . .

> Genevieve doing fairly well. . . . Found Genevieve much excited. The X-ray showed much improvement and she was allowed to swing out of bed and dangle her feet. It did seem very good to us.

On November 9, Genevieve came home from the hospital, having recovered very well from the broken bones and amazingly strong after more than a month in bed. From then on Gratia's main interest was to be with Genevieve, to take care of her and to prevent another fall. On Thanksgiving Day, the Buffingtons celebrated Gratia's birthday at home. It was the first time that Genevieve had come downstairs since returning from the hospital. After the event, Gratia wrote: "I'm quite tired tonight. A wonderful present from Wellington's family, a house coat, padded—blue with pink lining, just fits."

1950. In early June Genevieve Macdonald had a massive stroke; she died on the twenty-third of the month. Gratia bid her a tender farewell in her diary: "Genevieve died at 2:30 this afternoon. A beautiful earthly life ended. How I shall miss my dear companion."

Irene and Walter Hauser, along with Florence Livingston and other library friends, drove up for the funeral. Constance put on a lovely luncheon afterward. Added Gratia: "The Hausers stayed overnight and were a great comfort."

From Gratia's July diary: "Virginia went back [to Minneapolis] on afternoon train. Confided to us that she has fallen in love with Bob Shaw. I am glad. He is finishing his master's degree in journalism. It is always lonesome when Virginia goes back, especially now, with Genevieve gone."

At the end of the year, Gratia summarized in her diary the events that had meant the most to her.

> War in Korea and developing war throughout the world. Family: Connie born [daughter of Edwin and Peggy Buffington]; Genevieve dies; Constance, serious operation; Virginia gets en-

gaged; Gratia, eye operation. Many home repairs; Gilbert biggest business year. [Buffington] trip to California. Fur coat.

In this time of the Korean War, Robert MacGregor Shaw was working in Germany. Hence, in the fall of 1951, he and Virginia each traveled to London, to be married in an Episcopal church. Back in Duluth, Virginia's Great Aunt Gratia rejoiced exceedingly!

Sharing of Gifts

May I be no man's enemy, and may I be the friend of that which is eternal and abides. May I never quarrel with those nearest me; and if I do, may I be reconciled quickly. . . . May I wish for all men's happiness and envy none. . . . May I never fail a friend in danger. . . . May I always keep tame that which rages within me. May I accustom myself to be gentle and never be angry because of circumstances.

Translation of an early Greek prayer,
pasted by Gratia into her 1951 diary

1951. Life on Superior Street went forward in a somewhat quieter mode. Gratia recovered quite well from her eye operation and for a time enjoyed improved eyesight. In February she suffered a mild heart attack but was soon up and about, able to attend luncheons, lectures, concerts, and an occasional play. She was more often alone now, and she spent hours on end bringing into order her long-neglected stamp collection.

March brought Gratia sad news of Clara Baldwin—one of her oldest friends, her ally in a host of battles, beginning with Company Q at the university, then the State Library Commission, pensions for school librarians and a host of other reforms.

> **March:** Had word that Clara Baldwin was much worse. Dear Clara. . . . Had word tonight of Clara Baldwin's death this morning. She'd been suffering from a stroke for several years. Will miss her. . . . Read material for writing a memorial of Clara Baldwin, but eyes are bad.[35]

Then, on April 13, Gratia suffered a serious stroke. She was taken to the hospital and remained there for two months. Amazingly, she recovered almost completely except for a general physical weakness that made walking difficult. Gratia continued to write letters after the stroke, but she no longer kept a diary.

1952. Gratia's increasing blindness was now diagnosed as glaucoma, an advancing condition for which there was no cure. Her innate curiosity was still at work, though, and she set about to reconstruct a history of the disease. Confined to the house, Gratia no longer had access to library resources. Yet, somewhere out of the depths of her past, she remembered that the Babylonians had treated the disease two millenia before Christ. She knew it was mentioned in the Code of King Hammurabi, which was found inscribed on a block of stone, and she even recalled that this stone tablet was discovered in a castle ruin during her early years at the library.[36] She found great satisfaction in remembering all of this and more.

Gratia wasn't yet ready to give up this world, and she desperately wanted to be part of the lives of those she loved the most, especially granddaughter Alta Marie, who was now almost thirteen years old.

> February 17
>
> Dear Alta,
>
> I was so pleased with the letter about your aquarium. But your mother says it only holds a gallon and that is too small. I never raised guppies, but I know they are very small. I am sure

you would enjoy larger older fish. So I am telling Mother to get you a larger one, as large as you have space to have one, and the square-cornered ones are better than round ones. You should have some nice tropical fish. Tell Mother to get you what you want and send the bill up to me.

I cannot write much this morning. I am getting quite blind and I think I won't be writing much more. I will have to take care of my eyes. . . . My love to all of you, Mother.

And later:

April 2

Dear Alta,

I'm so pleased you have your fish aquarium. I hope you picked up just what suited you and that you have just the right setup, for it is a fascinating hobby. You are evidently like your father and like live things. I cannot write much this morning. I have had an attack of pneumonia, and although I did not have to go to the hospital, I do not get strong very fast and sleep much of the day. But I wanted to tell you to make out the bill for the fish equipment and send it to me.

Then I wanted to say to your father and mother how glad I am that they are joining the church. I wouldn't care what church, just so they are happy there, and like the minister. I hope they will give all the time and service they can so that they are real church supporters. Religion certainly needs revival in these corrupt times, when people seem to have no respect for honesty or truth. I guess we have been neglecting our Christian heritage, and we had better get back on the job.

I wish Wellington would get back to work with boys. I remember the tough little gang that appeared at our back door every Saturday morning to go hiking with him. I used to put up lunches for them. I remember the little boy that used to swear so and then confided to Well, "We need a prayer meeting." I remember too the bunch out in Washington that Wellington took under his wing, and they gave him a fountain pen when he left. Boys always liked him and they need leaders. He likes out-of-doors and has much to give boys that they need. . . . Love, Grandma.

Gratia sensed that she was on the threshold of eternity, and she wanted desperately to leave something of herself behind. Horace's ring she had given to Virginia years earlier, when Virginia was in high school. Now she looked through her belongings and found what she treasured even more—two Bibles, one belonging to her mother, the other to her father. Father's should go to grandnephew Edwin and Mother's to Virginia, and so she wrote to each of them, letters quite the same and in a handwriting clearer than it had been in months.

My dear Virginia,

This is your great-grandmother's Bible. I gave it to her and she used it many years, and I want you to have it.

If you were going to make a long tour, you would want a guide book. Well, you are going to take such a tour. You have no choice, it is an unavoidable, inescapable tour to the "world without end." Every human being must take it, and he has no choice as to the day nor the hour. You may have 80 or 90 years ahead and you may have a day. The trip is inevitable. This is the only "guide book." The highway is well marked. If a detour is made, the way back is well marked. The rules and laws of this country are clear.

The description is a little vague and no travelers have returned to tell us, but there is enough to give us faith to proceed. St. Paul says, "Eye hath not seen, ear hath not heard, neither hath it entered into the heart of man to conceive what God hath prepared for those who love him." And St. John tries to visualize, by talking of streets of gold and gates of pearl.

Have you ever tried to realize what <u>forever</u> really is, what is the <u>world</u> <u>without</u> <u>end</u>? Think hard, away into the <u>forever</u>; it staggers your <u>mind</u>, You cannot think <u>forever</u> and <u>ever</u>. Neither can you think of an end. Yet the directions to get there are simple. "What does the Lord require of thee, but to do justly, to love mercy, and to walk humbly before thy God." "He that believeth on the Lord Jesus Christ shall be saved."

But I am giving you the guide book. It is the only one. Get well acquainted with it and you will have no fear to start anytime without further preparation. And as the years go by, so they have with me, you will look forward to a radiant country, with radiant beings as your eternal companions, and the most congenial possible occupations.

I'll be waiting for you, Aunt Gratia.

But Gratia wasn't yet quite on the threshold of eternity. There were still some earthly joys left. In August Wellington and his family paid a visit, and afterward she wrote to him: "Your visit came and went so fast. It was like a dream. I was so glad you came."[37]

1953. For all useful purposes, Gratia was completely blind now. Yet once again, when moved to share her insights, she rose to the occasion. Using a thick black pen, she wrote to grandnephew Edwin Buffington, out in California.

April 16

Dear Edwin,

I cannot write very well for I am nearly blind, but I want to answer your last letter. I have written this letter at least a hundred times in my mind, and it is probably my last one. I am well and enjoy life, but my eyes are failing fast. . . .

You may not remember that in your last letter you said you did not think Steve [Edwin's son] should be turned loose in the Bible and asked my opinion. I would think it would be better to read it aloud. I knew a big businessman in Minneapolis who read it aloud every Sunday afternoon. He did not require anyone to listen, but his children gathered about him. And he did not let anything interfere—company nor engagements. He always read for an hour or two. I think he read the Bible through, skipping as much as he wished and reading with discretion. Anyway, things go over the heads of children and can be very simply explained.

It was much the same in my home except that we had family prayers and father read the Bible aloud. Then Lana and I learned much, memorized many Psalms, which I can repeat yet today. We also learned the Ten Commandments, the Sermon on the Mount and many chapters. We often spent Sunday afternoons in a contest seeing who could learn the most verses. We always learned the

International Sunday School lesson and repeated it to father every Sunday morning. Father believed we should learn the Bible, and Lana and I have always felt it a great asset. She could repeat whole chapters and so can I.

As I stand now on the threshold of eternity, as we all must do, I say to myself, "Underneath are the everlasting arms." "I will strengthen thee, yea, I will keep thee, yea I will uphold thee with the right hand of my righteousness." "I will take the wings of the morning and fly to the uttermost parts of the sea, even there shall thy right hand hold me," and many other promises. I could go on and repeat many more verses, but everyone should learn them for himself and hear the voice of God talking to him personally.

What is the Bible? It is the history of a primitive people, developed by the personal knowledge and direction of God. When did a nation begin with a perfect God and a perfect code of conduct like the Ten Commandments, or a national leader who said, "What does the Lord require of thee, but to do justly, to love mercy and to walk humbly before thy God."

But besides being the story of a nation being guided by its relation to its God, it is a soul guided by its master and developed by its close relationship to a perfect God and a code that has only perfection as its aim. No one can face into eternity and not wish that he had approximated more closely to the climate of that country revealed so clearly in the "Word of God."

I wish I could write more, but much has already been written and you can get plenty of instruction better than mine. I can only sum up that I think you cannot afford not to help your children understand God's message to the world through the written word, and to help them find a direct road to Him in their hearts. I am close to my earthly end, but I feel close, just a narrow gauge wall to the eternal life, whether we wish or not. Life has no end, it is indestructible as matter. Life never ends, it is continuous. Look at life that way and teach your children in the "way, the truth and the life."

I wish I could write more, but I could not say more anyway. I love you all, Aunt Gratia.

Indeed, these were Gratia Countryman's last written words, for she died on July 27, 1953, four months short of her eighty-eighth birthday.

Afterword

In accordance with Gratia Countryman's written instructions, her funeral was held in Minneapolis, at Westminster Presbyterian Church on Nicollet Avenue. It was at Westminster that she had kept her church membership in the last decades of her life.

Most of Gratia's immediate family were at the funeral—Wellington, Dorothy, and Alta Countryman, Constance and Gilbert Buffington, and Virginia Buffington Shaw—along with librarians, retired librarians, library board members and friends, not the least of them Blanche Molineux Scott, dressed in her signature black hat and black wool skirt.

Gratia's ashes were buried at Oakwood Cemetery in Nininger Township, next to her parents, brother Theo, and the two siblings who had died as infants almost a century earlier. Today a granite family monument marks the place.

In her Last Will, Gratia Countryman gave equal consideration to her nearest and dearest—son Wellington, niece Constance, and their respective children. But she also left a smaller portion of her estate to four institutions—the Minneapolis Public Library, the Greater University Fund, the State Women's Christian Temperance Union, and the Piney Woods Country Life School in Mississippi.

Gratia's death sparked an energetic effort, both on and off the library board, to establish a Countryman branch library as had been done for her predecessor, James Hosmer. This effort was combined with plans to build a new branch library in southwest Minneapolis. Property was purchased just off Minnehaha Creek, studies were done, architect plans commissioned, and a billboard sign erected on the site—"Minneapolis Public Library, Gratia Countryman Branch." It all came to naught, however, for lack of funds and perhaps for lack of sustained interest. The property was eventually sold. Since then, other branch libraries have been added to the Minneapolis library system, but none has carried Gratia's name.

Over the years, the name Gratia Countryman has generally faded from the collective memory of the community. Thus if there is an overall raison d'être for the tale told here, it is simply to record for posterity that such a woman once graced this corner of the world and for a moment in history made the public library the most significant institution in the entire community.

Selected Writings

"The Vocation in Which a Woman May Engage"

Gratia Countryman delivered this talk on June 16, 1882, at Hastings High School graduation exercises, Hastings, Minnesota. She was fifteen years old.

The question is not what vocation can a woman follow by which to gain a livelihood, as if the sphere of woman were so prescribed and narrow as to admit of little choice, but, from so many, what one will she choose through whose channel she may win bread and butter and clothes, possibly happiness, and fame.

During the past half century, woman, the weaker vessel, has been coming up out of the dead ashes of man's estimation of her capabilities and duties, and by her energies aided by the goodwill and wisdom of her more enlightened brothers, she has demonstrated the hitherto dim problem that woman is an apt scholar and imitator, in short, can do very many things that man can do.

In former days, though a woman might have done well in what she attempted, she was deprived of the credit due her; man considered her as a menial and gave her no opportunity to cultivate her talents, and if by any means she became noted, it was thought to be due only to her high station in life, or to some accidental circumstance. As in the reign of Queen Elizabeth, though by a wise administration she added greater glory to the English nation, yet it was thought to be only an accident of birth, for had she not been Queen Bess, she might have been a scullion in some Englishman's family. In the reign of Victoria things have changed; respect due to woman and woman's work has increased with advancing civilization and the spread of learning among the masses.

Man, in ignorance, kept woman a mere slave; man, enlightened has clearly seen that woman has a mind like unto his mind, possessing his hopes, aspirations, and pluck.

I would not have my speech run into woman's rights, or refer to her peculiar sphere, as compared with man's. All that will take care of itself, so long as she keeps within the limit of her duties and possibilities. And now we come to that word "possibilities."

For many years, it has been a practice among men, during the latter years of their college course, to choose the profession which they intend to follow. In our day, knowledge is being extended so fast and so far that if a man would accomplish anything, he must not only devote his time and talents to some particular science or profession, but he must choose that branch of his science or profession for which he is best adapted, and concentrate all his powers of body and mind in this one line of research. Then if a woman would become equally proficient in any art, science, or profession, must she not also choose for herself an occupation and pursue her studies thereafter with reference to it, instead of finishing her education in a general way?

Woman has but recently been admitted to some colleges and allowed to learn some profession, but if she applies herself faithfully to the avenues now open to her, she will be successful in others hereafter to be opened.

She has already become an educator, and the world has accorded her a grand place in this profession. She may also fit herself to become an educator of adults in the higher branches. It is a noble work to which she is peculiarly adapted, and let her but make it a life work, as do some men, and what a world of good she can accomplish, for has she not the forming to a great extent of the characters of the pupils placed under her charge? And though she may choose many another profession, yet if she will but throw all her energies into the work of teaching, she will succeed gloriously in this profession, where she might make but questionable progress in others.

May she not also become a banker? No one will say that there is not plenty of evidence to prove that woman's capacity for business is marked. She may not venture largely, but she will most likely venture carefully. She may therefore become a merchant. Every year her field of usefulness in this direction is being extended, and those who venture in this field are generally successful, commencing on a small scale, buying judiciously and wisely.

Again, is her sense of justice less acute than that of her brother? And if not, may she not also become a lawyer? She certainly would not be lacking in her ability to manage a case, as men generally very well know, for she clings to her point of argument to the last moment, and when all arguments fail her, does she not cling to her opinion just the same.

Convince a woman against her will,
And she's of the same opinion still.

Her deft fingers, her sympathy and cheering counsel, joined to medical knowledge would enable her to work cures and thus might she be able to make the noble profession of medicine profitable to her as to the other sex.

She may become an authoress. The cultivation of a naturally fertile imagination and the expression of her deepest thoughts and feelings may thus be distributed, and others besides her immediate acquaintances may be benefited.

But while we are thinking of our subject, avenues of pleasant and profitable labor multiply upon our thoughts. She may become a bookkeeper, or she may learn telegraphy and a host of employments worthy [of] her time and attention. In all these she may become excellent if she remembers that "thoroughness is the first element of success" in any undertaking.

Pushing out into the world where her inclinations may lead with faith, with firmness, with unflinching honesty of purpose and purity of character, she may hope to win wherever her brother expects to win.

And yet, these random remarks would not be well finished did we not say that whatever else a woman may choose as a means of gaining a living, she is not fully equipped unless she learns well the art of housekeeping. There are so many that push on to get rid of this, the crowning glory of woman's achievements. To make a loaf of good bread; to prepare with skill the table for a hungry family; to keep a clean and orderly house; to make a bed fit for the repose of a king; to sew; to darn; to mend; in short to be able to stand in such a relation to those under her charge, that it may be said of her as it was of the woman in the Bible, "She looketh well to the ways of her household, and eateth not the bread of idleness." And while she may have all other accomplishments, these she <u>must</u> have.

"Liberty"

Gratia Countryman delivered this suffrage talk on March 31, 1917, to the Intercollegiate Prohibition Association at Hamline University, St. Paul, Minnesota.

Several years ago, we rejoiced when a great oriental nation threw off the dynasty of oppression and stood forth a republic.

It had much to learn before it could be a real republic, but the great impulse of freedom was stirring, the right of self-government.

A few days ago, another startling and sudden thing happened in Europe. The most autocratic government in the world was overturned in a day, and the people shook themselves out of their shackles, opened their Siberian prisons, and stood up in the majesty of their human birthright. We were thrilled to the heart because we believe in liberty, or think we do. We talk a great deal about it, and a few Americans have it and the rest boast of it.

Twice have great events happened in our own country in the name of freedom. Once we threw off the yoke of England and wrote a constitution which should rest upon the consent of the governed. And again, before you and I can remember, they arose and in the name of liberty broke the shackles of Negro slavery, and enfranchised the black man, for the consent of the governed.

Now you and many thousands are striving successfully to break another tyrannical force—that of the liquor traffic, which has controlled our politics, chosen our lawmakers, filled our prisons, saddled us with costly institutions, killed millions of strong, splendid men, maimed and crippled millions of children, which had better never have been born.

The European war does not begin in blood guiltiness with this tyrant, nor will there be any more crippled and maimed after this war than are being caused every year in the shape of subnormal, idiotic, criminal children and utterly worthless, sodden, inefficient men and woman. We might as well be under the tyranny of war lords as under the tyranny of liquor lords. There will never be true democracy in this country until these shackles are broken, to which task this association, I take it, is pledged.

I assume therefore that you believe in democracy, that you believe the government should be controlled by the consent of the governed. If you do really believe it, then I have only to remind you that we are as yet but half a democracy. I enlist your entire sympathy with making it a complete democracy, for one-half of the governed have no part in the government. You rejoice with China and with newborn Russia in their reach after freedom; you must then rejoice in the efforts of your American women to grasp this precious thing—political liberty.

Democracy rests upon universal suffrage, the consent of the governed, of which women are a large intelligent and moral part. No matter how much one may argue pro and con about the enfranchisement of women, it all comes back to the principle of democracy and to whether men really believe in democracy. Over the whole world, the democratic principle is slowly creeping; it is enlarging its meaning as it sweeps forward; it is inevitably including the whole of humanity, its men and its women.

Miss Rankin, our first Congresswoman, said that in her campaign, she asked one man if he didn't believe that government rested upon the consent of the governed. Yes, he certainly did. Well, how about the consent of the women? Well, the government didn't govern the women. Well, how about that, if she broke the laws, she paid the penalty, and if she had property, she paid her taxes. But he flatly declared that the government governed the men and the men governed the women. And he never saw the base injustice of his position.

I do not know your nationalities, but many names of your officers are Scandinavian. Many of the men before me are descendants from the Scandinavian race. Let us look at your countries. Iceland was the first country to go dry and has given Icelandic women the full suffrage. Likewise in Norway, Denmark and Finland, women have the full municipal and parliamentary vote and are eligible to all offices. In Sweden women have full municipal suffrage. Do you think that America with her system of public schools and co-educational colleges is producing women less able than the Scandinavian woman? When the Scandinavian woman comes to our land of liberty, she loses her liberty. The Irish, the Scottish and the English women have municipal suffrage. New Zealand and Australian and the Western Canadian women have full suffrage and had better keep away from the land of the free if they wish to keep their freedom. Do you really feel that the American women, descendants of these older countries, are less able than the Irish woman, the Australian woman or the Canadian woman? Does the American democracy feel no pride in its womanhood that it can deny her the liberty which monarchies give her?

Who teaches the American youth? Who fills and upholds the churches, who spends the country's money, who runs the 20,000,000 homes of the nation, who is foremost in the social and philanthropic enterprises? Is the American woman not the foremost of all in her wide and laudable enterprises?

I stood at my window this morning and watched the First Minnesota Infantry go by and I said, Who reared and cared for these sons and taught them patriotism and duty? The women of this land, who are governed entirely without their consent.

Sometimes we American women feel like making a parody on Shylock's speech. Hath not a woman brains, hath she not justice, conscience, emotions and a strong sense of duty fed by the same impure food, subject to the same occupational diseases, killed by the same sweated industries as men are? When you harm her home, does she not cry out; when you ruin her children, does she not fight; when you try to close upon her the way of escape, will she remain passive? I've been talking recently about it to young men. I find them more conservative, more idealistic about it than older men. Their argument mainly falls under two headings. I suppose you may feel that public life unsexes a woman. Unsex her? How could you, for her sex isn't like an old glove that she might accidentally lose or throw away. She can't lose it; it was born with her. She will always feel attracted to you and she will always want a home with you. How can you feel so toward the girl who climbs trees with you, races with you, plays tennis with you and then suddenly is too precious to vote with you?

Her home work, her woman's work, is all tangled up with the community life. Pure food and milk supply, water supply, clean streets, protection from disease, school problems, child labor, moral conditions, cost of living, what are they but home problems? How many of our city ordinances, our state legislation, have to do with public health and living conditions. Isn't the liquor question a home question? Most women feel that it is. How can women unsex themselves when they are only trying to protect and make good homes. You say that public life (and by the way, most women aren't seeking public life, and those that must be active in the campaign for equality will be glad to retire when the cause is won)—you say that public life will destroy men's chivalry toward women. I have never heard that this was the result in the present enfranchised countries. They apparently feel more respect for her. But may I ask how much chivalry is being shown to the 10,000,000 wage-earning, self-supporting women in this country who must depend upon the kindness and chivalry of men? Do you think the records of the sweated industries, the white slave traffic, show any chivalry toward woman? What would the laboring man do without the ballot to protect himself? What are these 10,000,000 laboring women doing without it? Chivalry isn't protecting them.

When Booker Washington, who did so much for the lowliest class in our country, went to Europe to study conditions and methods, he reported that in every country as well as our own he found women the lowest down. You do not seek far for the reason: she has no weapon of defense. Yet for all this the criminal records of this country show that only five percent of the criminals are women. Ninety-five percent are men. Should lawbreakers be the lawmakers?

College men, you are open minded about almost everything; you are in the forefront in a great moral fight. Be open minded toward another great movement which is sweeping the world, democracy—this other moral movement: respect the woman who studies beside you, respect the woman who may someday rear and teach your sons, respect the sanity of the campaign for freedom which womenkind are making. Can you put yourselves in our place? If so, you will surely sow complete democracy. I'm for it.

"Maria Sanford," A Eulogy

Maria Sanford, 1836-1920, was in her time the most renowned professor at the University of Minnesota, 1880-1909. Unorthodox in her ways, she was controversial, yet inspired immense loyalty among her students. Professor Sanford lectured across the nation on subjects ranging from child labor to educational reform. She died April 21, 1920. Gratia Countryman presented this eulogy on May 9, 1920, at the memorial service for Maria Sanford. Surviving are Gratia's pencil notes.

Friendship has been the subject of many writers, from Plutarch to Hugh Black, and none can express the wonderful experience of friendship. When I think of Miss Sanford, I think of her as my friend. When the message reached me of her death, I didn't think first that a great woman had passed away, that the lamp of a splendid intellect had gone out. I thought first of my personal loss of a personal friend. There was a hurt in my heart, a quick stab, which only the loss of a friend could cause.

But I was only one of many, many, many who felt that sharp sting of personal loss. We were her friends and she was ours. She had that peculiar genius for friendship which few people possess. One may speak of each and all of her wonderful qualities, but those of us who were close to her and loved her think first of the great heart into which we were admitted.

I remember her now as I first saw her in the classroom, with her bright cheery ways and her clear ringing voice, but it wasn't the magnetism of her voice, it wasn't the cheerful temperament, it wasn't the literary appreciation, it wasn't the delicious humor, it wasn't the hearty laugh that drew us to her. It was the thing behind all these, which produced all these, the great unselfish heart of that dear woman that made us not only respect and admire her, but love her deeply and unfalteringly.

The secret of friendship is just the secret of all spiritual blessing, the way to get is to give. Miss Sanford was giving out all of the time. She had more than most women to give and her gifts multiplied with the giving, as the loaves and fishes, until she had wherewithal to feed the multitude. I have never known another person who seemed to have such a wealth to give out and who gave her spiritual blessings so unstintingly.

It would take too long to review the work she has done for women, for I believe that she has worked all of her life in furthering all opportunities for women. She was an ardent supporter of higher education for women when ardent supporters were needed. She has been an active suffrage worker, and helped in her own fine way to impress women themselves with the serious duties of citizenship. But some of her finest talks out through the state and elsewhere have been on purely domestic problems. No girl could listen to some of Miss Sanford's talks on home relations, on the beauty of character, without being stirred to the depths of her girl heart to do better. Miss Sanford knew girls so well, she knew the problems of young girlhood, she had a peculiar way of stimulating them and putting unforgettable thoughts into their minds. She had a way of reciting just the right little poems (and how full her head used to be of them) to just the right person when it would put courage and strength into their souls.

I am sure that not only her old college girls, but hundreds of girls whom Miss Sanford has addressed—high schools and farmers' institutes and women's clubs—can remember the homely advice, the practical little everyday talks that just fitted our common everyday needs.

"For naught that set me's heart at ease nor giveth happiness and peace" was low esteemed in her eyes.

We women think of her courage—

I remember a little episode so delightfully like her, over which we often laughed.

(Story of washing ceiling)

We women remember her unswerving sense of duty—

(I remember her sprained ankle.)

We remember her civic pride—

I believe she was one of the first to help clean up streets and set out trees.

We remember her unbounded energy—

Those of us who went to her sunrise classes.

We remember all the trails wherein she has been a living example unto us, but most of all we remember the generous, unselfish, responsive open heart of our dear friend.

"Fathers"

This essay appeared under the caption "Miss Countryman Says:" in The Parent-Teacher Broadcaster, *January 1932, published by the Minneapolis School Board.*

In the olden days there was no question about the father's place in the home. He was the seat of authority; he was a patriarch; he was distinctly the head of the family and was proud of his lineage and proud to hand down the family name and tradition to his sons. It was a bitter thing to bear the disgrace of a wayward son or daughter. But now discipline is more lax; many a father seems to lack a sense of deep responsibility if son goes wrong. He has not, through the years, kept the place of authority in his home nor the voluntary respect and comradeship of his children. Father seems too often to have abdicated in favor of mother, especially in matters relating to the children and to the conduct of the home. We do not underestimate the value of mother and her influential place in family government and discipline, but we feel sure that the many youth problems would not be so difficult if more fathers would not abdicate while the children are growing up.

"Father's Day" in the State University, in many churches, in various organizations has served to emphasize father's important place in the character-forming years of his children and to take him out of business cares into the realm of his children's interests. The distinction of founding Father's Day belongs to Mrs. John Dodd of Spokane, Washington, who conceived the idea as a tribute to her own father. In urging the support of such a day she says that Father's Day would call attention to such constructive teachings as:

The father's place in the home
The training of children
The safeguarding of the marriage tie
The protection of womanhood and childhood

So Father's Day is now recognized as well as Mother's Day. There is a delightful volume of short stories, *Father in Modern Story,* which features father quite as truly as the companion volume, *Mother in Modern Story,* features mother. For the family circle where reading aloud is not a lost art, nothing will provide a more enjoyable evening. Some one of these stories should fit into almost every father's life and experience and serve to stimulate a profound sense of his importance to his family.

Tributes to father have been less frequent than to mother, but there has recently been published a very interesting collection of poems called *Father, An Anthology of Verse,* which makes one realize that fathers awaken just as deep a sentiment and leave as lasting an impression as mothers. The book will be helpful for special occasions, but it will also be a delightful book for any father to own.

It would surely deeply interest fathers if they could realize just how they appear and appeal to their children. Do the children feel at home with him or do they fear him; do they respect and admire him, or do they think of him only as their source of money. Do they love and trust him or are they indifferent to him; do they take his advice or do they scorn his opinion. Last year in a certain town, the children from the fourth grade through the high school were asked to answer (anonymously) four questions about their fathers. The answers were printed in the September 1930 number of the *Child Welfare Magazine,* to be found in the Library. It would certainly interest fathers to read the opinion of the children themselves as to how they were filling their job as fathers, for this symposium of opinions would probably be the same in any town. Some of the replies indicated a pathetic longing for father's attention and sympathy, and others criticised an indifferent father. It is a serious thing, this living up to the keen, clear judgment of children, for they need something from their fathers which not even mothers can give.

> You may not worry much about
> Religion, which is right or wrong.
> But here's a thing, without a doubt
> To keep you straight and keep you strong.
> Here's your responsibility,
> The greatest mortal ever had—
> Just to be worthy, friend, to be
> Some youngster's dad.

Few men would fail their children in times of physical danger; they would brave any weather to get the doctor; they are broken hearted if the dread summons comes for their children. But the responsibility for giving far deeper protection is what father should assume. In the magazine, *Playground,* Volume 22, is an article by Henry Turner Bailey called, "The Man Who Put His Arm Around Me." He says that ought to be the boy's first thought about his father. The big man who carried him in his strong arms; who lifted him into his high chair, who held him in the twilight and told him stories, who held him while he learned to swim, who put his arms around him as he proudly sat beside him in church, and who kept his arms around him as he passed the dangerous straits between boyhood and manhood. And he adds: "If you fathers don't do such things for your sons and daughters you are losing half the fun of living. If you spend your time just making a living for them; if you spend your time at the Lodge or your club, then later you must not wonder why your boys and girls do not spend their evenings at home, or why they do not really care a rap about you." Boys want daddies who will play with them, grow up with them, be comrades with them as no one else on earth but dads can be.

There is an increasing number of men who are acting as leaders of boys, in the Boy Scout movement, in the Y.M.C.A. clubs and various organizations. They are coming to the Library watching for articles in magazines and for new books on character training helps. Many men are training and inspiring not only their own boys, but other men's boys. But it will bring a new day when every man is the comrade and inspiration of his own sons and daughters. There are many fine books and magazines in the Library for parents. One magazine especially, called *Parents,* would be useful in every home. And we would like to recommend a little book for fathers called *The Job of Being a Dad* by Frank Cheley, and another by the same author called *Dad, Whose Boy is Yours,* consisting of forty-eight little talks with fathers who want to be real dads to their real boys.

While we usually think of father's relation and comradeship with his sons, I want to add that there is no relationship in the home so wonderful as that between a daughter and an understanding father, and I am writing this with the memory of a wonderful father who was tender and sympathetic, who was a stimulus to every ambition, and a friend to be leaned upon with confidence and trust. Would that there were more such fathers!

Gratia in her bedroom at Wetoco Lodge, 1929
Source: Virginia Buffington Shaw

LIBRARY ANN'S COOK BOOK

Library Ann's Cook Book

Published in 1928 by the Minneapolis Public Library Staff Association

Gratia's Recipes

HALIBUT MOUSSE

2 pounds halibut
2 eggs
1 cup cream

Remove skin and bones from two pounds halibut; put it through meat chopper four times until it is a fine pulp. This will make about one cupful. Add two unbeaten eggs one at a time, mashing thoroughly into pulp, add cream, mixing thoroughly into pulp. Put into buttered mold and steam for an hour. Serve with a white sauce with either lobster or shrimps added. Will serve about six people as luncheon or supper dish. Very nice served with salad of peas and celery with clover-leaf rolls.—(Miss Countryman.)

RAINBOW MEAT LOAF

Use finely chopped cooked ham or veal or chicken. Place in mold a layer of meat one-half inch thick mixed in lemon jelly or plain gelatin, then a layer of finely chopped boiled eggs, soaked with gelatin, then another layer of meat, etc. Between layers may be placed strips of red pimentos or green peppers. Slice across layers to serve. Excellent for lunch served with creamed potatoes or peas and carrots.—(Miss Countryman.)

ITALIAN RAVIOLA

2 pounds round steak
3 large onions
1 large green pepper
1 can tomatoes
1 can mushrooms
3 pints water
½ pound bacon
1 cup grated cheese
1 tablespoon
Worcestershire sauce
2 packages wide noodles
Salt

Cut up steak, onions, and peppers into small pieces. Fry onions and brown pieces of steak, then with the salt and water, place steak, onions, and peppers in large iron pot and simmer for three hours. One hour before serving add tomatoes, mushrooms, cheese, bacon, noodles, and sauce. Cut bacon into fine pieces and crisp before adding, pouring grease and all into the pot. Serve hot with steamed rice (or baked potatoes).—(Miss Countryman.)

MACARONI AND CHEESE LOAF

- 1 cup cooked macaroni
- 1 cup milk
- 2 cups soft bread crumbs
- ½ cup butter
- 1 cup grated cheese
- 2 pimentos
- 1 green pepper
- 1 tablespoon chopped parsley
- ½ teaspoon onion juice
- 1 teaspoon salt
- 5 eggs

Chop macaroni fine, also pimentos and green peppers. Mix all together, folding the beaten eggs in last. Bake in a mold about one-half hour. Turn out of mold and serve with mushroom or tomato sauce.—(G. A. Countryman.)

APPLE ROLL

Make dough as for baking powder biscuit. Roll out one-half inch thick. Cover with finely chopped apples, sprinkled with sugar, cinnamon, bits of butter. Roll up like a jelly roll, then slice across about one inch thick. Place slices in baking pan, pour over them a cup or so of water and a cup of sugar and bake. Serve with whipped cream.—(Miss Countryman.)

FLORIDA DELIGHT

- 1 can peaches
- Plain sponge cake batter

Grease an iron skillet liberally with lard, cover about one inch deep with brown sugar and dot with butter. Place canned peaches flat side own over whole surface. Pour sponge cake batter over them, and bake until sponge cake is done. Turn out on platter, peach side up, and serve with whipped cream.—(Miss Countryman.)

SIMPLE TORTES

For each torte place four vanilla wafers, one on top of the other, with whipped cream between each one and on top. Set in icebox overnight. Just before using cover sides and top with whipped cream. One may also use chopped nuts with cherry on top.—(Miss Countryman.)

Notes

1. Mena C. Dyste, "Gratia Alta Countryman," 1965 master's thesis.

2. Nancy J. Rohde, "Gratia Countryman, Evangel of Education," 1974, manuscript in the Minneapolis Collection, Minneapolis Public Library.

3. First lines of Sonnet No. 8 by James Russell Lowell; Gratia's entry for Thursday, Thanksgiving Day, from her own daily calendar, on which she inscribed in ink a verse from literature for every day of the year.

4. See "Selected Writings" for entire speech.

5. Delta Gamma, a university sorority, has always carried the name Delta Gamma Fraternity.

6. Esther McBride Brown Christianson in a letter to Gratia's niece, Constance Buffington, August 2, 1953.

7. Josephine Cloud, December 1936.

8. Jessie McMillan Marcley, December 1936.

9. *A Bicycle Odyssey 1896;* see Bibliography.

10. Lana's grandson, Edwin Buffington, San Diego, January 5, 1993.

11. See "Selected Writings."

12. Irene Hauser, undated, and Rodney Loehr, 1992.

13. State Library Commission *News & Notes,* p. 53.

14. Letter from Gratia to her aunt, Lany Truax, May 17, 1917.

15. Letter to Herbert Putnam, May 31, 1917.

16. Interview with Virginia Buffington Shaw, February 1993, and with Wellington Countryman, October 1992.

17. During Gratia Countryman's tenure, Professor Loehr worked part

time in the library bindery throughout his high school and undergraduate university years.

18. Letter to Gratia Countryman, April 23, 1928.

19. *Minneapolis Times,* December 28, 1930.

20. *Minneapolis Times,* 1931.

21. *Minneapolis Times,* October 25, 1931.

22. Presented by University of Minnesota President Lotus D. Coffman.

23. *Minneapolis Times,* June 7, 1932.

24. Donald Norris, November 4, 1992.

25. *The Minneapolis Journal,* January 7, 1934.

26. From the "Minneapolis Newspaper Indexing and Microfilming" brochure.

27. THE INDEXER, Vol. 10, March 10, 1939.

28. October 26, 1938.

29. Herman Erickson, "WPA Strike and Trials of 1939," *Minnesota History,* Summer 1971.

30. Christopher Morley, *Friends, Romans . . . ,* The Ampersand Club, Minneapolis and St. Paul, 1940.

31. WPA "Newspaper Indexing Project Record of Accomplishment and Program Operation," prepared by Vera Mae Barrnes, January 27, 1943.

32. Gratia's day book for November 29, 1946.

33. Gratia Countryman, December 1946.

34. Reprinted in the "The Pine Torch," Piney Woods, Mississippi, January–February 1950.

35. This tribute appeared in *Minnesota Libraries,* June 1951.

36. Robert Shaw, July 1992.

37. From a letter to Wellington Countryman, dated August 17, 1952.

Bibliography

Major Sources of Unpublished Papers

These sources held virtually all of the private papers that became the kernel in this life of Gratia Countryman—letters, essays, diaries, daybooks, documents and other papers:

Family Archives: In the possession of Wellington Countryman, Virginia Buffington Shaw, and Edwin Buffington.

Minneapolis Public Library (MPL): Library Administration Archives and the Minneapolis Collection.

Minnesota Historical Society (MHS): Six boxes of Gratia Countryman papers, mostly public, some private.

Published References

Benidt, Bruce Weir. 1984. *The Library Book Centennial History of the Minneapolis Public Library.* Minneapolis: Minneapolis Public Library and Information Center.

Bobinski, George S., et al. (eds.). 1978. *Dictionary of American Library Biography.* Littleton, Colorado: Libraries Unlimited, Inc.

Countryman, Alvin. 1925. Countryman Genealogy, Part I and Part II. New York: Lux Bros. and Heath.

Countryman, Gratia. *A Bicycle Odyssey 1896,* compiled and edited by Jane Pejsa. 1994. Minneapolis.

DeLestry, Edmond L. 1923. "Passing of the Winchells," *Western Magazine,* Vol. 22, No. 6, December.

Drury, John. 1947. "In a Ghost Town, Ignatius Donnelly House," *Historic Midwest Houses.* Minneapolis: The University of Minnesota Press.

Dyste, Mena K. 1965. "Gratia Alta Countryman, Librarian." Master's Thesis, University of Minnesota.

Erickson, Herman. 1971. "WPA Strike and Trials of 1939," *Minnesota History,* Summer.

Hauser, Irene and Elftman, Robert. 1939. *Minneapolis Newspaper Indexing Project Manual of Instruction.* Minneapolis: WPA.

Hudson, Horace B. 1908. "Thomas Barlow Walker," *A Half Century of Minneapolis,* Minneapolis: The Hudson Publishing Company.

Kemp, James F. 1924. "Memorial of Horace Vaughn Winchell," *Geological Society Memorials,* March.

Library Ann's Cook Book. 1928. Minneapolis: Minneapolis Public Library Staff Association.

Morley, Christopher. 1940. *Friends, Romans . . . .* Minneapolis and St. Paul: The Ampersand Club.

Neil, Rev. Edward D. 1881. *History of Dakota County and the City of Hastings.* Minneapolis: North Star Publishing Company.

Pejsa, Jane. 1984. *The Molineux Affair.* Minneapolis: Kenwood Publishing.

Ridge, Martin. 1962. *Ignatius Donnelly: The Portrait of a Politician,* Chicago: The University of Chicago Press.

Rohde, Nancy Freeman. 1977. "Librarian and Reformer," *Women of Minnesota,* Barbara Stuhler and Gretchen Kreuter (eds.). St. Paul: Minnesota Historical Society Press.

Schofield, Geraldine Bryant, and Smith, Susan Margot. 1977. "Maria Louise Sanford, Minnesota's Heroine," *Women of Minnesota,* Barbara Stuhler and Gretchen Kreuter (eds.). St. Paul: Minnesota Historical Society Press.

Trenerry, Walter N. 1985. "High Stakes and Green Goods," *Murder in Minnesota.* St. Paul: Minnesota Historical Society.

Walker, David A. 1979. *Iron Frontier, the Discovery and Development of Minnesota's Three Ranges.* St. Paul: Minnesota Historical Society Press.

Wright, Mabel Osgood. 1903. *The Garden of a Commuter's Wife.* New York: The Macmillan Company.

Other Written Sources, Published and Unpublished

American Library Association Bulletin. Various years. Urbana, Illinois: University of Illinois Library, c/o Helen Ballew, Archivist.

Barrnes, Vera Mae. 1943. "Newspaper Indexing Project Accomplishments." St. Paul: WPA, January 27. Washington, D.C.: National Archives, c/o James S. Rush, Jr., Assistant Chief, Civil Reference Branch.

Business Women's Club of Minneapolis. 1919–1926. MPL.

Cloud, Josephine. 1936. "When Gratia Was a Girl," *Staff Stuff*, Vol. 12, No. 1, December.

Countryman, Levi, three boxes of papers. MHS; also family archives.

Countryman, Theophilus Russell. "Memoirs: The Cripple Creek Years 1892–1926," family archives; also MHS.

Delta Gamma Fraternity Archives, c/o Janet Christianson, Delta Gamma House, Minneapolis.

Evans, Sara M. 1989. *Born of Liberty, a History of Women in America.* New York: The Free Press, a Division of Macmillan, Inc.

Hamline University archives. Minneapolis: Methodist Church, c/o Thelma Boeder, Archivist.

Hennepin County Juvenile Justice Center, Adoption of Wellington Greenway, Minneapolis.

Hennepin County Probate Court, Estate of Marie Annette Todd, Minneapolis.

Hlavsa, Larry B. 1978. "A Brief History of Public Libraries in Minneapolis/St. Paul, 1849–1900." a Script. Minneapolis: University of Minnesota.

Library News and Notes. Various years. Originally Minnesota Library Commission, later, Department of Education, Library Development and Services, St. Paul.

Marcley, Jessie McMillan. 1936. "Memories of G.A.C.," *Staff Stuff*, Vol. 12, No. 1, December.

Minneapolis Journal. MHS, MPL, and family archives.

Minneapolis Morning Tribune. MHS, MPL, and family archives.

Minneapolis Public Library Board Minutes. MPL archives.

Minneapolis Times. MPL and family archives.

Minnesota Libraries. Minnesota Department of Education, St. Paul.

New York Times, October 22, 1933, and July 9, 1934. Minneapolis: University of Minnesota Library.

Nininger and Hastings. South St. Paul, Minnesota: Dakota County Historical Society, c/o Rebecca Snyder, Director.

Peripatetics Club documents, family archives.

Rohde, Nancy Freeman, "Gratia Countryman, Evangel of Education," a manuscript. MPL.

Ryan, Mary P. 1983. *Womanhood in America from Colonial Times to the Present,* Third Edition. New York: Franklin Watts.

St. Louis County Probate Court, Estate of Gratia A. Countryman, Duluth.
Twin Cities Library Club 1906–1984. MHS. Minutes c/o Mary Birmingham, Metronet, Minnesota Library Development and Services, St. Paul.
University of Minnesota archives. Minneapolis: University of Minnesota, c/o Penelope Krosch, Archivist and Head.
University of Minnesota Office of the Registrar. Minneapolis.
Walker, T. B., papers. MHS.
Woman's Club Minutes, 1907–1908, The Woman's Club of Minneapolis.
Women's Welfare League, 1911–1962. MHS.

Oral History and Other Oral Information, 1992–1994

Susan Hauser Bishop, Princeton, New Jersey; Edwin and Peggy Buffington, San Diego, California; Alice Brunat, Bloomington, Minnesota; Louise Christianson, Edina, Minnesota; Wellington Countryman, Des Plaines, Illinois; Harry Cummings, Eagan, Minnesota; Shirley Russell Holt, Minneapolis, Minnesota; Yvonne Hunter, Minneapolis, Minnesota; Professor Rodney Loehr, Bloomington, Minnesota; Marilyn McGriff, Braham, Minnesota; Hiram Mendow, Minneapolis, Minnesota; Donald Norris, Minnetonka, Minnesota; William and Jean Pearson, Lake Mille Lacs, Minnesota; Susan Rhetts, Minneapolis, Minnesota; Judge Noah Rosenbloom, New Ulm, Minnesota; Virginia and Robert Shaw, Edina, Minnesota.

Articles, Essays, and Talks by Gratia Countryman

1882. "The Vocation in Which a Woman May Engage," commencement speech, Hastings High School, Hastings, Minnesota, June 16. MHS.
1887. "University Notes," Hermean Society Oration, University of Minnesota, December 12. MHS.
1887. "The Drama of Today," University of Minnesota. MHS.
1887. "Famous Women," Hermean Society Oration, University of Minnesota, March 14. MHS.
1888. "Coeducation," Hermean Society Oration, University of Minnesota, May 7. MHS.
1888. "Influence of a Nation's Character Upon History," a talk, printed in the *Ariel,* University of Minnesota, June.
1889. "Safeguards of the Suffrage," commencement address, University of Minnesota, June 7.

1904. "State Aid to Libraries," speech to the American Library Association (ALA) Annual Conference, St.Louis, Missouri. MHS.

1904. Annual Reports, the Minneapolis Public Library, 15th through 47th, 1904–1936. MPL.

1905. "The Library as a Social Center," *Library News and Notes,* December. MHS.

1914. "What's Wrong with the Public Library?" a series of seven articles, answers to citizens' questions, *Minneapolis Morning Tribune,* November. Family archives.

1916. "Whence and Whither: an Appraisal," *Library News and Notes,* December. MHS.

1917. "Liberty," suffrage talk delivered at Hamline University, March 31, to the Intercollegiate Prohibition Association. Family archives.

1917. "Public Library, Dating to Days of '59, Makes Remarkable Record," *Minneapolis Golden Jubilee 1867-1917,* Minneapolis, June. Family archives.

1917. "Literature and the War." MHS.

1919. "Mothers of Tomorrow," delivered at Trinity Methodist Church, Minneapolis, May 11. MHS.

1920. "Maria Sanford," Memorial Service for Maria Sanford, May 9. Family archives.

1922. "Ambition and Persistent Effort," banquet of the YWCA Education Classes, May 19. MHS.

1922. "Americanization: The Library's Contribution," read before University of Minnesota Library Class, May 6. MHS.

1923. "Women and the Jury System," radio talk, March. MHS.

1924. "What Parent-Teacher Associations Can Do for Libraries," Second National Conference on Home Education, U.of M., Minneapolis, May 7. MHS.

1924. "What Parent-Teacher Associations Can Do for Libraries," *Library Notes and News,* June.

1925. "College Alumni Reading Courses," given at the opening meeting of the ALA Commission on the Library and Adult Education, Chicago, April 15. MHS.

1925. "What Parent-Teacher Associations Can Do for Libraries," *Cooperation in Adult Education,* Report of Second National Conference on Home Education, called by the United States Commissioner of Education, at Minneapolis, Minnesota, May 7, 1924.

1925. "Never Too Late to Learn," delivered before Minnesota Business Women's Convention at Owatonna, Minnesota, Spring. MHS.

1925. "Adult Education." MHS.
1926. "A Book Wagon for Every County," radio talk, April 29. MHS.
1926. "Our Trip to Europe," *Business Woman,* Business Women's Club, Fall. MHS.
1926. "Libraries and Schools," Campus Club talk, University of Minnesota, September 30. MHS.
1926. "Library Work as a Vocation for Women," *Women's Christian Association News,* Minneapolis, November 15. MHS.
1927. "The Library Profession," *Vocation Guidance Bulletin,* Minneapolis Board of Education, January. MHS.
1928. "School Libraries," draft of a talk, December. Family archives.
1928. "Public Library Administration of School Libraries," given at the Midwinter Meeting of the ALA, December; *Illinois Libraries,* Springfield, Vol. 11, No. 1, January 1929. MHS.
1928. "County Library Administration of County School Libraries," December. MHS.
1929. "Mr. Putnam and the Minneapolis Public Library," Herbert Putnam Testimonial Booklet, Washington, D.C. Family archives.
1929. "Spirit of the City," broadcast on WCCO Radio under the auspices of the Minneapolis Chamber of Commerce, January 23. MHS.
1929. "Minneapolis, My Home Town—Education," given at "Minneapolis—My Home Town" Night at the Foshay Tower, February 22. MHS.
1929. "Shall we have a Museum," *Parent Teacher Broadcaster,* March. Family archives.
1929. "Library Service to the Schools of Hennepin County, Minnesota," *School Life,* Bureau of Education, Vol. XIV, No. 8, April. MHS.
1929. "How the Public Uses the Library," May 14. MHS.
1929. "Contributions of County Libraries," Conference of State and County Supervisors of Rural Schools of the Midwestern States, Des Moines, Iowa, June 14. MHS.
1929. "County Libraries," given to the Iowa Library Association, October 16. MHS.
1929. "Talk to Freshman Students," presented at Andrew Presbyterian Church, Minneapolis, Fall. MHS.
1929. "The Library Welcomes Mr. Reed," given at banquet to welcome Mr. Carroll Reed, new Superintendent of the Minneapolis Public Schools, November 7. MHS.
1929. "Why Stop Learning?" *Parent Teacher Broadcaster,* Minneapolis, November. MHS.
1930 "Widening Horizons," *Woman's Club Bulletin,* January. MHS.

1930. "Library Work as a Profession," Woman's Occupational Bureau, Minneapolis, February 5. MHS.

1930. "The School's Best Friend," radio talk, County Library Service, Madison, Wisconsin, July 16. MHS.

1930. "Charles Reade's *Cloister and the Hearth,*" WCCO radio book review, October 6. MHS.

1930. "The A.L.A. Endowment Fund," presented to North Central Library Conference, October 17; also Twin City Library Club, April 23, 1931. MHS.

1930. "George Eliot's *Romola,*" WCCO radio book review, November 3. MHS.

1930. "Solve the Magazine Problem," *Parent Teacher Broadcaster.* MHS.

1930. "Rural School Libraries," talk to rural school educators. MHS.

1931. "George Eliot's *Adam Bede,*" radio book review, WCCO, January 12. MHS.

1931. "Making Plans for a Children's Room," presented at Library School, University of Minnesota, April 10. MHS.

1931. "The County Book Truck," presented at the Annual ALA Convention, June. MHS.

1931. "Hennepin County Library Services," *Ontario Library Review,* Ontario, Canada, August 31. MHS.

1931. "Welcome to the Library," *Parent Teacher Broadcaster,* September. MHS.

1931. "Administering the Public Library and the School Library as a Single Unit," Aberdeen, South Dakota, October 29; *South Dakota Library Bulletin,* Pierre, Vol. 17, No. 4, December. MHS.

1931. "Read About Home Interests," *Parent Teacher Broadcaster,* October. MHS.

1931. "School Libraries," draft of a talk, October. MHS.

1931. "Why Not Entertain at Home?" *Parent Teacher Broadcaster,* December. MHS.

1931. "Library and Adult Education." MHS.

1932. "Fathers," *Parent Teacher Broadcaster,* January. MHS.

1932. "Modern Homes Need Religion," *Parent Teacher Broadcaster,* February. MHS.

1932 "The Library and Adult Education for Women," talk to The Minneapolis Woman's Club, February. MHS.

1932. "County Libraries," Parent Teacher Association Meeting, Minneapolis, May 18. MHS.

1932. "Publicity," talk to the Parent Teacher Association, Minneapolis, May. MHS.
1932. "Books Have Curative Qualities," *Parent Teacher Broadcaster,* May–June. MHS.
1932. "The Place of the Library in the Modern School," given at Fargo, North Dakota, Agricultural College, July 15. MHS.
1932. "Library Service Hampered," *Parent Teacher Broadcaster.* MHS.
1932, "Christmas Seals," radio talk, WCCO, December 2. MHS.
1933. "Household Budget," Northwestern National Bank Lecture Series for Women, January 11. MHS.
1933. "Maria L. Sanford," a convocation talk, *Builders of the Name,* University of Minnesota, Minneapolis, February 16. MHS.
1933. "Libraries and Rural Life," February 28. MHS.
1933. "School Library Branches," March 1. MHS.
1933. "National Aspects of Library Service," given at the Library School, University of Minnesota, March 8. MHS.
1933. "Citizens' Councils," presented to Minnesota Library Association, June 17. MHS.
1933. "Present-Day Problems of the Library," radio talk, July 14. MHS.
1933. Acceptance speech, President of the American Library Association, Chicago, October 21; printed in the *ALA Bulletin,* December.
1933. "A Retrospect and a Forward Look," presented to Colorado Library Association, Ft. Collins, Colorado, November 17. MHS.
1933. "Library Extension," presented to Colorado Library Association, Ft. Collins, Colorado, November 17. MHS.
1933. "Facing the Future," *Library Notes and News,* Summer. MHS.
1933. "Library as a Lighthouse." MHS.
1933. "Reader's Advisory Service." MHS.
1934. "Shoulder to Shoulder," *ALA Bulletin,* Vol. 28, No. 3, March.
1934. "Building for the Future," *ALA Bulletin,* July.
1934. "Appreciation for A.L.A. Endowment," talk to Carnegie Corporation, Spring. MHS.
1935. "The School Libraries of the United States," an address before the Second International Library and Bibliographical Congress, Madrid, Spain, May. MHS.
1936. "Social Forces at Work Today," given at Crookston, Minnesota, February 4, and Sauk Center, Minnesota, May 4. MHS.
1936. "The Next Decade," presented to the Minnesota Library Association, Duluth, October 2. MHS.

1936. "Historical Sketch of the Library," *The Taxpayer,* Minneapolis, November.
1936. "Message from Miss Countryman," farewell talk to her staff, December 27. MHS.
1938. "The World Challenges Peace," address to the Annual Conference, Women's International League for Peace and Freedom, Minneapolis, April. MHS.
1941. "History of the Minnesota Library Association," read at the 50th Anniversary of the Minnesota Library Association, December. MHS.
1944. "This Changing World," *The Minneapolis Business Woman,* Business and Professional Women's Club of Minneapolis, February. MHS.
1945. "Religion in Soviet Russia," a talk at the Peripatetics Club. MHS.
1947. "Alexander Hamilton," a talk at the Peripatetics Club, March 31. MHS.
1947. "Educational Liberty, Newspapers, etc.," a talk at the Peripatetics Club, November 17. MHS.
1949. "World Government," a talk at the Peripatetics Club, Minneapolis. January 30; also at the Minneapolis Tourist Club, March 28. MHS.
1950. "Clara F. Baldwin, a Tribute," *Minnesota Libraries,* June. Family archives.
Undated. "The Bedouins," a talk at the Peripatetics Club. MHS.
Undated. "The Carolina Playmakers and the Folk Drama." MHS.
Undated. Sermon at Hope Chapel Girl's Club. MHS.
Undated. "Building for the Future." MHS.
Undated. "Extension System of the Public Library." MHS.
Undated. "Problems of Departmental Organization," ALA Midwinter Meeting, *Library Journal.* MHS.
Undated. "Need for County Libraries." MHS.
Undated. "Educating for Peace." MHS.
Undated. Talk on state of libraries, given to the Lion's Club. MHS.
Undated. "Recruiting for Library Work." MHS.
Undated. "What Is a Library, What Is a Librarian." MHS.
Undated. "Our Library School and the Accredited List of the A.L.A." MHS.
Undated. "American Social Problems.," MHS.
Undated. "What Libraries Might Do for the Music Profession," given before the Music League. MHS.
Undated. "Use and Abuse of the Public Library." MHS.
Undated. "Social Usefulness of the Public Library." MHS.
Undated. "Federal Aid to Libraries." MHS.

Index

Aanestad, Mr., 256
Abbott, Elizabeth, 187

Babcock, Prof., 109
Bailey, Elva, 233, 245, 248-9, 269, 296
Baker, Harry, 153
Baldwin, Clara, 69-73, 86, 91-6, 101-5, 117, 123-6, 135, 189, 203, 287, 297, 301-2
Banning, Margaret Culkin, 240
Bartleson, Charles, 115-6; Mabel 115-7, 235, 248
Bassett, Minnie, 34
Benson, Mr. 246
Berg, Anna, 196; Oscar, 196, 291, 295
Bishop, Susan Hauser 281
Black, Mrs., 233, 246, 250, 287
Blixt, Claus, 116
Borah, William, 239
Bowerman, George Franklin, 119-121
Boxell, Mrs., 245
Boyer, Dr., 299
Brandt, Mrs., 279
Bray, Elizabeth, 223, 225, 248
Brown, Lina (Reed), 86
Brunat, Alice, 188
Buffington, Constance, 300
Buffington, Constance Conger, 106-327 passim
Buffington, Edwin, 13, 195, 223, 243, 246, 288, 300, 304-305, 327; Gilbert, 173, 195, 221, 240, 244, 251, 256-7, 281-307; Peggy, 300; Steve, 305; Virginia (see Shaw)
Butturff, Mr., 44

Campbell, Mr., 94
Carnegie, Andrew, 158
Chamberlain, Alta (see Countryman); Octavia, 25; Royal, 21, 23, 25
Champlin, Mrs., 33
Cheley, Frank, 322
Christianson, Esther (Etta) McBride Fuller, 50-2, 56-61, 65, 70, 84
Cloud, Josephine, 79, 82, 327
Coates, Mr., 60
Coffman, Pres. Lotus D., 328
Conger, Charles T., 53-4, 83, 92, 106, 113, 222-3; Constance (see Buffington); Florence, 222
Conger, Lana (Lany) Countryman,28-244 passim
Countryman, Ada, 38, 41-3, 50, 114; Adda 140, 199, 297
Countryman, Alta Chamberlain, 17-298 passim
Countryman, Alta Marie, 264-9, 279, 286, 299-303, 307
Countryman, Amplius (Ampy), 19-222 passim
Countryman, Dorothy Whitstruck, 249-251, 265-7, 273, 279, 286, 293, 303, 307
Countryman, Gratia Alta, 9-328 passim
Countryman, Jason Melville, 25-6, 192; Lana (see Conger)
Countryman, Levi, 2-298 passim

Countryman, Martha, 145, 149; Minnie Martha, 23-5, 192; Peter, 43, 58
Countryman, Theophilus (Offie, Theo), 19-307 passim
Countryman, Wellington Greenway, 12-307 passim
Crafts, Letitia, 120-4, 155, 158
Crary, Dr., 24-5
Crays, Jennie, 102

Dayton, D. Draper, 106, 127, 157, 164, 197; Louise Winchell, 127, 157
Decker, Mrs. Wilbur F., 230
Deutsch, Prof. Harold C., 283; Marie, 283
Dodd, Mrs. John, 320
Dodge, Prof., 52
Donnelly, Ignatius, 15-8, 22, 103
DuBois, Mr., 273; William, 273
Dunlap, Vera, 86
Dyste, Mena C.. 11-2. 327

Erickson, Mrs. Philip, 236

Field, Barbara, 13
Fischer, Mr., 43-4
Fiterman, Dolly, 159
Folwell, Pres. William W., 218
Ford, Pres. Guy Stanton, 270
Frost, Celia 91
Fuller, Gratia Countryman Brown, 132

Gale, Edward C., 125, 156-7, 236; Samuel C., 157
Gideon, Mrs., 110
Gillis, Johnnie, 29-34, 38
Ging, Kitty, 116, 235
Glenn, Lt. Edward, 70-4

Hall, Prof., 52
Hamp, Mr., 60
Hanchett, Dr., 22
Hauser, Irene Melgaard, 258-60, 267, 273-5, 281-3, 287, 290-2, 295, 298, 300, 327; Jane (see Pejsa); Susan (see Bishop); Walter U., 273, 281-3, 287, 291-2, 295, 298, 300
Hayward, Harry, 115-6, 235
Hitler, Adolf, 261-3, 269
Hoover, Pres. Herbert, 218
Horton, Roy, 287
Hosmer, James K., 87-91, 100, 103, 110-1, 117-9, 125-6, 140, 308

Iturbi, José, 299

Jacobson, Mrs., 123
Jamieson, Judge, 145, 147, 159
Jones, Marian, 204, 206

Kellogg, Clara, 92-6, 101; Frank B., 218
Kittleson, Harold, 10, 14

Landon, Alf, 239
Lavell, Richard, 161-3
Lewis, Glenn, 215, 235, 237, 281-3; Lewis, Mr. (teacher), 31, 8
Lynskey, Louise (Baucher), 86, 100
Livingston, Florence, 91, 283, 291-2, 300; Hiram, 211, 278, 283, 291-2
Loehr, Prof. Rodney, 201. 327

Macdonald, Genevieve, 213-300 passim
Magee, Annie (Moore), 174-7, 270-3
Mann, Leonora, 91
McBride, Etta (see Christianson)
McKnight, Sumner T., 158
McMillan, Jessie (Marcley), 327
Mead, Harry, 33
Merritt Brothers, 46
Molineux, Blanche (see Scott); Roland, 274
Morley, Christopher, 270, 328
Moses, Mr., 248
Mussolini, Benito, 262

Nininger, John, 16
Norris, Donald, 219-220, 328
Northrop, Pres. Cyrus, 70-1, 76, 81, 87, 118, 124, 143, 157, 210, 241

Oren, Mabel, 235

Parks, Amelia, 174-5, 177
Patten, Katherine, 86, 136, 139, 143; Mrs., 137, 152
Pearson, Jean, 290; William, 290
Pejsa, Arthur, 14; Jane Hauser, 10, 14, 273, 281, 298
Pillsbury, Gov. John S., 159
Porter, Lil, 47

Putnam, Herbert, 80-92, 100, 118-9, 125, 179, 210, 241, 327

Quinlan, Elizabeth, 207, 282

Ramsey, Gov. Alexander, 16
Randall, Mrs., 151
Rankin, Rep. Jeannette, 314
Ratzlaff, Gratia Countryman, 132
Rich, The Rev. Mr., 31-3
Rockwood, C.J., 127
Rohde, Prof. Nancy J., 12, 327
Roosevelt, Pres. Franklin D., 232, 239, 261
Root, Lizzie, 29-34, 38
Rosholt, Ruth, 91, 169
Ross, Miss, 176
Ryan, Jack, 146, 150-4

Sanford, Anna, 149-152; Prof. Maria, 317-9
Scott, Blanche Molineux, 273-5, 281, 287, 290-2, 298, 300, 307
Shaw, Robert, 300-1, 328; Virginia Buffington, 12-3, 256, 281, 286-298, 301, 304, 307, 327
Siegel, Margot, 13
Smith, Ada, 73, 77; George, 287; Miss, 29; Mrs., 43
Spear, Lois, 86
Stalin, Joseph, 232
Starr, Augusta, 210
Stassen, Gov. Harold E., 267
Stillman, Norton, 14
Stone, Jacob, 118-9, 158
Strong, Rufus, 247-9, 252, 255
Struzyk, Deborah, 13
Stuhr, Susan, 298

Tee, Dr., 198
Todd, Marie, 111-299 passim
Todd, Mrs., 146-7, 150-1, 163, 173
Truax, Lany Countryman, 145, 327

Vik, Dr., 287
Vincent, Pres. George Edgar, 218
Vitz, Carl, 237, 281

Waite, Judge Edward F., 176-7, 248

Walker, Archie, 236; Thomas Barlow (T.B.), 80, 83, 87-8, 120, 130, 135, 155-9, 180-191, 209-10, 226-7, 285
Waller Family, 153
Ward, Barbara, 286; Dr., 286-7, 297
Washington, Booker T., 316
Wiley, Grace, 224, 226-8, 234
Williams, Mr., 44
Wilson, Agnes, 170-5, 205-6; Bess, 238-9; Pres. Woodrow, 179; Wellington (see Countryman)
Winchell, Prof. Alexander, 46, 63-4; Avis, 106; Charlotte, 46, 102
Winchell, Horace V., 45-304 passim
Winchell, Ida Belle Winchell, 63-4, 83-4, 88, 105, 135, 197; Ima, 45-7, 53, 106; Louise (see Dayton); Prof. Newton, 45-6, 63, 226; Royal Winchell, 88
Woodman, Clara, 92-6, 101
Woolley, Pres. Mary, 143
Wright, Mabel Osgood ("Barbara"), 128-130